OVERTHROW A
FASCIST REGIME
ON $15 A DAY

Wayne Madsen

Published by:
TrineDay
PO Box 577
Walterville, OR 97489
1-800-556-2012
www.TrineDay.com
publisher@TrineDay.net

Library of Congress Control Number:

Madsen, Wayne
Overthrow a Fascist Regime on $15 Dollars a Day—1st ed.
p. cm. (acid-free paper)
Includes index.
(ISBN-13) 9780977795369 (ISBN-10)0977795365
1. Political Corruption—United States.

FIRST EDITION
10 9 8 7 6 5 4 3 2 1

Printed in the USA
Distribution to the Trade by:
Independent Publishers Group (IPG)
814 North Franklin Street
Chicago, Illinois 60610
312.337.0747
www.ipgbook.com

For my friends and family who helped me get through the last seven years of fascist hell in Washington, DC.

Table of Contents

Introduction

The Internet has become the last vestige for the free and independent press. Arrayed against this last remaining outpost of a free and vibrant Fourth Estate are mega-corporations that mix current events and entertainment into a perception-managed blend of "infotainment."

In 1985, when I was a Lieutenant in the U.S. Navy and working at the National Security Agency's National Communication Security Assessment Center set up by President Reagan to secure the U.S. telecommunication infrastructure from a host of threats, including the Soviet Union, I could not nor would not have believed that some fifteen years later I would become an anti-war activist writing about the fascist tendencies of the White House.

It is probably also certain that in 1985, CIA officer Ray McGovern did not think much about a future in anti-war activism while he was preparing President's Daily Briefs for President Reagan. Nor did Cindy Sheehan, who was raising her five-year old son Casey in 1985, believe that she would become the public face of the anti-war movement after her son was killed at the age of 24 while serving in an illegal and contrived war in Iraq.

In fact, in 1985, just a decade after the Vietnam War debacle, hundreds of thousands of Americans could not have foreseen a future of political anti-war activism. In a mere 25 years, America forgot the lessons of Vietnam and worse, allowed themselves to be lured into another war — a war about oil on behalf of a clique combining neofascists and "neoconservatives" bent on world domination by an imperial United States, something they called the "New American Century."

This book is a reflection of shoestring budget political activism during seven years in neocon-occupied Washington, DC, one of the country's most expensive and elitist cities. Beginning in 2000 during the election campaign that propelled George W. Bush into the presidency, the following chapters, which reflect on reporting through a virtual Iron Curtain surrounding Washington from 2000 to 2007, concentrate first on the author's activities in trying to keep George W. Bush from attaining the presidency, including personally helping in the effort to prevent his re-election, and lastly, in assisting in the marginalization of his and his support base's political power in the 2006 election and afterward.

To go from an executive level position with a Fortune 500 company in 1997 to an austere lifestyle as a political activist and independent investigative journalist was never my goal. But when the specter of another corrupt Bush administration loomed on the horizon, there was no other choice. With the help of many friends and colleagues, meetings at coffee shops and local pubs soon blossomed into full-time activism.

The first thing one experiences when taking on the Bush cartel is the sudden diminution of paid gigs. In Washington, this occurs when phone calls or a simple aside mentioned at a meeting results in editors or executive directors no longer being interested in a freelance journalist's stories and other services, such as advisory board memberships with non-profit organizations. That results in tightening the belt financially and literally living on $15 a day (not counting rent, which is sky high in the DC area).

Of course, it helps to live in a bargain (for DC anyway) 439 square foot efficiency apartment across the Potomac in Arlington, Virginia, when operating a shoestring-budget political resistance movement against the most dangerous president in American history. Most groups with lofty or more realistic political goals, depending on how much money they have, locate their offices on Pennsylvania Avenue east of the U.S. Capitol if they are on a small budget, or near the White House if they are raking in premium dollars in support.

In any event, 439 square feet is luxurious condo living compared to the 64 square foot prison cell where Nelson Mandela spent much of his life in Robben Island's notorious detention facility for political prisoners. And 439 square feet is immense when stacked up against the broom closet-sized cells where prisoners of the East German Stasi spent months and years in confinement.

This book contains excerpts of articles written by the author from the confines of the 439 square foot center of rebellion 4.28 miles from the White House. With the so-called mainstream media not only in the hip pocket of the Bush administration but actually embedding its journalists in the military, the hunger for independent news and views from Washington was almost without precedent in recent history. The haughty corporate media considered any journalism not printed on the pages of the *Washington Post* or *New York Times,* or emanating from the infotainment cable "news" channels, to be within the realm of "conspiracy theories" and unprofessional journalism.

The criticisms of Web-based journalism represent the death rattles from a dying media. Newspapers and the 24-hour "news channels" have been losing market share to the Internet.

For whatever reasons, the corporate media have not seen the steady drift towards fascism in the United States and around the world. Seemingly endless wars based on lies, fraudulent and "engineered" elections, as well as corruption on a scale that makes Watergate look like a misdemeanor, are consistently ignored by the corporate media.

However, the Internet, ironically developed by the U.S. defense industry to provide continual packet switch communications in the event of a nuclear war, became an effective bulwark against the Bush administration's attempt to censor the news and lure the American public into a managed perception of reality as defined by administration propagandists.

I wrote the following on July 4, 2003, deep in the dark days of the Bush regime:

Amid the fireworks, parades, Wal-Mart sales, professional sporting events, and other commercialized and phony tributes to what was once a holiday celebrated not only across America but around the world, Americans have very little to be proud of.

With a President whose lack of mental acuity would qualify him as mentally handicapped under the provisions of the Americans with Disabilities Act of 1990—signed by Bush 41—the system of U.S. constitutional government and international comity is unraveling at the seams.

An elite group of neo-fascists in Washington, London, Canberra, Rome, Jerusalem, and Madrid are seeking to return independent nation states to colonialism. Republicans in the U.S. Congress and Texas are seeking to disenfranchise hundreds of thousands of African-Americans and other minorities by redistricting them into Bantustan-like congressional districts. Religious kooks like Senate Majority Leader Bill Frist and Pennsylvania Republican Senator Rick Santorum want a constitutional amendment to ban gay marriage. Add that to the proposed amendment to make illegal the burning of cheap, Chinese prison-made American flags and one can begin to see the end of sane government as we have known it.

Three and a half years later, Bush was on the ropes politically, a wounded but dangerous lame duck. And Frist and Santorum were gone from the Senate. In the dark days of 2003, no one could have predicted the demise of the Senate Majority Leader and his Whip. But an angry American public spoke loudly in 2006 — Frist's 2008 presidential ambitions were in tatters, and he withdrew from the race, while Santorum was roundly defeated for re-election, and relegated to mouthing nonsensical talking points on Fox News.

After the election, the purge of the arch-neocons began. The first to go was Defense Secretary Donald Rumsfeld followed by U.S. ambassador to the UN John Bolton. By May, World Bank president Paul Wolfowitz was fired over a gal-pal scandal. Vice President Dick Cheney's former Chief of Staff I. Lewis "Scooter" Libby had been convicted of perjury and obstruction of justice, though his prison sentence was later commuted by President Bush. However, with Cheney still in place, neocon influence still weighed heavily on Bush administration actions, especially in foreign policy.

This book steps through the good and bad days of the Bush regime from the vantage point of a small but determined group of political dissenters and supporters of a free press in the nation's capital. These unsung heroes came from all age groups, backgrounds, religions, races, and even political bent. They were old friends and new. There were officer and enlisted military veterans like Steve C., Steve M., Greg, Tim, Ron L., John H., and Ron F. Tassi. Fellow journalists like John C., John P., George F. Alan, Joe, Andy, Len, Jim, Ed, Gus, Kas and Yoichi helped with their support and encouragement.

Many of my closest friends helped me start the WayneMadsenReport.com in May 2005. WMR was designed to chisel through the wall of disinformation and non-news built around Washington, DC by the Bush administration, their "perception managers" in the corporate media, and special interests, and convey to the rest of the nation and the world, in a manner copied from Drew Pearson's and Jack Anderson's "Washington Merry Go-Round," unvarnished news and opinions from the nation's capital. It is never easy to invent a new mousetrap, but by mid-2007, WMR had survived and was gaining readership around the nation and the world.

There were pals from times and occupations past: Duane, Juhani, Dave H., Tom, Jeff, Lynn, and Craig. From Capitol Hill, there was Jim, Kathie, and Representative Cynthia McKinney. I cannot fail to mention a former U.S. Senator and a federal judge. And last but not least, there were the morale builders, the psychologist-bartenders who could help put things into perspective with the suitable drink for the right occasion. Thank you Buzz, Casey, Mike, Jack, and Rich.

Many in the new crop of journalists in Washington, DC consider journalism to be gabbing on their phones from their office suites to friends and sources and then surfing the Internet. In fact, journalism in the nation's capital still consists of making personal contacts and developing sources without the threat of electronic eavesdropping. I have met with sources in wooded forests, on baseball fields surrounded by the chain link fences of backstops, in museums, coffee shops, and bars. Especially bars. President Gerald Ford once commented that he didn't understand why reporters were always making fun of his famous pratfalls, adding, "Everyone knows reporters get all their exercise from sitting on bar stools." In fact, what may be lost in exercise opportunities is often more than compensated by valuable information.

I would be remiss if I did not mention the bravery and decency of the many truth-tellers, sometimes called "whistle-blowers," all of whom paid heavy prices for their veracity and tenacity. A final day of reckoning for the neocons will prove all of these truth-tellers correct — "Dean" of whistle-blowers Ernie Fitzgerald, Joe Wilson, Sibel Edmonds, Greg Ford, Russ Tice, Ken Ford, Jr., Frank Grevil, Iqbal Hakim, Dr. David Kelly, Tony Shaffer, Jill Simpson, Bunnatine Greenhouse, General Janis Karpinski and so many others. One day they will be all be vindicated and the neocon liars will pay dearly.

Hopefully, the lessons learned in Washington in the first decade of the 21st century can be used in the future whenever any similar menace looms over a democratic society.

And it must also be stated that in the summer of 2007, the United States was not yet out of perilous territory. The Democratic-controlled Congress was dragging its feet on taking severe actions against the Bush regime, even in the face of overwhelming evidence that George W. Bush, Dick Cheney, Alberto Gonzales, Karl Rove, and others had systematically violated the Constitution and a number of laws. Many wondered if the Democratic Congress was acting as an unindicted co-conspirator in failing to bring about the impeachment of the President and Vice President.

However, the best weapon against fascists and neocons is the truth. This book provides the history of one small effort to disseminate the truth and shows how accurate information is anathema to the corporate elitists and their political drones.

The last seven years of battle against the Bush regime and the corporate-controlled media sometimes seems like a grotesque nightmare. However, it has been a real battle and not an experience prone to exaggeration or the imagination. For one independent journalist, the battle was waged on a shoestring budget with the support of a few dedicated and like-minded friends from different backgrounds and walks of life.

And yes, some battles can be fought on $15 a day.

Chapter 1

The Firewall Against Bush

*You're putting out stuff that is unbelievable, George, and it's got to stop...
I don't know if you can understand this, George, but that really hurt. You
should be ashamed. You should be ashamed.*
— John McCain to George W. Bush , February 16, 2000

The experience of working with a then-maverick Republican
to deny another Bush residency in the White House was
a lesson in "Dr. Jekyll and Mr. Hyde politics." Senator
John Sidney McCain, Vietnam War prisoner-of-war icon and so-
called GOP maverick, radically changed from 2000 to 2007. The
McCain of 2007 was nothing more than a sycophantic George
W. Bush apologist for all the failed neoconservative policies that
dragged the United States into one of the worst military debacles
in its history.

However, in the election campaign of 2000, McCain was seen
as the only realistic "firewall" to prevent George W. Bush from
being anointed as the Republican candidate. For a Bush to claim
the nomination is to place him three-quarters of the way to the
White House, such is the power that this political family exercises
over the American body politic.

Many of the McCain volunteers were dedicated to denying
Bush a run for the White House. Some had worked in the H.
Ross Perot campaign in 1992, a political movement that almost
propelled the Texas billionaire into the White House as the first
independent President of the United States. Others recalled the
lackluster one-term presidency of George H.W. Bush and his
being up to his ears in the Iran-Contra scandal. They wanted

no part of another Bush administration. Moderate-to-liberal Republicans, independents, and Democrats all banded together in 2000 to ensure McCain was the GOP candidate. A defeat for George W. Bush would be a defeat for the Bush family — a signal that America was casting a vote of no confidence in the Bushes and everything they stood for — political power, greed, political dirty tricks, intelligence connections, and business fraud.

In 2000, McCain spoke as a person who was out to cleanse Washington, DC of its lobbyists and other power brokers who pushed their agendas through Congress and the White House as returns for large political donations. It was something I had witnessed in my battles during the 1990s with the Clinton administration over the privacy issue.

As much as the right-wing Republicans despised Clinton, he delivered on so many GOP key issues it could be said that he was the one of the best Republican presidents they ever had. On the North American Free Trade Agreement (NAFTA), the Telecommunications Reform Act, the Communications Assistance to Law Enforcement Act (CALEA), and other business-friendly, pro-surveillance and anti-labor policies, Clinton worked with the GOP Congress to sign the pro-Big Business bills into law.

McCain was right in 2000 about the influence of lobbyists on public policy. I had seen it firsthand in my work with the Electronic Privacy Information Center (EPIC) in pointing out how the Clinton administration was selling out the privacy interests of the American people to industry lobbyists. I wrote about this duplicity on the part of Clinton in 2000:

> Polls now show, more than ever before, that Americans are concerned about personal privacy. Internet surfers are leaving electronic trails of digital data about their buying, travel, reading, and sexual habits that circling bands of direct marketing vultures are eager to pick apart and consume. The Clinton administration walks and talks like born-again privacy advocates. However, when one peers under the rock that the administration claims to be its

"progressive" privacy policy, the vermin and other bottom feeders readily become apparent.

One major personal data collector is Acxiom. It is a huge data mining company that has amassed 20 million unlisted consumer phone numbers and routinely sells them to direct marketers. As a personal data reseller, Acxiom combines the phone numbers with other personal data culled from sources like the Internet. The result is an electronic dossier, undreamed of by George Orwell, being available to nosy telemarketers.

Acxiom is headquartered in Conway, Arkansas. After seven years of dealing with various Arkansas swindlers, rubes, and political shysters who descended upon the nation's capital after Clinton's election, one has to be a bit inquisitive about such a firm's link to the administration's policy-making machine.

Founded in 1975, Acxiom now maintains one of the world's largest reservoirs of personal information. Acxiom's chief executive officer is 55-year-old Charles Morgan, a bona fide "Friend of Bill." Shortly after Clinton's election in 1992, Morgan told the Direct Marketing Association's trade periodical *DM News* that Clinton would be a good friend of the direct marketing industry. He said Clinton "has been a strong supporter of our company and is a very strong proponent of companies like ours, which are information-based, and I would perceive him to be even-handed and rational about our industry." Morgan, who had been appointed to a number of Arkansas state commissions by then-governor Clinton, has advised Clinton on a number of issues relating to the direct marketing industry. None of this advice has been good for the cause of privacy in the United States.

Although Morgan was thankfully not named Chairman of the Federal Trade Commission (FTC), his advice to Clinton has been extremely apparent. Direct marketing industry self-regulation has been a cornerstone of the Clinton administration, even in the face of overwhelming evidence that this policy does not work. However, the FTC continues to insist that industry can police itself. Their stance is supported by a number of industry shills who have wormed their way into administration positions, including in the White House. Charles Morgan and people like him have been elated over Clinton's laissez-faire attitude on consumer privacy. It is noteworthy that this policy has resulted in threats of a data embargo being imposed by the more privacy-conscious Europeans against the United States. In reaction, the Clinton administration has acted as a virtual lobbyist for the direct marketing industry in blocking

Europe's attempts to protect its citizens' personal information from the data vultures in the United States. Taxpayers' money has been used by a traveling band of Commerce Department officials to strong-arm politicians and bureaucrats in Brussels, Berlin, Paris, The Hague, London, Madrid, Lisbon, Helsinki, Rome, and Copenhagen. Their efforts have largely failed.

During the changeover from Bush to Clinton in 1992, the Direct Marketing Association (of which Acxiom has always been a major player) was actually involved with Clinton's presidential transition team. In the lead-up to Clinton's inauguration, the DMA noted Clinton's long association with direct mailing campaigns in Arkansas. It is worthwhile to note that these campaigns included targeting investors with solicitations to invest in retirement properties in places like Whitewater and Castle Grande. After millions of dollars of retirement nest eggs were bilked by Mr. and Mrs. Clinton, they moved to Washington after a successful political campaign that relied heavily on direct marketing.

It is worth judging a policy-maker like Clinton by examining the friends he keeps. In Arkansas, Morgan started a group called the "Good Suit Club," a loose-knit association of business people dedicated to public-private partnerships to better education and jobs growth. Morgan and his friends supported a number of Governor Clinton's initiatives. This was just the kind of group both Clintons favored — a nebulous group supporting an obscure set of principles. The "Good Suiters" must have looked like an Arkansas version of the present "Third Way" club of Clinton, Tony Blair, and Gerhard Schroeder. Morgan's "Good Suits" also included Jackson Stephens, the chairman of Stephens Inc., an investor in Little Rock's Worthen Bank along with the now infamous Riadys of Indonesia. Add to the club Craig T. Smith, who would later become Clinton's White House political director at the height of the Lewinsky scandal. Smith later chaired the Washington-based and direct mail-intensive Gore 2000 campaign until the Vice President moved his headquarters to Nashville in October 1999.

The FTC and Federal Communications Commission have consistently pointed out that Acxiom's compilation and trafficking in unlisted phone numbers is not illegal. Knowing of the close ties between Acxiom and Clinton this should come as no surprise. Moreover, the Acxiom-Clinton connection will be with us for a long time to come. The Little Rock downtown development authorities are currently planning two new additions to the city's vista: a brand new building that will serve as Acxiom's corporate headquarters with the nearby Clinton Presidential Library in its shadow.

Clinton's dubious ties to the direct marketing industry took on even more ominous overtones when retired NATO Commander, General Wesley Clark of Arkansas, who was considered close to the Clintons, was appointed to the board of Acxiom in December 2001, a few months after the 9/11 attacks. Later, Clark lobbied the emerging homeland security infrastructure in the Bush administration for personal data collection contracts. Clark maintained his Acxiom board membership even after he announced his plans to run for the Democratic nomination for president on September 17, 2003. Clark finally left the Acxiom board on October 9, 2003. These developments were just further indications that the Clintons were no friends to the cause of privacy and individual rights.

The "Straight Talk" Express

In retrospect, something was radically wrong with the McCain "insurgency." McCain 2000 had all the telltale signs of a rump campaign designed to give Bush a good run but not endanger the political scion. As I wrote for *CounterPunch* on February 19, 2004, the McCain "Straight Talk" campaign was doomed from the start:

> I witnessed the futility of using highly compensated political mercenaries with the McCain campaign, for which I volunteered in 2000. Many of McCain's paid staffers were long-time Republican National Committee insiders who were still chumming it up with their old friends who also happened to be working for Bush. How many campaign strategies and secrets were passed on to the Bush campaign over drinks at Washington's Congressional Club (right next door to the Republican National Committee) is anyone's guess, but the effect on the McCain campaign was disastrous.... McCain surrounded himself with the pros and rarely listened to the volunteers. McCain's insurgency

campaign collapsed and, to make matters worse, a few years later he became a virtual cheerleader for the Bush neocon platform and its worldwide hegemonic agenda.

John McCain scored an impressive 16-point victory over George W. Bush in the New Hampshire Republican primary on February 1, 2000 and stood a good chance of denying the Bush family the keys to the White House. Although it seems unbelievable in retrospect, McCain constantly spoke of Bush cronies and "dirty money" as being the driving forces behind the prodigal son's presidential campaign.

Bush's South Carolina campaign, including political dirty tricks such as push polling and the media propaganda operations of Karl Rove and a band of wealthy fundamentalist Christian and business groups, in addition to long-serving South Carolina Senator Strom Thurmond, ensured that Bush would trump McCain in the February 19 South Carolina primary. As I wrote on November 1, 2002 in *CounterPunch,*

R ove's operation proceeded to target McCain with false stories — McCain was a stoolie for his captors in the Hanoi Hilton (this from a lunatic self-promoting Vietnam "veteran"); McCain fathered a black daughter out of wedlock (a despicable reference to McCain's adopted Bangladeshi daughter); Cindy McCain's drug "abuse"; and even McCain's "homosexuality."

After Bush beat McCain 53 to 42 percent in South Carolina, all eyes landed on Michigan and another key Southern state, Virginia. In Michigan's February 22 primary, McCain turned the tables on Bush, beating him 51 to 43 percent and winning 52 of 58 delegates. McCain also swept all 30 delegates in his home state of Arizona. Although Rove, Michigan Governor John Engler, and televangelist tycoon Pat Robertson attempted to engage in South Carolina-style smear tactics against McCain in Michigan, tactics that would become known as "Swiftboating" in the 2004 campaign against Senator John Kerry, McCain was poised to trump Bush.

Virginia became an important state in the primary race. With its 56 delegates up for grabs in the winner-take-all state, Virginia was a must-win for McCain to keep his momentum going. The Bush camp knew the stakes too. It marshaled all its Christian fundie resources — from Pat Robertson's headquarters in Virginia Beach, to Jerry Falwell's seat of power in Lynchburg, to the deep-pocketed Christian Fellowship mansion in Arlington — in order to ensure a win for Bush. Oddly, up until his win in New Hampshire, McCain did not even have a state campaign operation in Virginia, even though his national campaign headquarters was located in Alexandria. The McCain advisers totally wrote off southwest Virginia where no one was assigned as campaign coordinator in Roanoke, an area that was very receptive to McCain.

Rather than using volunteers in Virginia to gather the required signatures to get on the primary ballot, McCain's professional political staff opted to use a professional petition firm. The firm used was the same one McCain's paid advisers opted to use in gathering signatures in South Carolina, another state where volunteers stood ready to gather signatures for the Arizona Republican. It was yet another example of the chasm between paid political hacks and more committed volunteers.

After his February 1 primary win in New Hampshire, McCain set up a Virginia primary campaign just weeks away from the important February 29 primary. Named as Virginia chair of the McCain campaign was Paul Galanti, McCain's fellow prisoner of war in Hanoi. The selection of Galanti, who set up shop in Richmond, would be a fateful choice for McCain.

Ron Fisher, a fellow Naval Academy Class of 1958 pal of McCain, who helped the would-be President pass his academy electrical engineering course, formed, on a shoestring budget, the Northern Virginia McCain headquarters in rented office space in the Washington, DC suburb of Falls Church. Recognizing that if McCain bested Bush in Virginia, the Bush campaign would be dealt a deadly body blow, I contacted Ron and volunteered my services. It was apparent from the start that Fisher's Northern

Virginia efforts had no support from either Galanti's group in Richmond or the national McCain campaign headquarters in Alexandria headed by two professional political insiders, Rick Davis and John Weaver. Davis was McCain's campaign manager and Weaver, a former colleague of Karl Rove, was top strategist. From the outset, the individuals who surrounded McCain appeared more interested in currying favor with those around George W. Bush than in getting their man elected. McCain campaign signs were so hard to come by in Virginia that Fisher bought $7000 in signs with local funds collected from contributions. The same signs available in nearby Alexandria were not made available to the critical northern Virginia campaign.

To make matters worse, the national McCain headquarters actually tried to shut down the northern Virginia headquarters, which was attracting moderate Republican, independent, and Democratic volunteers. Shortly after setting up the northern Virginia headquarters, Fisher heard from hundreds of people in Iowa, the earliest caucus state, volunteering to help McCain in that state. McCain's political advisers decided to sit out the Iowa caucuses, handing the state's delegates on a silver platter to Bush.

As the February 29 Virginia primary election drew nearer, the organization at McCain's Alexandria and Richmond operations became more incompetent. One day, an older man strolled into the Alexandria headquarters and offered his services to the campaign. The receptionist, the daughter of one of McCain's Naval Academy buddies, smiled and took the man's card. She told him the campaign would get back to him. Weeks went by before someone noticed the man's card on the desk. It was that of Melvin Laird, the Secretary of Defense under Richard Nixon.

Things went much differently at the northern Virginia headquarters. When he arrived to make volunteer phone calls, everyone recognized Ronald Reagan's National Security Adviser Robert McFarlane. The northern Virginia headquarters also received a call from Nebraska Senator Chuck Hagel, a McCain supporter. Hagel wanted a McCain yard sign. He could not get one from McCain's national headquarters. The northern Virginia headquarters delivered Hagel a sign that had to be paid for from local funds.

It was clear that many of McCain's top strategists pulled their punches in Virginia. The question remains as to why. It is a well-known Karl Rove tactic to infiltrate the opposition's campaign in order to weaken it from within. The McCain national and Virginia campaigns, in Alexandria and Richmond, respectively, bore all the markings of having been penetrated at high levels.

At a straw poll meeting conducted in Arlington, Virginia by the GOP, McCain was represented by his brother Joe. Joe, a tough defender of his brother, was matched up against Bush's stand-in, South Carolina's elderly senior senator Strom Thurmond. Although four GOP senators had endorsed McCain, the campaign saw no need to have one of them represent their candidate in Arlington, a part of Washington, DC's important media market.

While McCain's campaign organization in Virginia was weak at the top, that did not stop the Arizona Senator from attacking both Pat Robertson and Jerry Falwell. That should have equated to more votes from moderates in northern Virginia, the Tidewater region of Norfolk and Hampton Roads, Richmond, and Roanoke. However, McCain's advisers wrote off Roanoke, and the northern Virginia's campaign headquarters was targeted for being shut down. The fix was in.

Bush won Virginia's modified open primary, 53 percent to 44 percent for McCain. (Bush also trumped McCain in Washington State, 58 percent to 38 percent.) Although political observers claimed that McCain did not draw enough Democratic support, he won populous Arlington County, 61 percent to 39 percent for Bush. Although the religious right in Virginia turned out in force for Bush, putting him over the top, a concerted effort to get out the independent and Democratic vote in northern Virginia could have made the difference. The loss in Virginia spelled the end for McCain's presidential campaign.

On "Super Tuesday," March 7, 2000, Bush locked up the nomination with wins in California, New York, and Ohio. McCain's 20-percent-plus wins in Vermont, Massachusetts, and Rhode Island were too little, too late. McCain's two-point win over Bush in the latter's birthplace state of Connecticut was a Pyrrhic victory for McCain. Vice President Al Gore locked up the Democratic nomination the same day. McCain would no longer be the firewall to stop Bush. That mantle was now in the hands of Al Gore.

On May 9, 2000, Bush and McCain met in Pittsburgh. After the personal sparring during the primary campaign, their post-meeting news conference was awkward at best. Asked if he had any difficulty in endorsing Bush after such a nasty campaign, McCain laughingly responded, "I endorse Governor Bush. I endorse Governor Bush. I endorse Governor Bush. I endorse Governor Bush. I endorse Governor Bush."

However, what McCain was saying publicly was not what he felt privately. A close McCain relative told me that after the Pittsburgh meeting, he asked McCain how the meeting went. McCain's response was, "I'd rather spend another year in the Hanoi Hilton than fifteen more minutes with that idiot." The Bush-McCain meeting had lasted 90 minutes.

McCain's Virginia campaign chairman would surface in another presidential campaign. In 2004, Galanti was a key member of the Bush-Rove operation known as the "Swiftboaters." These veterans accused Democratic presidential candidate John Kerry of lying about his Vietnam combat record. Galanti even suggested that Kerry's post-war opposition to the Vietnam War caused Galanti to be abused as a prisoner of war in Hanoi. The charge was as false as it was laughable. McCain would become one of Bush's chief cheerleaders for the disastrous Iraq war. McCain's fellow war-cheerleader would be the man Al Gore chose as his Vice Presidential candidate, Connecticut's former Democrat, now Independent Senator, Joe Lieberman.

The "Fixer"

Bush's selection of Cheney as his running mate in 2000 was all but inevitable. In a July 22, 2000, article for the *American Reporter*, I wrote,

As the world remains transfixed on the Governor's Mansion in Austin, Texas for signs of pontifical white smoke heralding George W. Bush's selection of a running mate, it is important to reflect on the business dealings of the current front runner for the Veep job. Dick Cheney, the man Bush selected to cull the herd of potential running mates down to a single candidate, is reported to have settled on himself for the number two spot.

The Bush camp is currently touting Cheney as some sort of statesman-level icon. After serving as Secretary of Defense in Bush the Elder's administration and rescuing Kuwait's oil from the clutches of Sadaam Hussein, Cheney went on to become Chairman of the Board and Chief Executive Officer of Halliburton, Inc., an oil drilling firm based in Houston. Halliburton owns the construction firm Brown & Root Services (BRS), a company involved in a number of shady U.S. intelligence operations in Africa and elsewhere.

Considering the fact that Bush the Elder lives in Houston and was involved with both the oil business and the CIA, the Bush, Jr.-Cheney ticket must be a dream team for the old man [it would later become a nightmare], his friends in the oil industry, and the folks who work at the George Bush Intelligence Center in Langley, Virginia (formerly known as the CIA Headquarters).

The GOP has a knack for reaching into the past to find candidates to lead the nation into the future. In 1996, the party anointed Bob Dole, a veteran of World War II, to preside over a nation entering the 21st century. Now it is rumored that Governor Bush has not only reached back to his father's administration but the gloomy post-Watergate era, to pick Cheney, a former Chief of Staff for President Gerald Ford.

Cheney's links to the defense and intelligence sector are all the more suspect considering the role of Halliburton and BRS in some of the world's most volatile trouble spots. In 1998, while conducting research in Rwanda for my book, *Genocide and Covert Operations in Africa 1993-1999*, a member of a U.S. military team reported that BRS was "into some real bad shit" in that beleaguered nation.

BRS provided "infrastructure support" for the U.S. military and the Tutsi-led Rwanda Patriotic Front (RPF) government led by Major General Paul Kagame.

It was such "infrastructure support" that enabled Rwanda to launch two American-supported invasions of the neighboring Democratic Republic of the Congo. The first was aimed at unseating Zairean dictator Mobutu Sese Seko and replacing him with Laurent Kabila, while the second was directed at toppling Kabila himself. The two invasions resulted in the deaths of hundreds of thousands of Congolese and Rwandan refugees.

While special commissions appointed by the governments of Belgium, France, and the Organization of African Unity have charged their own citizens and diplomats with purposeful or tangential complicity in central Africa's turmoil, no American panel has ever probed the involvement of the U.S. government, military, and business in Africa's woes. If such a panel were to look into American misdeeds on the continent, Dick Cheney, the man in charge of Halliburton and BRS, would have to be called and asked, "What did you know about events in Rwanda and when did you know them?"

Under Cheney's leadership, BRS and Halliburton have been part and parcel of the Pentagon's operations around the world. BRS provides construction and other "infrastructure support" to U.S. troops in Bosnia, Kosovo, Macedonia, Croatia, Albania, Greece, and Hungary.

Infrastructure support for the Kosovo Liberation Army (KLA), has permitted that organized crime-influenced guerrilla force to commit heinous human rights violations against Serbs, Rom (gypsies), anti-KLA Albanians, and Slavic Muslims in the province.

Halliburton, in its "integrated solutions" for West Africa, has provided support for offshore oil drilling platforms in the Gulf of Guinea and South Atlantic Ocean. The Halliburton-Gulf-Chevron-Mobil-BP Amoco teams have ensured that ruthless dictators have either risen to or remained in power to ensure the free flow of oil from West Africa's offshore waters.

Leaders like Equatorial Guinea's Obiang Nguema Mbasogo use the revenues generated from offshore oil to enrich themselves and their families and ruthlessly suppress ethnic and political opposition. The same holds true for the regimes in Congo (Brazzaville), Gabon, Cameroon, and Angola.

BRS provides support to the oil industry in Angola's enclave of Cabinda, which is seeking independence from Angola. Supported by BRS and American mercenary companies like AirScan of Titusville, Florida and MPRI of Alexandria, Virginia, the Front for the Liberation of the Cabinda Enclave (FLEC) is kept in check, often brutally and bloodily, by the Angolan army.

So if, as all readings indicate, Governor Bush has chosen Cheney as his running mate, we can expect a Bush-Cheney administration to be a return to yesteryear. The CIA, the oil industry, and the military back together fighting a Cold War that no longer exists, with the victims being the unfortunate citizens of countries attempting to get their fair share of the wealth generated by natural resources like oil.

Cheney's practice of immersing Halliburton in all sorts of overseas politics would eventually bring his attention to another country with which he had some past experiences: Iraq.

After McCain and Lieberman turned out to be de facto Trojan horse candidates for George W. Bush, Al Gore recognized how the neoconservatives and right-wing had compromised two campaigns in 2000, his own and McCain's. The experience would change Al Gore from Democratic centrist to a tough-minded anti-war progressive.

Chapter 2

The 2000 Election Disaster

The early warning signs of 9/11: "If this were a dictatorship, it'd be a heck of a lot easier, just so long as I'm the dictator."
George W. Bush, December 18, 2000

From July 31 to August 3, 2000, the GOP met in Philadelphia to formally nominate George W. Bush and Dick Cheney to be President and Vice President, respectively. I covered the convention for an online publication, *American Reporter*. The convention featured millionaire Republicans, many of whom were oil tycoons from Texas, coming to Philadelphia on private jets, charter flights, and limousines. They were Bush's "haves and have mores" and they would dictate the immediate future of the United States of America.

While the Republican politicians and media celebrities were ensconced in Philadelphia's most posh hotels, I stayed with my sister Judy in suburban Elkins Park. The difference between Bush's "haves and have mores" and those who lived in the blighted neighborhoods of north Philadelphia, clearly seen from the SEPTA commuter train on the way to center city, could not have been more stark.

The GOP policymakers had plans for those who lived in poor neighborhoods like north Philadelphia. After they seized control of the White House, federal assistance programs would be slashed, public education would be strangled, and voting rights for minority groups would be curtailed. The Republican fat cats who met at swank parties in train dining cars brought into Philadelphia for the convention put the finishing touches on their plans for America. Those plans would turn the federal government into a wholly owned subsidiary of Big Oil, Big Banks, Big Pharma, and the military-intelligence complex.

On July 29, McCain addressed the progressive "Shadow Convention" organized by Arianna Huffington at the University of Pennsylvania. When McCain expressed his "sincere conviction" of support for Bush, the crowd of union activists, progressives, and Democrats heckled the Arizona Republican, prompting his threat to walk off the stage. After calming the crowd, Huffington convinced McCain to finish his speech. McCain's condemnation of big money in politics and promotion of campaign finance reform drew cheers from the progressive crowd.

I wrote about McCain's appearance at the Shadow Convention, having covered it for the Hollywood, California-based *American Reporter*:

Senator John McCain spoke at the opening session of the Shadow Convention last week in Philadelphia, drawing boos and catcalls as he endorsed George W. Bush. "I am obliged, not by party loyalty, but by a sincere conviction," McCain emphasized, "to support my party's nominee, Governor George Bush of Texas." His comment was met with a flurry of jeers from both liberal activists and McCain's own supporters. Of the latter, many were veterans of McCain's bruising primary campaign against Bush.

McCain's uncharacteristic praise for the Texas Governor surprised Ron Fisher, the former chairman of McCain's northern Virginia presidential campaign. Fisher, a Naval Academy classmate of McCain's, said the senator seemed to be under "a lot of pressure" from the Bush camp to enthusiastically support the Texas Governor.

In his speech, however, McCain did not once mention the name of Bush's vice presidential running mate, oil executive Dick Cheney. In the days prior to Bush's selection of Cheney, a number of GOP leaders were overtly and covertly backing McCain for the number two spot.

McCain's speech was also punctuated by heckling from an eclectic group of activists holding three-sided signs similar to those bearing the names of states and territories seen at the official conventions. The signs bore slogans like "Disaffected,"

"Disappointed," "Disrespected," and "2 Poor 4 Access." Some individuals shouted that McCain was supporting the alleged relocation of some of Arizona's Hopi and Navajos in order to allow coal mining on their reservations.

Most delegates, however, demanded that the hecklers shut up and allow McCain to finish his speech uninterrupted. Arianna Huffington, the driving force behind both the Philadelphia and Los Angeles Shadow Conventions, also came to McCain's defense, asking the more disruptive delegates to show some courtesy to the former presidential candidate. Her rebuke resulted in standing applause from a large majority of the convention in a segment not aired by most of the television networks.

McCain anchored himself to George W. Bush. Whatever else he stood for was overshadowed by his odd enthusiasm for Bush. McCain's support for Bush and neoconservatism was an anchor that, in the future, would drag McCain down with Bush as the nation began to later reject the Republican Party and neocon ideas and principles.

The GOP convention was more a coronation of Bush than a nominating event. Texan Republicans, with their trademark Stetsons, cowboy boots, and arrogant demeanor, wildly declared that Bush was some sort of savior for the nation.

I recall running into Michigan Governor John Engler on Arch Street, across from the Philadelphia Convention Center. I asked him why he, as Bush's Michigan chairman, ripped off a number of McCain delegate seats in what was supposedly a "winner-take-all" primary. He replied that some people came into Republican headquarters claiming to be McCain delegates and the Michigan Republicans had to vet their credentials. I asked him whether that decision should have been left up to the McCain campaign and not Bush partisans, including him. At that point one of his aides approached and grabbed him for a "meeting."

I also wrote about the Bush campaign's McCain delegate-grabbing tactics for the *American Reporter*:

On July 29 McCain released all of his current 170 committed delegates to Bush, having previously lost 70 additional delegate seats to Bush as a result of GOP gerrymandering. Most of these seats were lost in "winner-take-all" states that McCain won in the primaries.

Michigan, for example, was one such state. McCain won its 58 delegates. However, Governor John Engler, a Bush supporter, would not have been able to lead his state's delegation to the Philadelphia convention. So the Michigan GOP apparatchiks merely expropriated 12 of McCain's delegates.

Engler explained his delegation's situation to this reporter during a chance street encounter in downtown Philadelphia. Engler said 46 of Michigan's delegates were pledged to McCain but other McCain delegates walked into GOP offices in his state demanding seats merely because they claimed to be McCain delegates. He said the Bush campaign was justified in claiming the 12 seats because there were questions about the legitimacy of those prospective delegates.

What appears illegitimate, however, is that under GOP rules, the 12 Michigan seats were reserved for McCain supporters and not Bush loyalists. Under such a scenario, prospective McCain delegates like Ron Kinder of California could demand seats in the "winner-take-all" California delegation. Although Bush won California, McCain piled up an impressive number of votes as well.

Kinder, however, must view the GOP convention proceedings from seats reserved for non-voting guests.

Similar delegate grabbing occurred in the other states in which McCain won all the seats: Arizona, Massachusetts, Connecticut, and Rhode Island. In those states, Governors Jane Hull, Paul Celucci, John Rowland, and Lincoln Almond — all Bush supporters — simply grabbed seats away from duly elected McCain delegates, giving them to themselves and their political cronies.

The ease with which McCain's campaign folded like a cheap tent every time it was challenged by the Bush machine made me even more certain that some of McCain's people were working with the other side. But I never realized that the number one Bush strategist was someone who specialized in infiltrating the opposition's campaigns to wreak havoc. His name is Karl Rove, and the country would later learn more about this Bush "Svengali" and his tactics.

But there was one convention guest who really riled me. On August 1, McCain addressed the convention. Although the First Union Center appeared large on television, the basketball venue is surprisingly small when you are on the floor. Helping to gauge audience reaction were small binoculars I had carried with me. Sitting in the VIP box for McCain's speech were the McCain family, President Gerald Ford and his wife Betty, Bob and Elizabeth Dole, Nancy and Maureen Reagan, and George H.W. and Barbara Bush. McCain made several references to his insurgent campaign. He said, "It is easy to forget in politics where principle ends and selfishness begins. It takes leaders of courage and character to remember the difference."

Throughout the speech, McCain was applauded by everyone in the VIP box. Even George H.W. Bush applauded the man who would have denied his son the White House. I was looking at the former President and his wife through the binoculars when I noticed something I would never forget. While former President Bush was applauding one of McCain's lines, Barbara Bush reached over and grabbed his hand. Watching her lips, it was clear she said, "That's enough George."

McCain then said something that turned my stomach, "My friend, Governor Bush, believes in an America that is so much more than the sum of its divided parts.... He wants nothing to divide us into separate nations. Not our color. Not our race. Not our wealth. Not our religion. Not our politics. He wants us to live for America, as one nation, and together profess the American Creed of self-evident truths." After such a hate-filled Bush campaign, McCain's words rang hollow. Mr. Straight Talk had sold out. Little did I realize at the time, but McCain's sell-out in Philadelphia would have dramatic consequences for the future — for some teens who would later join the military, and for others, some fathers, mothers and even grandparents dying and wounded on the battlefields in Iraq and Afghanistan.

On the evening of the roll call vote for president on August 1, the GOP hoped to have Bush nominated by unanimous acclamation. It was not to be, thanks to a single McCain holdout from Massachusetts. When the roll call was held, Massachusetts recorded a single vote for McCain. It was not easy to seek out the man who refused a request by McCain's wife Cindy to vote for Bush. When I waded into the Massachusetts delegation and asked a woman sitting next to the Massachusetts sign where the person was who voted against Bush, she refused to tell me. It was clear that whoever the holdout was, the Massachusetts delegation was warned by the Bush camp not to identify the offending individual.

Thanks to someone from the nearby Utah delegation who had heard my question, the man who bucked the Bush machine and voted for McCain was pointed out to me. He was sitting alone in the Massachusetts delegation. He was Dr. Dwight Stowell, a dentist who was enthusiastic about by McCain's stand against the bewildering amount of special-interest money poured into political campaigns, he told me that he was not very popular after casting the sole vote for McCain. In fact, he said he was afraid of "being shot." I took the comment as a joke. Years later, I remembered the comment and felt in my gut that Dr. Stowell may not have been joking after all. On August 3, as the convention prepared to hear Bush's acceptance speech, I went back to the Massachusetts delegation to seek out Dr. Stowell for a comment. I could not find him. I was told he had left Philadelphia for Massachusetts after casting his vote for McCain. I had a bad feeling about his quick departure and what was going on behind the scenes with the Bush camp. A few years later, my nascent fears were realized, as the new administration continued its tradition of strong-arming and intimidation.

Thanks to the generosity of Bell South media relations director and former Associated Press managing editor Bill McCloskey, there were ample amounts of cold beer in the Bell South media tent to numb the effects of Bush's acceptance speech and McCain's sell-out to Bush. I got the distinct impression that some of the old-timers gathered in the media tent who had covered Bush's father and the scandal of Iran-Contra knew that if the junior Bush won the election, the country was in for some deep trouble. Their fears were not misplaced.

On August 4, while standing on the platform at Philadelphia's 30th Street Station to return to Washington, I noticed a couple and their two children standing in line in front of me. Examining their luggage tags I noticed their name was "Bush." I recognized the man as Marvin Bush, the youngest brother of George W. Bush. Trying to be magnanimous, I told Marvin that he must be proud to have seen his brother nominated for president the previous evening. His response? "Yeah."

This was a family that considered America to be its private domain and its people as the servants for them and their fat-cat friends. Years later, my path would somewhat cross with Marvin's again. I was the only journalist to investigate the unusual death of his maid/governess at his Alexandria, Virginia home.

I did not plan to cover the Democratic convention in Los Angeles scheduled for a few weeks later from August 14 to 17. It was too late to get a hotel room. However, as things turned out, my old friend Dave, with whom I went on a People-to-People trip to the USSR almost a decade earlier, had just relocated to Los Angeles and he had a spare room right next to the Doubletree in Westwood, a convention hotel housing the Iowa delegation that had buses going to the Staples Center, the downtown convention venue. With a discount $220 round-trip airplane ticket in hand and a free place to stay, I was on my way to the second nominating convention. It would be as disappointing as Philadelphia.

There was also something unsettling about how the two major political conventions were tied to corporate-named sports complexes: the First Union Center in Philadelphia and the Staples Center in Los Angeles. America had become a wholly-owned subsidiary of Big Business. Was the Ford Lincoln Memorial or the Microsoft Washington Monument far behind?

Vice President Al Gore had an easy time with former New Jersey Senator Bill Bradley in the primary campaign. The Al Gore of 2000 was pro-free trade and pro-military/industrial complex. Bradley ran on a traditional progressive Democratic set of principles. While many political observers saw Gore running to the center-right in the primary they expected him to run more liberal in the general election. That was until August 7, when Gore chose Connecticut Senator Joseph Lieberman, a darling of the pro-business Democratic Leadership Council (DLC) as his running mate.

Arrayed in a fenced off protest area across from the Staples Center were some of the same progressive groups that protested Bush in Philadelphia. There was a sense that both the Republicans and Democrats had sold out to the richest people in the country. The establishment by police and federal law enforcement agencies of a "First Amendment Zone" at the Democratic convention was a disturbing omen for the future.

While waiting to board buses at the Staples Center on the evening of August 14 to be taken to a California Welcome Party at Paramount Studios sponsored by Governor Gray Davis for convention delegates, guests, and media, our group was subjected to a barrage of Los Angeles cops with riot sticks. They had previously cleared the First Amendment Zone of all the protestors and decided to turn their attention toward the delegates waiting for buses. Marching in a phalanx, the cops forced everyone off the street in front of the Staples Center and onto sidewalks. The reason given was that President and Mrs. Clinton were leaving the arena for the Paramount function and the cops were clearing the area.

I found myself, along with an older gentleman, being shoved with a billy club onto the sidewalk. When we managed to get on the bus, where we waited three hours to finally arrive at the Paramount reception, we spoke to one another about the bullying treatment. The older man said he was an official guest at the convention and found the manhandling by the cops outrageous. It turned out he had been a close adviser to Pennsylvania's former Democratic Governor Milton Shapp. We both bemoaned the state of America's democracy — and this was little over a year from 9/11.

While there was hope that Gore might move back to more traditional Democratic values after defeating Bradley, Gore's support for free trade and selection of Lieberman turned off the progressive movement. On July 28, 2006, I wrote in an op-ed piece in the *Miami Herald*, "In 1988, Lieberman welcomed the support of William F. Buckley, Jr. and other staunch conservatives in his first Senate race against progressive Republican Lowell Weicker. With their aid, Lieberman barely edged the popular Weicker." The op-ed was in support of Connecticut Democratic challenger to Lieberman, Ned Lamont. Lamont defeated Lieberman in the Democratic primary only to be trounced by Lieberman in the general election with strong Republican support, including active help from the Bush White House. It was another example of Lieberman's lifelong dalliance with the GOP and conservatives.

Weicker, a liberal, Nelson Rockefeller Republican, had ruffled feathers since his condemnation of Nixon administration abuses as a member of the Senate Watergate Committee. Lieberman owed his seat to Buckley, a right-wing Republican. This same man was selected by Gore to be his running mate. On the Republican side, there were two right-wingers, George W. Bush and Dick Cheney. On the Democratic side, there was also a right-winger, Lieberman. Progressives looked at the field and shook their heads in disgust. Many political observers trumpeted Lieberman because he was the first Jewish candidate on a national ticket. However, if that was Gore's primary reason for his decision, there were other, decidedly more progressive Jewish candidates, including Minnesota's Senator Paul Wellstone and Wisconsin Senator Russ Feingold. Gore had been hoodwinked by the corporatists and the right-wing.

On the night of August 16, 2000, Lieberman delivered his acceptance speech at the Staples Center. He made a special point of mentioning John McCain's operation for skin cancer. The applause from the Democrats indicated that McCain still had some goodwill among the opposition party. However, it would soon emerge that Lieberman and McCain agreed on many more things than did Lieberman and the man at the top of his ticket, Al Gore.

Earlier, as Lieberman was wading through the crowd on the convention floor, I was caught up in a sudden mob rush. As I turned around to see what was causing the commotion, I felt a sharp elbow jab to my left kidney. I said, "Watch where the fuck you're going." Then, I realized the elbow wielder was none other than Lieberman. I stared at him and there was no "excuse me" or "I'm sorry." I wondered why Gore would put such an asshole on his ticket. The same interests who would later control the Bush White House manipulated Gore. In effect, the neocons had three loyalists on the tickets of both parties: George W. Bush, Dick Cheney, and Joe Lieberman. In case the planned 2000 vote fraud failed to materialize, Lieberman would carry their water in a Gore administration.

Little did Gore realize that his campaign manager Donna Brazile would later emerge as Lieberman's chief supporter in his 2006 Democratic Senate primary race against Gore's fellow anti-war challenger Ned Lamont, and in Lieberman's later independent challenge against Democratic Senate nominee Lamont. That would place Brazile and other top DLC colleagues on the same side as George W. Bush in supporting the pro-war Lieberman over the anti-war Lamont. The Republicans would also pull the rug out from under their own Republican candidate, Alan Schlesinger, to avidly support Lieberman in the general election.

On June 19, 2006, I was present at the Washington, DC launch of a new Web-site, thedemocraticstrategist.org. The three main Democrats who launched the new Web-site were Democratic pollster Stan Greenberg; Ruy Teixeira of the Center for American Progress; and Bill Galston of the Brookings Institution and a founder of the Third Way movement, the ideological basis for the anti-labor and anti-progressive "triangulation" policies of Bill Clinton.

The DLC slant of this new operation was best exemplified by what the speakers said about the Connecticut Democratic primary race between Lieberman and the anti-war Lamont. Greenberg confessed that he was a friend of Lieberman and was working for his re-election. Brazile also said she was a friend of Lieberman and that she considered him a "man of true principles" and her "rabbi."

The choice of Lieberman by Gore would have dire consequences in an election where some apparent voting fixes had already been set in place. A number of disenchanted Democrats would vote for Green Party candidate Ralph Nader. It would help Bush barely win with the electoral vote even though he would lose the popular vote.

Much has been written about how George W. Bush; his brother, Florida Governor Jeb Bush; Karl Rove; Florida Secretary of State Katherine Harris; and other GOP operatives criminally conspired to steal the 2000 Florida presidential election and, thus, the White House. However, little attention has been paid to the role of the news media in Bush's "Grand Theft Election" of 2000. I wrote about the media's complicity in the April 17, 2003 edition of *CounterPunch*:

> It is a sad state of affairs when a movie actor must tell a group of assembled journalists that they missed the mark on covering a huge voting scandal in Florida's 2000 presidential election. Speaking at the National Press Club on April 15, actor Tim Robbins exhorted the media to investigate why 50,000 mostly African-American voters were scrubbed from the electoral rolls before Election Day. Robbins added that there is a Pulitzer Prize out there for the journalist willing to step up and fully investigate the scandal.
>
> The voter registration scandal involved a contract awarded by then-Florida Secretary of State Katherine Harris to Data Base Technologies (DBT) Online, later a subsidiary of ChoicePoint, a firm that has given generously to Republican coffers over the years. After examining the registration files, DBT identified 173,000 ineligible voters. However, at least 50,000 voters were groundlessly dropped from the voters' rolls. So on Election Day, thousands of African-Americans, who would have voted for Al Gore, were told by Florida election officials they could not vote. It was as if Jim Crow returned to Florida after a long hiatus.
>
> After Robbins challenged the press gathered at the National Press Club to investigate the election scam in Florida, National

Press Club President Tammy Lytle, Washington Bureau Chief of the *Orlando Sentinel,* interrupted the actor: "As someone who represents a major Florida newspaper, I can tell you we looked into that." Robbins, knowing he was being fed a plethora of equine excrement, responded, "Really, I'd like to read that."

Robbins, of course, knows better. Robbins referred to the miserable status of American journalism when he cited the "Aussie rags" in the United States, a reference to Rupert Murdoch's growing and more menacing media empire. The *Orlando Sentinel* would never investigate Bush family malfeasance anywhere or anytime.

A newspaper that owes its very existence to the capital of American artificiality, Disney World, along with its gaudy central Florida clones, is hardly capable of launching a major investigation of the mass and systematic disenfranchisement of African-American voters. In fact, the *Sentinel*'s readership, locked behind their splendid little gated communities or holed up in their sterile condominiums, would not stand for the paper rocking the boat by suggesting that Jeb Bush and his purported girlfriend, Katherine Harris, criminally conspired to throw Florida's 25 electoral votes into George W. Bush's column. The *Sentinel* has shown what kind of editorial "independence" it maintains by repeatedly endorsing — election after election — George H.W., George W., and Jeb Bush.

I also wrote about the Florida election scam in the March 2002 issue of *Multinational Monitor:*

In 1998, Florida's Secretary of State Katherine Harris undertook to cleanse the state's electoral rolls of unqualified voters. The $4 million job of sifting through the rolls and purging them went to DBT Online (now known as Database Technologies), the Boca Raton, Florida-based subsidiary of Choice Point, Inc. Choice Point had originally spun off from the giant credit data firm Equifax. Using the massive criminal history, credit, motorist, insurance and other personal files amassed by its parent Choice Point and CDB Infotek, another Choice Point subsidiary, DBT determined that a number of Florida voters, mainly African-Americans, were not qualified to vote when, in fact, they were.

Those ruled ineligible to vote included 8,000 Floridians listed as felons in a Texas database. However, many of the individuals were guilty of only misdemeanors and therefore should not have been stripped of their voting rights under Florida rules.

Choice Point later admitted that it made a mistake when it provided the erroneous list from Texas to Florida. If even a small percentage of the disenfranchised African Americans had been able to vote, both the Florida election and the electoral college could have been tipped in favor of Vice President Al Gore.

November 7, 2000 began as any other presidential election day — pollsters were predicting a close election — but with Florida fixed and Ralph Nader drawing away more than expected numbers of disenchanted Democrats, the Bush camp was confident that election engineering and other malfeasance would win them the White House. I was at the National Press Club as the returns came in. As expected, Bush swept the South and picked up crucial Ohio, the prairie states, and the Rocky Mountain States. Gore took the Northeast, Upper Midwest, and Pacific coast. In the wee hours of the morning, Florida, first called for Gore, then deemed too close to call, and then given to Bush by a razor-thin margin, swung the overall win column to Bush. Little did America realize it, but it was witnessing a political coup d'etat, albeit one without tanks in the streets.

Years later, I was told by a Democratic Party and Gore campaign insider what took place that fateful election night between Bush and Gore. It will be recalled that when Florida was declared for Bush after having been declared for Gore, the Vice President, who was at his Nashville, Tennessee campaign headquarters, phoned Bush at his hotel venue in Houston and conceded. Just prior to Gore making a public concession, the returns showed Florida as being too close to call — a mere 600 votes separated Bush and Gore in Florida — and Gore phoned Bush back. Bush responded to Gore, "Let me make sure if I understand. You're calling me back to retract your concession?"

Reports at the time stated that Bush was "not happy" to receive Gore's phone call. However, according to Democratic Party sources who were with Gore in Nashville and could hear Bush on the phone, the conversation became menacing towards Gore and his family. In what amounted to a tantrum, Bush reportedly called

Gore a "son of a bitch," spoke about the presidency as being part of Bush's "legacy," and made veiled threats against Gore and his family. Bush victory celebrations were already underway at the Houston hotel and at the Governor's Mansion in Austin at the time the phone calls were made.

Gore challenged the election results in Florida. What would follow would be a series of court rulings that would eventually end up in the U.S. Supreme Court, a court that would appoint Bush President in a 5-4 decision. All the time, Bush family cronies from all over the country descended on Florida to threaten, cajole, and engage in the political chicanery that is the hallmark of Bush politics.

Bush, ever cocky, began making inane and painful comments I later called "POTUSoids" in a November 21, 2001 Internet article:

POTUSoids result in the painful burning of the ears and incessant itching of the eyes every time the current POTUS of POSTCON America speaks. POTUS is Secret Service-speak for "President of the United States." POSTCON America is privacy-speak for "post-Constitutional America" — a state that has actually existed since December 12, when the U.S. Supreme Court in Bush v. Gore voted 5-4 to "select" the current POTUS. It has been downhill ever since for the country and its constitutional form of government.

Let's review some more severe POTUSoid flareups:

On December 18, six days after the "Supremes" selected POTUS, Bush said the following about his new job after meeting with the top four congressional leaders:

I told all four that there are going to be some times where we don't agree with each other, but that's OK. If this were a dictatorship, it would be a heck of a lot easier — just so long as I'm the dictator.

Then this POTUSoid is repeated on July 27, 2001 months after being sworn in:

A dictatorship would be a heck of a lot easier, there's no question about it.

Then this irritating POTUSoid from July 22, 2001:

I know what I believe. I will continue to articulate what I believe and what I believe — I believe what I believe is right.

Another pre-selection POTUSoid from the campaign:
It's going to require numerous IRA agents.

That October 10, 2000 POTUSoid was made about almost-POTUS Gore's tax plan. Now, if I'm not mistaken, the IRA — Irish Republican Army — was considered a terrorist group. Doesn't that make them "evil ones"? Why would evil ones need to collect taxes?

Another pre-selection POTUSoid made in Saginaw, Michigan:
I know the human being and fish can coexist peacefully.

Wait a minute! What about the sharks that killed and injured all those swimmers this past summer? They sound a hell of a lot like evildoers to me! Why do 22 terrorist groups rate an evil rating while those damned sharks get a free pass? A real head scratching POTUSoid there.

Here's another POTUSoid that actually results in gastric reflux:
Well, I think if you say you're going to do something and don't do it, that's trustworthiness.

That's from August 30, 2000, but consider that POTUS swore the following oath on the Bible on January 20, 2001: "I, George Walker Bush, do solemnly swear that I will faithfully execute the office of President of the United States, and I will to the best of my ability, preserve, protect, and defend the Constitution of the United States."

That's not trustworthiness. Hell, that could be an evil doer's act. I wonder what St. John of Ashcroft of the Pentecostal Church of our system of questionable justice might say? (Missouri Senator John Ashcroft, defeated for reelection by the deceased Governor Mel Carnahan, killed in a plane crash just prior to the 2000 election, would become Bush's Attorney General).

An August 3, 2001 Crawford, Texas POTUSoid:
My administration has been calling upon all the leaders in the — in the Middle East to do everything they can to stop the violence, to tell the different parties involved that peace will never happen.

Sounds like at least one of them understood that message loud and clear!

Then there are written POTUSoids, like POTUS's new executive order dealing with the release of papers of past presidents:
absent compelling circumstances the incumbent president may independently order the archivist to withhold privileged records.

And that's what POTUS did in signing Executive Order 13233 — which bars the release of 68,000 pages of Reagan administration documents already cleared for release by the Reagan Library. Well, this POTUS sure wouldn't want us all to find out about the slimy things Daddy POTUS did back in the 1980s with Noriega, Bank of Credit and Commerce International (aka, Bank of Crooks and Criminals International), Iran-Contra, and even providing covert CIA assistance to people like that major-league evil doer Osama bin Laden. No, we don't want to know any of that stuff — and we won't in POSTCON America.

Sometimes a POTUSoid can be quite close and personal as was this one experienced by Russian President Vladimir Putin in Slovenia on July 23, 2001:

You saw the President yesterday. I thought he was very forward-leaning, as they say in diplomatic nuanced circles.

Probably Putin was "leaning forward" instead of "forward leaning" — thinking to himself, "How could this dumbshitsky have ever been elected President of the United States?"

A "L'etat c'est moi" POTUSoid from July 2, 2001:

Well, it's an unimaginable honor to be the President during the Fourth of July of this country. It means what these words say, for starters. The great inalienable rights of our country. We're blessed with such values in America. And I — it's — I'm a proud man to be the nation based upon such wonderful values.

Well, what POTUS wants, POTUS gets! His values, his nation. What are the current immigration rules for Australia?

This POTUSoid was extremely painful to the people over at the National Geographic Society:

We spent a lot of time talking about Africa, as we should. Africa is a nation that suffers from incredible disease.

This POTUSoid was very painful to the eyes more than the ears:

There's no such thing as legacies. At least, there is a legacy, but I'll never see it.

No, but we will. For many, many years to come.

How about this POTUSoid from before selection?:

I know how hard it is for you to put food on your family.

Well, your Daddy knows something about that and the Prime Minister of Japan, now doesn't he?

Here's a POTUSoid that hurts but also triggers laughter:

Rarely is the question asked: is our children learning?
Yep.

And the POTUSoid that eats right down to one's gall bladder:
The great thing about America is everybody should vote.
Right... and they should all be counted!

By the summer of 2001, Bush's poll numbers were dropping like a lead weight. In fact, with congressional elections due in 2002, the Democrats were confident that they would regain control of the Congress and Bush would become a failed one-term president like his father. However, there were other forces at work that would ensure Bush's re-election and would prop him up during his first term as the most powerful president in the history of the nation.

The Houses of Bush and Clinton: Tied together by an umbilical oil pipeline

During the final days of the Clinton administration an event took place that would show the links between the Houses of Bush and Clinton. It was Clinton's pardon of American financier and international fugitive Marc Rich. The deal was worked out by Rich's attorney, a man who would later come to symbolize the corruption of the Bush administration — I. Lewis "Scooter" Libby. I wrote about Clinton's pardon in early 2001 and the links this had with Bush's agenda:

> The brouhaha concerning ex-President Clinton's apparent pardons-for-cash scandal is only the tip of an iceberg that reveals the former First Family as a clan rubbing shoulders and accepting money from an international network of Russian mobsters, KGB operatives, agents of influence for the Mossad, and questionable international businessmen. And when one begins to peer deeply into the Clinton family's connections to their wealthy financiers, images of the Bush family and their associates also soon come into focus.

Senator Hillary Clinton's brother Hugh Rodham received some $400,000 for arranging last minute presidential pardons for two ex-convicts. However, some of Hugh's past business dealings have also placed him in the company of criminals. Two years ago, Hugh and his brother Tony traveled to the small autonomous Georgian republic of Ajaria, nestled on the Black Sea between Turkey and Russia. The potential for making quick profits in the Caucasus region, a hotbed of organized crime activity, seemed to entrance the "Brothers Rodham." Ajaria is a virtual personal fiefdom of Aslan Abashidze, an important rival of Georgian President Eduard Shevardnadze.

Abashidze has a fondness for fast boats — a must for any serious smuggler, especially when considering Ajaria's seldom patrolled coastline. After having received the Rodham boys in his presidential palace, Abashidze convinced them they should invest in a cartel to corner the hazelnut market. U.S. intelligence officials later succeeded in convincing Clinton to warn his brothers-in-law away from the deal.

Any joint venture involving Abashidze would have likely also involved his close friend Grigori Loutchansky, a Georgian-born Israeli citizen who spent most of his adulthood in Riga, Latvia and is now influential in Ukraine. He heads up the Austrian-based firm Nordex, a company involved in imports and exports of things like oil, natural resources like aluminum, and, allegedly, nuclear weapons materials. Loutchansky was also a key player in Motorola's $5 billion Iridium low-earth orbit satellite network. Iridium has now gone bankrupt and there are plans afoot to de-orbit the communications satellites, sending them into a trajectory that will char them to a crisp in Earth's atmosphere. Loutchansky and Nordex are thought by many people, including former U.S. National Security Adviser Sandy Berger and former CIA Director John Deutch, of being involved in more suspicious activities involving Russian crime syndicates. Between the time the Soviet Union began to crumble and the Russian Federation emerged, Marc Rich and Loutchansky made billions of dollars from selling Russian oil and aluminum from faltering Soviet-era and local mafia-controlled state enterprises to the West.

Therefore, it is no surprise that Loutchansky is on an official watch list maintained by the U.S. State Department. That means he is ineligible to get a U.S. visa. However, that did not stop him from entering the United States back in 1993 to attend a White house dinner with Bill Clinton, and getting a private two-minute meeting. Loutchansky's invitation was arranged by a New York real estate developer and syndicated radio talk show host named Sam Domb, who had contributed $168,000 to the Democrats. Apparently, Loutchansky's own deep pockets, estimated to be worth in excess of $2 billion, snagged him an invitation to return to Washington in 1995 to attend a fundraiser with Clinton at the posh Hay Adams Hotel. However, Loutchansky decided to pass up that particular soiree.

Loutchansky also had another chum who had donated a large sum of money to the Democrats. He is Roger Tamraz, a wealthy Lebanese-American who reportedly forked over $300,000 to the Democrats in 1995 and 1996. He apparently promised another $400,000. That sort of money got him six separate meetings with Clinton. Tamraz's big interest was getting Clinton's support for the construction of an oil pipeline from Azerbaijan to Turkey. Tamraz also had interesting links to some former KGB security officers for President Boris Yeltsin. It seems that Clinton was not the only leader fishing for campaign contributions. According to the *Washington Post*, the KGB officers told Tamraz in Milan that they could use $100 million cash on the barrelhead for Yeltsin's own presidential campaign.

Construction of trans-Caucasus oil pipelines also involved a wealthy Chechen businessman named Khozhakhmed Nukhayev. Rumored to be one of the most influential Chechen mafia bosses, Nukhayev became Vice Prime Minister in the Chechen government of Zemlikan Yandarbiyev following the April 1996 missile-attack assassination of President Dzhokar Dudayev — an assassination involving a complicated electronic pinpointing process thought to be impossible without the support of U.S. communications spy satellites.

After the Yandarbiyev government fell, Nukhayev became president of the US-Caucasus Chamber of Commerce, which established its headquarters in Washington. Nukhayev spent some time in Houston talking to oil executives. Interestingly, the Vice President of the Chamber was Fred Bush, a close friend of former President George Bush but no relation to the ex-President or his family. The big bankroller behind the Chamber was none other than the Saudi billionaire Adnan Khashoggi, who had proven himself an invaluable asset to the United States during the Iran-Contra affair.

One of the major deals the US-Caucasus Chamber of Commerce was pushing for was the construction of a pipeline between Baku, Azerbaijan to Ceyhan, Turkey. This had the support of Nukhayev, Khashoggi, and Tamraz. BP-Amoco, Bechtel, Exxon Mobil and Vice

President Dick Cheney's old firm, Halliburton, are principal players in the deal. Another principal interlocutor for the Azerbaijani pipelines was the US-Azerbaijan Chamber of Commerce. It was, until recently, headed by Richard Armitage, now Colin Powell's number two man at the State Department. Armitage, who once represented the interests of Texaco, was assisted in heading the Chamber by Reza Vaziri of R.V. Investments. A principal of that firm is former Bush Chief of Staff John Sununu. R.V. Investments has interest in a lucrative gold mine in Azerbaijan.

Cheney's Chief of Staff, Lewis "Scooter" Libby, Jr., won a libel suit on behalf of Armitage. The suit was filed against a book author who contended that Armitage, while stationed in Southeast Asia during the Vietnam War, was involved with Golden Triangle drug baron Khun Sa in drug trafficking.

The counsel for Armitage's US-Azeri Chamber was none other than the son of former Secretary of State James Baker. And Libby's name appeared in a *New York Times* op-ed piece by former President Clinton, who ratted him out as a former lawyer for Marc Rich. From e-mail turned over to the House Government Reform Committee, it appears that Libby, who was with the law firm Dechert LLP, had more than a cursory attorney-client relationship with Rich. In fact, Cheney's Chief of Staff represented Rich for eight years. No wonder Mary Matalin, Cheney's Communications Director, said she wants to move forward and not look back.

A December 26, 2000, e-mail from former Clinton counsel and Rich attorney Jack Quinn to Robert Fink, another Rich attorney with the firm Piper, Marbury, Rudnick, & Wolfe, reads as follows: "Moreover, based on your reaction to the possibility of raising this with Scooter [Lewis Libby], and based on my conversation with Mike Green on how Scooter is likely to feel compelled to react, and the fact that Scooter already knows what we are doing [the pardon] and could easily volunteer if he saw a way to be helpful, I would pass on that as well."

Yes, John McCain was right when he spoke of the vicious cycle of Washington influence peddlers. When you peel away the Clinton layers in the onion you discover the Bush layers. A list of GOP doyens who are involved with Azerbaijani oil and the pipeline reads like a "Who's Who" of the Republican Party — in addition to Sununu, there is former Reagan aid Michael Deaver, former Secretaries of State Henry Kissinger and Lawrence Eagleburger, former Senator (and friend of Marc Rich) and Reagan Chief of Staff Howard Baker — and just for good measure, two Democrats who have politically supported Republican administrations: former U.S. ambassador to Moscow Robert Strauss and Carter National Security Adviser Zbigniew Brzezinski.

Another proposed Azeri pipeline would connect Baku to the Ajarian port of Batumi, much to the delight of Abashidze and Loutchansky. The former would receive payments from the pipeline to enrich him while the latter could boast to his Ukrainian friends in the government in Kiev that they would be guaranteed an endless supply of Azerbaijani crude by Black Sea tankers from Batumi.

Perhaps the involvement of so many friends of Bush in the Caucasus intrigue was one reason President George W. Bush wants to "move on" from the Clinton pardon scandal. If one starts to investigate all the ties of the Clintons and Rodhams to Marc Rich and his colleagues in the Caucasus oil and import-export business, major connections to Bush loyalists begin to appear. The role of the Central Intelligence Agency is also not to be underestimated. The agency, which is now headquartered in the "George Bush Center for Intelligence" in Langley, Virginia, apparently held a briefing in 1997 attended by former Secretary of State Madeleine Albright. A secret CIA team had recently traveled through Chechnya, Azerbaijan, Dagestan, Georgia, Ajaria, Ingushetia, Turkmenistan, and Kazakhstan disguised as oil engineers. Their finding was that the Caucusus and surrounding regions were number one priorities for the United States.

As with past exploits of the CIA, it does not matter if organized crime is involved in something that involves a high priority for the U.S. intelligence community: cooperation will occur. It is no wonder, therefore, that Clinton's defenders cite nebulous "national security interests" in his pardon of Marc Rich. If George H.W. Bush had been re-elected in 1992, he almost most certainly would have used similar reasons for pardoning Rich upon leaving office in 1997. After all, Rich was a man Bush could respect, a man who, when oil was being sold on the international market for $140 a ton, found Russian suppliers willing to sell it at $5 a ton. Knowing the high stakes involved with Caspian region oil, the reasons Rich and his friends can curry favor with the Clintons and the Bushes are, simply stated, oil, oil, and oil.

The Baku-Ceyhan pipeline received the personal endorsement of both Bill Clinton and Madeleine Albright. It was a critical project for Turkey, which saw the Ceyhan terminal as bringing a number of jobs to the impoverished region of Turkey near the Syrian border.

And Turkey had a powerful new ally in Israel. Marc Rich, who has now been revealed as an agent of influence for the Israeli Mossad, had a great deal of expertise in oil. He brokered the sale of Russian oil from mafia-tainted Russian corporations. A seasoned sanction-buster, Rich sold Iranian oil to Israel and Nigerian and Iraqi oil to South Africa. He dealt with two other countries subject to United Nations sanctions: Libya, and Serbia. The fugitive American resident of Switzerland also carried both a Spanish and Israeli passport. Several international law enforcement experts agree that almost every major Russian mafia boss now carries an Israeli passport.

Rich's ex-wife Denise had the perfect entrée to the Clinton administration. She had donated about $1 million to the Democrats, a fact that not only would lead Clinton to granting a pardon to Marc Rich but would present his and his colleague's plans for exploiting the Caucasus oil in a favorable light.

With the United States firmly supporting the Caucasus chieftains in their pipeline project, the millions lavished on the Clintons turned out to be well worth their investment. It also turns out that Hillary's brothers were not just working for hazelnuts. And in the end, the interests of the oil companies — with their well-worn connections to Bush and Clinton, Russian organized crime, and the intelligence services of the United States, Russia, and Israel — will prevail.

I was present at Bush's inauguration on January 20, 2001. It was a cold and dark day, with an icy rain pelting the onlookers. On the inaugural stage were George W. Bush; his father George H.W. Bush, outgoing president Bill Clinton, and Dick Cheney. Vice President Al Gore seemed to be the only guy outside of the "club" — a syndicate that stretched from Texas through Arkansas and into Washington, DC to points abroad, including Saudi Arabia, Switzerland, Israel, and other areas that had attracted the interests of multinational bad actors.

The protestors were out in force. Some managed to hit Bush's limousine with oranges and eggs. There was a sense that Bush and his gang would bring ruin to the nation. They could not have possibly foreseen how right they would be nine months later on one bright and sunny morning in New York, northern Virginia, and rural western Pennsylvania.

Later in the day, I was riding the Washington Metro system as tuxedoed Republican men wearing cowboy boots and their expensively-coiffed wives in their evening gowns began boarding the trains to attend various inaugural balls around the city. I heard more than one of these well-heeled Republicans pronounce in bellowing voices, "This is our town now." I knew then there would soon be trouble, though I could not fathom what this new administration, which took power in an electoral coup, had in mind for the United States. On that dismally gray January evening, a bitterly cold and damp winter wind blew through Washington — it was a definite omen of bad times on their way.

**EMBASSY OF
THE STATE OF KUWAIT
ISLAMABAD — PAKISTAN**

بسم الله الرحمن الرحيم

سفارة دولة الكويت
اسلام آباد — باكستان

8th August, 1993

<u>TO WHOM IT MAY CONCERN</u>

It gives me great pleasure to certify that Lajnat Al-Dawa Al-Islamiah (I.D.I.) is a Kuwait based charitable relief organization.

It has performed a tremenduos work by giving Free of Cost humanitarian assistance to the Afghan Refugees in their hour of trial and tribulation. Because of their dedication and selfless devotion for the welfare of the humanity, the people of Kuwait in general and the philanthropists in particular have reposed great confidence in this organization by making substantial contributions.

It also gives me pleasure to write that this organization responded immediately at the call of the Government of Pakistan for assisting them in accommodating the Afghan Refugees by offering humanitarian assistance to them and to the destitutes in large.

KUWAIT EMBASSY

Post Desert Storm Kuwaiti embassy letter vouching for terrorism-connected "charity."

Chapter 3

9/11, the Patriot Act
&
Our New Fascist Regime

*The Patriot Act has increased the flow of information within our government
and it has helped break up terrorist cells in the United States of America.
And the United States Congress was right to renew the terrorist act — the
Patriot Act.*

—George W. Bush, Washington, D.C. , September. 7, 2006

Without the attacks of 9/11, there would have been no Patriot Act, no Iraq War, no trashing of the United Nations, no upending of the U.S. intelligence community, no Department of Homeland Security, and no second administration for George W. Bush and Dick Cheney. Moreover, there would have been no critical role in government or policy making for those who benefited most from 9/11, those who were charter members of Project for the New American Century and who pined for a "new Pearl Harbor": Donald Rumsfeld, Paul Wolfowitz, I. Lewis "Scooter" Libby, Zalmay Khalilzad, Richard Perle, William Bennett, and Cheney himself.

The Patriot Act "wish list" — a smorgasbord of fascist programs

There is no doubt that the Patriot Act represented a wish list for the most right-wing elements in America's legislative offices and corporate boardrooms — the perfect laws for anyone wishing to impose a fascist regime on the United States.

There were some major signs in the months before 9/11 that the Bush administration, while outwardly showing little concern for "al Qaeda" and Osama bin Laden, was, nevertheless, planning to invest huge amounts of money in the military-intelligence complex for exotic ways to track the American people.

One such area of investment was biometrics — the use of some personally-identifiable physical attribute to track individuals. I wrote about the Bush administration's early interest in biometrics in March 2001, a half year before the 9/11 attacks:

Representatives of various U.S. government agencies trumpeted the benefits of biometric identification at the Biometrics 2001 Conference held in Arlington, VA on March 22. The conference was co-sponsored by AFCEA International and the Department of Defense Biometrics Management Office (DBMO). The DBMO's Director, Phillip Loranger, announced his desire for the Pentagon's new Biometrics Fusion Center in Bridgeport, West Virginia to become the "repository for all DoD biometric data bases." Loranger's boss, Army Lt. Gen Peter Cuviello, the Army's Director of Information Systems for Command, Control, Communications, Computers and Intelligence (C4I), said that although he did not see the Biometric Fusion Center growing in size to compete with the FBI's Integrated Automated Fingerprint Identification System (IAFIS), which is also located in West Virginia, he could see fusing data into his center from non-DoD players like the FBI.

The Army considers its mandate to pursue biometric technology to be Public Law 106-246, section 112, which was signed by President Clinton on July 13, 2000. That law states that "to ensure the availability of biometric technology in the DoD, the Secretary of the Army shall be the Executive Agent to lead, consolidate, and coordinate all biometrics information assurance programs of the DoD..." Dr. Joseph Westphal, the acting Secretary of the Army, paid a visit to the Biometrics Fusion Center shortly after he assumed his post in early March.

Dr. Don Prosnitz, the Chief Science and Technology Advisor to the Department of Justice stated a primary goal of his department was to consolidate the FBI's IAFIS and Immigration and Naturalization Service's IDENT fingerprint ID system. There are also plans to combine fingerprint and DNA databases into a common system. Prosnitz feels the public will eventually trade off any qualms about the government maintaining their fingerprints in a database for easier access through immigration lines. He said biometrics is ideal for an immigration system that processes 530 million travelers a year at a rate of 1.5 million each day. There are also plans by the Justice Department to permit the Drug Enforcement Administration, the U.S. Marshals Service, and the Bureau of Prisons to use a joint fingerprint database to handle drug felons from point of arrest to incarceration. Echoing the Pentagon officials, Prosnitz claimed the Congress was pushing for the consolidation of biometric databases throughout the government.

However, not all government employees are happy with biometrics. Jack Applebaum, a Systems Development Engineer for the State Department's Bureau of Diplomatic Security, said that some tenants within U.S. embassies abroad object to having their faces scanned and entered into a database. In addition to their opposition to facial recognition access systems, they are opposed to any type of voice recognition system. The embassy tenants, widely believed to be clandestine operatives of the NSA, CIA, the joint NSA/CIA Special Collection Service, DEA, Defense Intelligence Agency, and FBI, are concerned about operational security vulnerabilities from the collection of facial images by digital imagers and the electromagnetic signals (TEMPEST radiation) emitted from biometric devices.

Concerning privacy matters, Loranger claimed that after a thorough legal, social, and cultural review by the Department of Defense involving RAND Corporation, there was a determination that First, Fourth, and Fifth Amendment rights were not impacted upon by increased biometric usage. That sentiment was echoed by Jeffrey Dunn, the Chief of Identification and Authentication for the National Security Agency (NSA), a leading participant in biometric application development in the Federal government and private sectors. Dunn said that his analysis shows that when a system "is explained well, it will be accepted."

One of the testing grounds for the Pentagon's biometrics applications is South Korea. Kenneth Scheflen, the Director of the Defense Manpower Data Center, said that the importance of biometric-based smart cards became apparent when a criminal ring in Korea was discovered selling a package of U.S. military base ID cards, ration cards, and license plates for $1500 each. Scheflen claimed that military members and retirees are more accepting of biometrics because they receive benefits in return for cooperation. He also said the military "owns" its members and can order them to do anything it wishes. Scheflen admitted that military dependents pose a special legal issue and, therefore, the military has decided not to subject them to biometric identification at the present time. Scheflen revealed that former Deputy Defense Secretary John Hamre wanted the fingerprint cards of all former U.S. military members computerized but because of the quality of the prints, the unique fingerprint minutiae — the numerical values of print whirls, ridges and other features — could not be extracted with any degree of accuracy.

Dr. Steven King, a Special Adviser on Critical Infrastructure Protection to the Deputy Undersecretary of Defense for Science and Technology, said that a voluntary pilot biometric iris identification access program at the Army Research Laboratory in Adelphi, Maryland met with varying degrees of success. Iris identification was chosen for its richness of features. The iris of the human eye contains unique freckles, pits, rifts, striations, and corona — and the irises of the left and right eyes are different as well. The Army Lab discovered that although facial recognition systems had a 25 per cent error rate for moving targets and a 0.7 per cent error rate for stationary subjects, the error rate for iris systems was as high as 6 to 7 per cent for stationary targets. This was caused by the glare and glint from eyeglasses, unregistered glass eyes, contact lenses, and even ethnic differences. King said that of the total Adelphi laboratory work force, some 1 to 2 per cent would object to an employee-wide biometric identification system on privacy grounds.

Exhibitors participating in the Pentagon confab included Lau Technologies, the developer of the "Face in the Crowd" facial identification system used to scan the images of 100,000 spectators at this year's U.S. football Super Bowl in Tampa, Florida. Lau, which traces its beginnings to doing engineering work for the Defense Department on weapons like the Bradley Fighting Vehicle, has spun off a publicly-traded company called Viisage, the marketer of Face in the Crowd. The facial recognition system will be used at the 2002 Winter Olympics in Salt Lake City, Utah.

According to a company official, Viisage owns a database containing millions of drivers' license photographs from as many as thirteen states. Some of the seed money for Lau/Viisage and other facial recognition companies like Identix and Visionics Corp. comes from the Defense Advanced Research Projects Agency (DARPA). DARPA is funding such research as part of its Human ID at-a-Distance (HID) Program. Moreover, it is working with NSA on HID research and development.

Identix is working with Florida Secretary of State Kathryn Harris to develop a fingerprint identification-based voting system for military members. The system, known as iTRUST, uses Federal encryption and authentication standards, including public key infrastructure (PKI) standards. A major investor in Identix is Motorola, a company with historically close ties to the NSA. Identix claims that there is no way to link an identifiable fingerprint with a cast vote. Harris's military experiment may be used to justify using the Internet-based system statewide. Identix claims that Congress is pushing the biometric industry to come up with a fraud-proof federal voting technical standard.

Lau/Viisage is similarly involved in the technical development of electronic voting. Its system was recently used in Uganda's presidential election to verify voter eligibility. Nevertheless, there were still a number of claims of voter fraud in the balloting. In addition, Visionics' systems were used to identify registered voters in last July's Mexican presidential elections. Visionics facial recognition systems are also used by football stadiums in the United Kingdom and by the London borough of Newham.

Facial recognition systems may soon become more commonplace at the world's airports. The International Civil Aviation Organization (ICAO) has recommended facial recognition as the primary biometric to be used globally. This came out of a study by ICAO's New Technologies Working Group.

In the first few months of the Bush administration the privacy-invasive technology to track Americans and people around the world was on the shelf and ready to be sold. All that was needed was some watershed event to open the floodgates to such technology being sold to Uncle Sam.

In fact, the entire blueprint for the future homeland security infrastructure, warrantless eavesdropping, and infringement on personal liberties was spelled out in June 2000 in a congressionally-mandated report on counter-terrorism. Moreover, some of the key commissioners who came up with new ways to surveil the American people would become part and parcel of the neocon march to war in Iraq.

I wrote about the counter-terrorism proposals over a year before 9/11:

On June 5, 2000, the National Commission on Terrorism, established by Congress in 1999, released its final report titled "Countering The Changing Threat Of International Terrorism." Among other recommendations, the Commission calls for increased powers for the FBI and NSA to conduct electronic eavesdropping. Specifically, the Commission wants streamlined procedures for FBI surveillance requests to be presented to the Foreign Intelligence Surveillance Court (FISC). Currently, the Department of Justice Office of Intelligence Policy and Review (OIPR) requires, in addition to probable cause, evidence of wrongdoing or specific knowledge of a political group's terrorist intentions before forwarding a surveillance application to the FISC. Also, the commission wants past activities of a political group to be considered when determining whether the probable cause threshold is met.

The Commission also wants the federal government to fully reimburse FBI special agents and CIA field officers for personal liability insurance if they are sued for violating the rights of U.S. or foreign citizens.

The report also calls for increased funding for the NSA. The report states, "The National Security Agency (NSA) is America's most important asset for technical collection of terrorism information, yet it is losing its capability to target and exploit the modern communications systems used by terrorists, seriously weakening the NSA's ability to warn of possible attacks." The Commission also calls for greater sharing of intelligence between nations on cyber-crimes.

Another recommendation calls for a more effective national system to monitor the activities of foreign students in the United States. The proposed monitoring system would include information on what classes foreign students take. For example, if a student changes his or her major from English literature to nuclear physics, the monitoring system would alert federal law enforcement and intelligence agencies. Also, countries currently eligible for the U.S. Visa Waiver Program would have their status suspended or ruled ineligible for such a designation. The report calls for Greece to be suspended and Pakistan to be ineligible. The report states "Greece has been disturbingly passive in response to terrorist activities." Held up to particular scorn is Greek support for the Kurdish Workers Party (PKK). The report also calls for the FBI to station reporting officers around the world who would provide terrorist intelligence to U.S. law enforcement and intelligence communities. The CIA would maintain its current network of reporting officers.

The Commission also calls for the transfer of all authority to the Department of Defense during a "catastrophic terrorist attack" or "prior to an imminent attack." The U.S. military would direct all federal, state, and local authorities from a unified command structure.

Former Ambassador Paul Bremer chaired the National Commission on Terrorism. He served as U.S. ambassador to the Netherlands from 1983 to 1986 and from 1986 to 1989 was Ambassador-at-large for Counter-terrorism. Other commission members included retired Army General Wayne Downing, the former Commander-in-Chief of the U.S. Special Operations Command and James Woolsey, former Director of Central Intelligence.

Out of the 120 people interviewed by the Commission, only one represented the civil liberties community. The remainder included such individuals as White House Counter-terrorism czar Richard Clarke, FBI Director Louis Freeh, CIA Director George Tenet, former CIA Director Bob Gates, journalist Steve Emerson, terrorism guru Yonah Alexander, Undersecretary of State Thomas Pickering, and former National Security Adviser Brent Scowcroft.

June 2000 also revealed some details about the NSA that would be an omen of things to come. In June 2000, I wrote about NSA eavesdropping on Americans, including First Lady Hillary Clinton and former President Jimmy Carter:

The Electronic Privacy Information Center (EPIC) in Washington, DC is in possession of several formerly classified documents indicating that the National Security Agency (NSA) instituted special procedures to handle communications intercepts dealing with the activities of Hillary Rodham Clinton and the independent Bosnian peace negotiations of former President Jimmy Carter. Additional documents point out that NSA instituted special handling procedures for intelligence reports about 1996 U.S. presidential and congressional candidates. These are contained in an internal NSA memo issued five months before the election.

The released documents, originally requested in 1999 by House Permanent Select Committee on Intelligence Chairman Porter Goss and refused by the NSA's General Counsel on the ground that disclosure would violate attorney-client privilege, were ultimately turned over to the oversight committee. EPIC filed a Freedom of Information Act request for the documents and when that request was refused, a lawsuit was initiated in the U.S. District Court for Washington. Although most of the more than 100 pages of documents are heavily blanked out, the information released points to the complex manner in which certain intercepted communications involving U.S. citizens find their way into NSA intelligence reports.

The two NSA memoranda dealing with Mrs. Clinton and President Carter and so-called minimization procedures for communications intercepted concerning them are "smoking guns" to many intelligence agency observers. They argue that for NSA to have special regulations for two identified U.S. VIPs may mean that the agency has an extensive watch list for others as well.

The Clinton memo is as follows:

8 July 1993 NSA Memo from P052 Subj: Reporting Guidance on References to the First Lady.
Mrs. Clinton may be identified in reports only by title (currently, Chairperson of the President's Task Force on National Health Care Reform) without prior approval when that title is necessary to understand or assess foreign intelligence and when the information being discussed relates to her official duties.... As with other senior officials of the Executive Branch, no reports may be published concerning Mrs. Clinton's private life or activities absent evidence of criminal wrongdoing and even then only after review by senior NSA management and the OGC.
Formerly Classified CONFIDENTIAL — HANDLE VIA COMINT CHANNELS ONLY

The Carter memo:

15 December 1994 NSA Memo from P0521. Subj: Reporting Guidance on Former President Carter's Involvement in the Bosnian Peace Process.

The current U.S. Administration has cautiously welcomed this development [Carter's invitation by Bosnian Serb President Radovan Karadzic to participate in efforts to end the war], but has made clear that Former President Carter would be traveling to Bosnia as a private U.S. citizen and not as a representative of the U.S. Government.... Since Former President Carter will not be officially representing the U.S. Government, any reports that reflect either his travels to Bosnia or his participation in efforts to end the war may identify him only as a 'U.S. person.' Only if Former President Carter eventually becomes an official envoy of the U.S. Government in this activity, could he then be identified as a 'former U.S. President.'

Formerly classified SECRET — HANDLE VIA COMINT CHANNELS ONLY

One particularly disturbing NSA memo deals with the 1990 death in Guatemala of a U.S. citizen, Michael DeVine and the 1991 disappearance of the Guatemalan husband of Jennifer Harbury, also a U.S. citizen. The memo indicates that NSA was not to turn over raw signals intelligence traffic to federal investigators who were trying to determine whether US intelligence agencies, including the NSA and CIA, knew in advance of Guatemalan government involvement in the murder of DeVine and the likely murder of Efrain Bamaca Velasquez (Mrs. Harbury's husband). There is strong evidence that elements within the CIA knew in advance of the murders. The NSA memo raises the possibility that if a law enforcement investigation involves criminal activities by U.S. intelligence agencies (e.g., CIA), NSA has a policy of not cooperating with the investigation.

The DeVine/Bamaca Velasquez memo follows:

31 March 1995 NSA Memo from P0522 to A05, B05, G Chief of Staff, and W9G Subj: Guatemala — Prohibition on Search of Raw Traffic.

[NSA IG has] asked that DDO secure any information concerning events in Guatemala from January 1987 to the present relating to Michael DeVine, a U.S. citizen, and Efrain

Bamaca Velasquez, the husband of a U.S. citizen, Jennifer Harbury.... NSA is not authorized to collect SIGINT for law enforcement or investigative purposes."

Formerly classified SECRET — HANDLE VIA COMINT CHANNELS ONLY"

September 11, 2001

On the morning of September 11, I was on my way from Arlington, Virginia to downtown Washington to attend the weekly staff meeting at the Electronic Privacy Information Center (EPIC). Before 9/11, the cause of privacy in the electronic and computer age was something I considered the major issue for our time.

I was listening to the radio when the first plane struck the World Trade Center. After turning on the TV, I witnessed the second plane strike. While on my way to the Metro station, my longtime friend, a Captain in the Navy whose office was in the Navy Annex, across from the Pentagon, phoned and said, "They hit the Pentagon." He described a chaotic scene in the area of the Pentagon with workers from the Navy Annex and the Pentagon running away on the streets from the area in something resembling a Japanese monster movie.

After I arrived at EPIC, the mood seemed more somber than expected. However, it was then I learned that the twin towers of the World Trade Center had both collapsed. What about the cause of privacy after an event like this? I said, "I think we should all drink the purple Kool Aid now."

The attacks of September 11, 2001 would change America forever. Although America flirted with fascism during the Civil War, the infamous Palmer raids during World War I, the "Red Scare" days of Senator Joseph McCarthy, and Richard Nixon's abuses during Watergate, none compared to the post-9/11 imposition of an imperial presidency on the American people.

On September 27, 2003, I wrote an op-ed in the *Miami Herald* on the abuses of the Patriot Act:

It is indeed a slippery slope when some on the right say that vandalism carried out by destructive environmental activists be defined as acts of terrorism.

Congress hastily passed the anti-terrorist Patriot Act in October 2001 during a time when it was under siege by a real bio-terror anthrax attack. Many members of Congress, on both the left and right, now regret not examining closely the long-term effect of the Patriot Act on the constitutional rights of Americans.

Following an arson attack against a condominium under construction in San Diego, the vandalism of sport utility vehicles at four Los Angeles area auto dealerships and the freeing of 10,000 minks from a farm near Seattle, the Justice Department is labeling such attacks "ecoterrorism."

There are calls by some in Congress, particularly Rep. Scott McInnis, R-Colo., that "ecoterrorists" be treated in the same manner as members of al Qaeda. To expand the Draconian Patriot Act and the proposed future "Patriot II" and "Victory" acts to cover arson, vandalism, destruction of private property and trespassing would propel the United States dangerously closer to the type of society envisaged by George Orwell in *1984*.

It is a hallmark of totalitarian regimes around the world to elevate simple crimes to "crimes against the state." In many lands, those who merely practice their religion or join a labor union are labeled national security threats by the authorities and are tossed into jail. It is clear that Attorney General John Ashcroft and his zealous allies in Congress have environmental activist groups such as the Earth Liberation Front, Earth First and the Animal Liberation Front in their gun sights.

But to argue that these groups pose the same level of threat as al Qaeda and Jemaah Islamiya is ludicrous. The environmental vandals are not in the category of worldwide networks that aim to kill thousands by setting off bombs and releasing dangerous toxins.

A number of people in the United States and abroad began to wonder if 9/11 was crafted by the criminal Bush family and their compatriots to bring about a fascist regime in the United States. Parallels between 9/11 and Adolf Hitler's Reichstag fire were often cited. Some world leaders also contemplated the Bush regime's involvement in the attacks. As I wrote in WayneMadsenReport.com in May 2006:

The first skeptics to question what role the Bush administration played in the 9/11 terrorist attacks were a few cabinet ministers in the governments of America's NATO allies. They included German Science and Technology Minister Andreas Von Bulow and British Environment Minister Michael Meacher. They were joined by Belgian European Parliament Member Paul Lannoye and, later former Italian President Francesco Cossiga.

However, in recent months the former cabinet ministers have been joined in their skepticism about the "official" version of the 9/11 events by Venezuela's President Hugo Chavez and Iran's President Mahmoud Ahmedinejad.

In March, Chavez said Venezuela will open an official investigation into the 9/11 attacks. Now, Chavez has been joined by Ahmedinejad, who in a recent letter to President George W. Bush, asked, "Why have the various aspects of the [9/11] attacks been kept secret?" Ahmedinejad indicated that the attacks could not have been carried out without the knowledge of the U.S. "security services."

The fact that the Venezuelan and Iranian leaders suspect Bush administration complicity in 9/11 is interesting. These leaders have at their disposal two highly capable intelligence agencies. A major priority of the intelligence services of Venezuela and Iran (DISIP and VEVAK, respectively) is counter-intelligence against the United States. However, that is not likely where Venezuela and Iran may have gleaned information about who was behind the 9/11 attacks.

Venezuela and Iran are members of the Organization of Petroleum Exporting Countries (OPEC) and a major priority of their intelligence services is collecting information on oil deals, including the Bush administration negotiations with the Taliban in Tashkent and Berlin prior to 9/11 that quickly went sour and likely provided the impetus for the Muslim insurgents to attack New York and Washington on 9/11.

VEVAK, a sworn enemy of the Taliban and al Qaeda, had successfully penetrated the Taliban's and Pakistan's security services and would have been well aware of the attack plans and any U.S. foreknowledge of them, including knowing about money movements from Pakistan to the hijackers in Florida.

DISIP was well aware of the smuggling of cocaine from Colombia, trans-shipped on a Saudi diplomatic Boeing 737 through Venezuela, by Saudi Royal family members who then used the proceeds to support al Qaeda's attack on America.

As more and more governments are wrested from the control of the global neocons — Italy, Britain, Mexico, and others — additional intelligence may be obtained from various espionage agencies that will prove that the Bush administration was not an idle bystander in the events that led up to 9/11.

On September 11, 2005, the fourth anniversary of the 9/11 attacks, *WMR* reported,

George H.W. Bush's Operation Desert Storm made Kuwait safe for an important part of "al Qaeda's" financing operations. Documents dating to 1993 and obtained from European intelligence sources by WMR indicate that after U.S. troops ran Saddam Hussein's forces out of the oil rich emirate, Kuwait became a significant base of operations for Osama bin Laden and his "al Qaeda" support network. Kuwait was the headquarters for an Islamic "charity," Lajnat al Dawa al Islamiyah, a group designated by the Treasury Department as a "specially Designated Global Terrorist (SDGT) organization." Lajnat gave financial support to Khalid Sheikh Mohammed, "al Qaeda's" chief planner of the 9/11 attacks, which occurred exactly four years ago. Mohammed's brother ran Lajnat's operations in Peshawar, Pakistan.

Lajnat has been linked to Chicago-based businessman Sulaiman al-Ali, an individual who the FBI said was a central money mover for such terrorist-funding front organizations as the International Islamic Relief Organization, Sana-Bell, Inc., Global Chemical Corporation, the Saar Foundation (which had close links with Karl Rove's friend and adviser Grover Norquist), BMI, Inc. (an investment bank), the International Institute of Islamic Thought, Safa Trust, P-Tech (a Boston-based software company having active contracts with the FAA and NORAD on 9/11 and which was tied to "al Qaeda" via links between its director Yaqub Mirza and "al Qaeda" financier Yasin Kadi), and the Muslim World League.

Although these groups primarily funneled Saudi money to terrorist organizations like "al Qaeda" and Hamas, it was Lajnat that transferred primarily Kuwaiti money from the emirate to "al Qaeda" operations in Pakistan. According to documents obtained by WMR, Lajnat had the firm support of both the Kuwaiti and Pakistani governments. The first document is a letter, dated Aug. 3,

1993, from the Pakistani ambassador to Kuwait certifying Lajnat al Dawa al Islamiyah (LDI) as a charitable organization. The second is a letter from the Kuwait embassy in Pakistan stating much the same. A third letter is from the U.S. accounting firm of Ernst & Young giving LDI a clean bill of health from an audit.

From April 14 to 16, 1993, former President George H.W. Bush visited Kuwait to accolades and awards from the Kuwaiti government for his role in "freeing" Kuwait from Saddam Hussein. It was also during Bush's trip to Kuwait that Saddam was accused of plotting to assassinate the elder Bush, an unsubstantiated charge that would influence junior Bush's decision to invade and occupy Iraq ten years later and one that prompted President Clinton to launch 27 cruise missiles to strike Iraqi targets in retaliation.

In fact, after the "liberation" of Kuwait from Iraqi forces, the emirate quickly became an important base for "al Qaeda" financing, an activity of which George H.W. Bush as both an ex-President and ex-CIA director, as well as a close confidant of the Kuwaiti government, should have been fully aware as part of his periodic intelligence briefs by the CIA.

Clinton said he struck Iraq with the cruise missiles as a result of "compelling evidence" that Bush was the target of an assassination plot by members of the Iraqi Intelligence Service. However, the CIA in 1993 was headed by James Woolsey, an individual who later associated himself with the same neocon elements who helped develop the phony reasons for George W. Bush's war against Iraq, including placing trust in convicted embezzler and "Curveball" patron, Ahmad Chalabi and his Iraqi National Congress (INC). Woolsey served as a paid consultant for the INC. In fact, it was Woolsey who presented the report to President Clinton that Iraq was behind a foiled car bomb attack on senior Bush in Kuwait.

Based on the bogus reports the neocons have generated within the last few years, there is no reason to believe that Woolsey was on the level in 1993 or in 2003. In fact, it was Kuwait that had its hands involved in funding terrorism through its support for Lajnat, which in turn funded Osama bin Laden and "al Qaeda" in Pakistan and Afghanistan. And this support occurred after "al Qaeda's" fingerprints and the involvement of its patrons in Khartoum, Sudan were discovered in the first attack on the World Trade Center earlier in 1993.

Ex-President Bush's close links with a government — Kuwait (in addition to Saudi Arabia) — a government that supported a group that funded "al Qaeda" and the 9/11 attacks on the United

States suggest that Mr. Bush may have had information concerning Kuwaiti (and Saudi) support for planned terrorist activities against the United States prior to 9/11. The business activities of ex-President Bush and those of George W. and Marvin Bush with the Kuwaiti government deserve a thorough investigation by U.S. law enforcement into the possible aiding and abetting of terrorist-supporting states that helped finance terrorist attacks against the United States. These would not be high crimes and misdemeanors but acts of treason. On the fourth anniversary of 9/11, 3000 souls call out for justice.

Following the 9/11 money trail

O n December 4, 2005, WMR reported,

S audi money funded 9/11 attacks. U.S. intelligence insiders have confirmed that NSA intercepts of financial communications prior to 9/11 showed that Saudi and Chinese money, funneled through Cyprus, helped fund "al Qaeda" units in Afghanistan and arms deals between Saudi Arabia and China. Cyprus is a major nexus for financial transactions of the Russian-Ukrainian-Israeli Mafia.

One sure method to uncover covert operations is to "follow the money." The tactic worked for the investigations of Watergate, Iran-Contra, Bank of Credit and Commerce International (BCCI), and Enron. Following the money that financed 9/11 is no exception. A number of expert witnesses to the financing of 9/11 made contact with me. They represented a cross-section of financial specialists from New York, Dubai, and Houston. In January 2006, I wrote about one aspect of the financing of 9/11 — and a link to the Bush criminal syndicate:

R esearchers and investigators have uncovered links between a Miami bank that collapsed in 2002 amid a fraud scandal that was highlighted by billions of dollars in questionable cash, fraudulent loans and money movements linked to the Bush family, and businesses linked to funding pilot training for the 9/11 hijackers.

After the collapse of Hamilton Bank of Miami, the Federal Deposit Insurance Corporation (FDIC), an entity that was transformed by the Bush administration from a regulatory agency into an investment center, and the Israel Discount Bank assumed liability for the insured accounts. The FDIC assumed liability for half the accounts and the Israel Discount Bank took over the other half. Three Hamilton branches were reopened by the Israeli bank as "IDC." Insiders report that Hamilton Bank was involved in joint (and possibly rogue) U.S.-Israeli intelligence and money laundering operations.

In 2002, the *Miami Herald* reported that bags of cash from Latin American political leaders would routinely be flown to Hamilton Bank for money laundering. The *Herald* reported that one of Hamilton's customers was then-Panamanian President Mireya Moscoso. Hamilton maintained an office in Panama. According to court documents filed by the Office of the Comptroller of the Currency, Hamilton's dubious loans to Maximo Haddad, the owner of the Mexican construction firm PYCSA that built a private toll road in Panama and the owner of two offshore companies, Perpetual International Holdings and Alderly Management; Manuel Cohen, the Panamanian Consul General in Miami and the managing director of Alexander H Finance Co.; failed banks in El Salvador and Ecuador; Metrobank International (Vanuatu); Metrobank Panama, and a Florida drapery and window covering firm with subsidiaries in Texas, Venezuela, Brazil, El Salvador, Australia, Mexico, Spain, and Puerto Rico "appeared to have no legitimate business purposes." Hamilton Bank has been described by intelligence insiders as a front operation for intelligence-related activities that may include, in addition to money laundering, weapons and drug smuggling.

On June 8, 2007, I re-visited the Hamilton Bank story on the *WayneMadsenReport* after speaking to some well-placed sources familiar with the failed bank's operations in Florida:

A diplomatic source has told WMR that Hamilton Bank, which collapsed amid a huge fraud scandal in 2002, laundered billions of dollars into the United States. After Hamilton's failure, the Federal Deposit Insurance Corporation (FDIC) and the Israel Discount Bank assumed liability for the bank's accounts.

The diplomatic source told WMR that one of Hamilton's major customers, Panamanian-Mexican construction tycoon Maximo Haddad, routinely flew large amounts of cash and bonds in and out of Florida and that Hamilton was used as a money laundering operation. Haddad also served as Panama's Honorary Consul for Tampa, although he lived and continues to live in West Palm Beach.

In 2004, after the Drug Enforcement Administration (DEA) discovered large amounts of cash and bonds during a search of Haddad's plane in Florida, the State Department requested Panama to ask Haddad to resign. Panama's embassy in Washington also wanted to avoid the embarrassment of having one of its diplomats declared *persona non grata*. Eventually, the U.S. government stripped Haddad and Manuel Cohen, Panama's Consul General in Miami and business associate of Haddad, of their U.S. visas. The DEA search of Haddad's private plane came on a tip from the FBI, which had been conducting surveillance of Haddad.

WMR has learned that some of the laundered cash came from two private toll roads operated by Haddad in Panama, the North and South Corridors.

Another bank associated with Haddad, Laredo National Bank in Texas, also reportedly laundered Juarez Cartel drug money into the George W. Bush 2000 presidential campaign. Laredo's owners were chief donors to George W. Bush's campaigns.

No criminal charges were ever brought against Haddad. Haddad's attorney, former southern Florida Justice Department prosecutor Alexander Angueira, according to our sources, intervened with Alberto "Al" Cardenas, the Cuban-American GOP lobbyist and former Chairman of the Florida Republican Party, to quash the case against Haddad and Cohen. Cardenas, a close friend of Jeb Bush, is now a top campaign supporter of GOP presidential candidate Mitt Romney. Former Assistant Secretary of State for Western Hemisphere Affairs Roger Noriega, who now works for Cardenas, is conducting outreach to the Hispanic community on behalf of Romney.

Large sums of the Panamanian money ended up in the pockets of top Republicans, including Jeb and George W. Bush.

In January 2006, WMR reported that Hamilton House in Nassau, Bahamas helped launder $10 million from the Saudi Royal family, via Switzerland, to fund Saudis in the United States. Some of the money was used to pay for flight training for some of the 9/11 hijackers. We have learned that Haddad also maintains a residence in Nassau, but it remains unclear if there are links between the failed Hamilton Bank and Hamilton House in the Bahamas.

In July 2005, I had written about additional 9/11 financial links:

In 1995, a $10 million transfer was made to Houston. The source was the Saudi Royal family. The funds were transferred to Nation's Bank via Banca Svizzera Italiana via SWIFT. On September 28, 1995, a $50,000 check was cashed at NationsBank of Pasadena, Texas. It allegedly originated from the $10 million of transferred funds from Saudi Arabia and the payee was "Fayyaz Ahmed." Fayyaz Ahmed, aka Fayez Ahmad, was also named as one of the hijackers aboard United 175 that crashed into the South Tower of the World Trade Center.

The account from which the $50,000 was paid was in the name of Treatment Services of the Southwest Corporation, 14359 Torrey Chase Blvd., Suite D Houston TX 77014-1635, in North Harris County —check number 266-406556-1; Tax ID # 76-0455993. Much of the funds eventually ended up in Phoenix, later the location of some of the 9/11 hijacker trainees.

Ahmad also used the aliases Banihammad Fayez Abu Dhabi Banihammad, Fayez Rushed Ahmed, Banihammad Fayez, Rasid Ahmed Hassen Alqadi, Abu Dhabi Banihammad Ahmed Fayez, with the FBI officially tagging him as one Fayez Rashid Ahmed Hassan al Qadi Banihammad. Fayyaz Ahmed had been a resident of Delray Beach, Florida. The FBI later said that the "Fayyaz Ahmed" who cashed the check in Pasadena was merely a student paying for college tuition but the note on the check states "contingent for travel expenses." Dallas, Texas was also one of the locations used by the hijackers for flight simulator training. One of the flight training "tasks," the hijackers trained to do was to maneuver planes between World Trade Center 1 and 2.

According to information recently obtained by *WMR*, the facts about the money transfer are maintained in the Superior Court of Arizona, Maricopa County, "In the Matter of the Proceeds of Account 41C-07029 RDC Holdings Co., Inc." The FBI in Arizona has investigated the case but may be under pressure not to follow certain leads that could lead to the Bush family and their business associates.

According to a source close to the case, the $10 million was moved from Bluelake World SA, a Switzerland-based firm, via Topaz Liberty and Andromeda International (both Panamanian firms), to the account of Southwest Services of Houston, the account from which Fayyaz Ahmed was paid $50,000.

Another intermediary for the funds transfer was reportedly Hamilton House of Nassau, Bahamas, a possible off-shore entity of Hamilton Bank in Miami. The financial network that moved the $10 million to Arizona and Texas reportedly has close links to Potomac Capital, a Geneva-based entity set up by CIA Director George H.W. Bush in 1976.

The Bush financial networks involved with Metrobank and Hamilton also involve the entry of illegal foreign money into the 2004 Bush-Cheney campaign.

On December 11, 2006, I followed up on the 9/11 financing:

WMR has learned from one of its sources in New York that the Federal Reserve Bank of New York actively covered up massive money laundering by the Hong Kong and Shanghai Banking Corporation (HSBC) United Arab Emirates branch through its branch in New York. The money laundering consisted of questionable money movements through Dubai that involved individuals linked to "al Qaeda," including those connected to the 9/11 terrorist attacks on the United States.

WMR reported additional information on the Dubai connection on March 1, 2006:

Internal documents from the UAE Central Bank in Dubai detail huge money laundering operations in the UAE according to financial industry insiders. Moreover, the Sharjah branch of HSBC Holdings PLC was tied to international arms trafficker Victor Bout, indicted in Belgium for money laundering and named in various UN reports as a chief embargo buster in Africa and Taliban-controlled Afghanistan.

American citizen Iqbal Hakim, a native of India, was the chief examiner for the UAE Central Bank. Hakim, yet another whistle-blower who has been ignored and mistreated by the Bush administration and threatened by Bush's Persian Gulf potentate friends, discovered a suspicious $343 million per year money flow through an HSBC personal account in Dubai. The transactions were investigated by the FBI and the Bureau of Immigration and Customs Enforcement but no prosecutions resulted.

From the same report:

Carlyle [The Carlyle Group] has its fingerprints on the Dubai Ports World deal to assume control of six major U.S. ports from Peninsular and Oriental Steam Navigation Company (P&O). After Treasury Secretary John Snow left CSX Corporation as its chairman, CSX Lines was sold to Carlyle, which renamed it Horizon Lines. David Sanborn, who was a CSX executive under Snow, became director of European and Latin American operations for Dubai Ports World and arranged to sell the Dubai state-owned firm CSX port operations in South America and Asia. Sanborn was then appointed Assistant Secretary of Transportation for Maritime Administration (MARAD), the oversight agency for U.S. shipping and ports.

The Dubai Ports World deal to take over U.S. port operations was signed off by the Committee on Foreign Investment in the United States (CFIUS), chaired by Sanborn's old CSX boss Snow. Perhaps not coincidental to the lucrative port deals, the Dubai Investment Corporation recently invested $100 million in The Carlyle Group. And Dubai Ports World's deal involves taking over operations at more than just six U.S. ports — New York, New Jersey, Philadelphia/Camden, Baltimore, Miami, and New Orleans.

Vice President Dick Cheney's old company, Halliburton, has some interesting partners in its work in occupied Iraq. On December 11, 2005, *WMR* reported on links between Halliburton/Kellogg, Brown & Root and a Viktor Bout-owned airline based in Moldova, Aerocom/Air Mero. Bout's airlines have also reportedly been involved in flying low-wage earners from East Asia to Dubai and on to Iraq where they work for paltry salaries in sub-standard living conditions. Halliburton/KBR has sub-contracted to a shadowy Dubai-based firm, Prime Projects International Trading LLC (PPI), which "trades" mainly in workers from Thailand, the Philippines, Nepal, India, Pakistan, and other poor Asian nations.

In 2004, after a Filipino PPI worker was killed in a mortar attack on Camp Anaconda in Iraq, the Philippines government of Gloria Macapagal-Arroyo ordered PPI, which is based at P.O. Box 42252, Dubai, UAE, to send overseas Filipino workers home from Iraq and Kuwait and banned it from further recruiting in the Philippines. Some of PPI's recruiting included running ads on the Internet. In addition to the other south Asian employees, the Philippine workers were employed by PPI under a Pentagon sweetheart umbrella contract let to KBR under the LOGCAP (Logistics Civil Augmentation Program) III program.

Although little is known about PPI, it reportedly has been linked to Halliburton/KBR for a number of years and has been associated with Halliburton contracts in the Saudi Arabia, Kuwait, and the Balkans during the time when Dick Cheney headed the firm. PPI has also been involved in operations at Guantanamo Bay, Cuba, where Filipino workers were involved in building the prison housing suspected "al Qaeda" prisoners.

Inside sources report that PPI has some high level financial partners, including the al Nahayan royal family of the United Arab Emirates and Vice President Cheney.

There were a number of suspicious "suicides" in the international banking industry after 9/11. On July 31, 2005, *WMR* reported the following:

This weekend brought two strange deaths involving recently retired top banking officials — one in New York and the other in Europe. On July 30, it was reported that former Citigroup board member Arthur Zankel fell from the window of his 9th floor Manhattan apartment. Zankel retired from Citigroup's board in 2004 and was said by his longtime friend and colleague, Citigroup Chairman Sanford Weill, to have been suffering from depression. Hours later, Wim Duisenberg, the retired head of the European Central Bank, was found dead in his swimming pool at his villa in Faucon, in southeastern France. Duisenberg retired in 2003. On July 29, Milan prosecutors announced indictments against subsidiaries of UBS, Deutsche Bank, Citigroup, and Morgan Stanley as part of the investigation of the financial collapse of the Italian dairy mega-corporation Parmalat. Duisenberg was backed for the head of the European Central Bank by the German banking establishment, including Deutsche Bank.

On July 24, 2006, almost a year later, *WMR* reported on another suspicious death in Europe:

On July 21, former Parmalat board member Gianmario Roveraro, kidnapped on July 5 in Milan after attending a meeting of the right-wing Catholic sect Opus Dei, was found dead under a highway bridge near Parma, his body dismembered by a chainsaw in what appeared to be a ritualistic murder for which the Opus Dei is well noted. Roveraro's death is similar to that of Opus Dei-linked Milan banker Roberto Calvi whose body was found under the Blackfriars Bridge in London in 1982 after the bankruptcy of Italy's second largest bank, Banco Ambrosiano. Calvi was the bank's chairman and was considered the Vatican's banker. Financial problems involving money laundering and the bank were first discovered by a Bank of Italy audit in 1978.

A number of Vatican observers believe that Pope John Paul I was murdered in 1978 after he discovered the role of the Ambrosiano Bank and the Mafia in the Catholic Church's finances. The Milanese Calvi and Roveraro were both reported to be members of Opus Dei. Opus Dei always refuses to admit who are its "supernumeraries" or members. Dan Brown's *The Da Vinci Code* was widely condemned by the Catholic Church as pure fiction and blasphemy. However, the recent murder of Roveraro and the current trial of five men in Rome for the murder of Calvi (first determined by London police to be a suicide), are bound to put the Fascist-linked Opus Dei back in the media spotlight.

Roveraro was awaiting indictment for his role in the $17.7 billion collapse of the Italian dairy giant Parmalat. The financial collapse of the firm mirrored the largest corporate failure in history, that of Enron. Three men have been arrested and charged with kidnapping Roveraro.

Practicing a form of fraudulent business practice also conducted by Enron, Parmalat filed for bankruptcy in December 2003 after a $5.06 billion account held by a Cayman Islands subsidiary tied to the Bank of America was found not to exist. Enron also operated fraudulent off-the-books subsidiaries in the Cayman Islands, and a British banker named Neil Coulbeck, who was involved with those Cayman accounts, was recently found dead under suspicious causes in an East London park.

Roveraro's murder came on the heels of a July 14 decision by a New Jersey state appellate court to reject a motion by Citigroup to dismiss a lawsuit that the re-organized Parmalat brought against the financial giant. Citigroup unsuccessfully argued that the New Jersey court had no jurisdiction in the matter. Parmalat is suing Citigroup in New Jersey state court in Hackensack and 50 other banks in Federal Court in Manhattan. In addition to Citigroup, Parmalat is suing the Bank of America, as well as auditors Deloitte Touche Tohmatsu and Grant Thornton International.

As *WMR* reported last July, the financial collapses of Parmalat and Enron and the involvement of Citigroup are linked by investigations on both sides of the Atlantic. Roveraro's and Coulbeck's twin deaths follow by almost a year the suspicious deaths, mere hours apart, of Citigroup's Arthur Zankel and the European Central Bank's Wim Duisenberg.

There was definitely a large international money trail regarding suspicious financial transactions surrounding principal players in the 9/11 attacks. On May 22, 2007, *WMR* reported yet another incident involving dubious financial transactions with an Enron connection:

*W*MR has received documents sent to one of the presidential campaigns from Leonard D. Wallace, a former business associate of former Enron Vice Chairman J. Clifford Baxter, that provides details of al Qaeda and the 9/11 attacks being financed through Citigroup/Citibank. The document states that Baxter, who was to appear before a congressional committee to testify on Enron's dubious business practices, died from a reported suicide on January 18, 2002.

According to the document received from a Baxter associate, the former Vice Chairman of Enron was planning to expose Citigroup's knowledge about Saudi banks that were funding the terrorists who were responsible for carrying out the 9/11 attacks, *including* some Saudi banks in which Citigroup had a financial stake.

Wallace writes, "This cover-up of criminal misconduct has certainly been perpetrated both at 1600 Pennsylvania Avenue, Washington, DC and at Citigroup's 399 Park Avenue address in New York City." The document goes on to state, "Alberto Gonzales, and the U.S. Department of Justice that he heads, have successfully blocked any investigation of Citigroup, despite evidence that has been presented to them."

Wallace also writes, "I was brought into this spider web of greed and illegality by J. Clifford Baxter, a business associate of mine who was at one time vice chairman of Enron. Through his relationship with Robert Rubin at Citigroup's Chairman's Suite in New York City, in August 2001, I became privy to a series of

61

business transactions planned by Citigroup that I began to realize were not only illegal but also aiding international terrorism from Saudi Arabia. I complained to Citigroup's senior executives and their board, and Cliff told me and others that he was going to expose this bank fraud of Citigroup and Saudi banks. Then, about 30 days after my first letter to Citigroup's chairman, Cliff suddenly died on January 18, 2002 from what is to this day still considered a very questionable suicide."

In a letter dated February 14, 2005 to Attorney General Alberto Gonzales, Wallace presents the background of his case: "I had a prior association in a $1.5 billion armored vehicle project with J. Clifford Baxter, the former Enron executive who died mysteriously in January 2002. As a result of that project, there are two public companies that can corroborate my participation and the integrity with which I conducted myself.

"In August 2001, Cliff told me that he was involving me in securing $5 billion in loans and the subsequent investment of these funds. The collateral was to be located at Citibank Singapore, and he said that he would provide me with 4 pages of posting instructions."

The loan deal eventually was handed over to a Citibank Miami vice president — on September 10, 2001. Wallace writes, "During the next 100 days, up until mid-December, Citigroup, through its headquarters and elsewhere, clearly orchestrated a well-coordinated conspiracy whose major impacts were going to be the defrauding of another bank and the acquisition of ill-gotten gains that would be received and/or distributed to others by Citigroup's senior management. It was represented to me by Citigroup officials and their documentation that the 'others' included Account 98 activities, which I later learned were synonymous with the funding of terrorist organizations.

"Citigroup Singapore supplied a false inventory and authentication about Federal Reserve Bonds that supposedly were being used as collateral for the $5 billion loans. Citibank headquarters in Manhattan and Citibank Miami confirmed the authenticity of these bogus bonds. The posting instructions they provided me referred to Account 98s to be managed by unknown operatives in Saudi Arabia at SAMBA Bank, of which Citigroup was a major stockholder." [*WMR* previously reported on and provided a canceled SAMBA (Saudi American Bank) check written to a group affiliated with Hamas. This editor was personally told by a former chief of Mossad in October 2002 that if one wanted to find out where al Qaeda received its funding, one need not look further than the six largest U.S. banks, one of which is Citigroup.]

So, just what is al Qaeda, really?

It has often been said that if George W. Bush and the neocons did not have al Qaeda, they would have to invent it. Perhaps they did. On September 10, 2004, the eve of the third anniversary of the 9/11 attacks, I wrote about the background of al Qaeda. The organization that the neocons love to invoke had some interesting roots, connections that linked al Qaeda to past right-wing support networks for anti-Communist Afghans.

Osama bin Laden:
A Texas Republican In Muslim Clothing

When Ronald Reagan passed away a few months ago, eulogies poured into Washington from around the world. One eulogy was conspicuously absent — that from America's international Public Enemy Number One and arch-terrorist Osama bin Laden. Speaking at a Cato Institute seminar on the War on Terrorism on September 8 in Washington, Professor Walid Phares, a Middle East expert at Florida Atlantic University, offered for the first time a quote attributed to bin Laden that his colleague has penned in a forthcoming book. Bin Laden told Phares's colleague in Saudi Arabia in the 1980s, "I like Reagan. He believes in God. He's helping us. He's better than the others." The fact that George W. Bush considers himself the heir to Reagan's legacy and his policies, in addition to the fact that he never misses a chance to speak of his own devotion to God (even more so than Reagan ever did) and has brought almost every one of Reagan's cowboy operators into his administration, must also place him in the eyes of bin Laden as "better than the others."

Washington's heavily corporate-funded Cato Institute, a citadel of conservative and libertarian policy-making, is the least likely place one would expect to hear the Bush foreign policy wrung through the ringer. However, Cato has emerged as a key player in a conservative counter-attack against the neoconservative foreign policies enacted by Bush's inner circle of national security and defense advisers who have corrupted Republican ideology to the point where it would be unrecognizable to Barry Goldwater, Senator Bob Taft, Dwight Eisenhower or Richard Nixon.

Osama bin Laden has always been there for the opportunist Republicans and their neoconservative symbiotes and they have always been there for him. No wonder after Bush's initial post-9/11 bravado that he would catch bin Laden "dead or alive," the man who once ran most of his late father's Saudi construction company, and its business dealings with Bush family favorites Adnan Khashoggi and Manuchehr Ghorbanifar, Osama was allowed to escape during the Battle of Tora Bora.

Which brings us to Richard Perle and his merry band of neoconservative agents of influence for Israel. Not only did Perle attempt to get Khashoggi to invest in his Trireme Partners (an enterprise he set up with Henry Kissinger) but he and his disciples in the Pentagon's Office of Special Plans attempted to use Ghorbanifar to re-open an intelligence back channel to Iran, unused since the Iran-Contra scandal of the Reagan administration. Ghorbanifar, a friend of neoconservative Svengali, Michael Ledeen, once failed twelve of fourteen questions on a CIA-administered polygraph test. He only passed on the two questions about his name and nationality. Ghorbanifar has only surfaced in U.S. government circles after Israel or its agents of influence inside and outside the U.S. government brought pressure to bear.

The fact that bin Laden would identify with a conservative Republican president should come as no shock. After all, it was Reagan and his cabal of neoconservatives and extreme right-wing Cold Warriors who arranged for bin Laden to receive economic and personnel assistance from Saudis and weapons from the Egyptians and Israelis during the Afghan mujaheddin war against the Soviets. It was George H.W. Bush, who, in 1980, went to Paris to negotiate a deal with the radical Iranian Islamists to keep the U.S. hostages at the Tehran embassy hostage past the November election to ensure that there would be no "October Surprise" (i.e., a release) that would benefit President Jimmy Carter at the polls. (It is clear that in his heart of hearts President Carter, a living icon of American statesmanship, had this in the back of his mind when he constantly referred to the "extremism" of the current Bush administration in his speech to the Boston Democratic convention.)

It was Reagan and his administration that established a virtual anti-Soviet "aircraft carrier" along the Afghan-Pakistani border with the help of Pakistan's Inter Service Intelligence Service (ISI). It was at one non-descript guest house in Peshawar, in the heart of this American-nurtured remote forward operating base, that Afghan and Arab mujaheddin graduates of Saudi Wahhabist religious schools and indoctrination centers would congregate and discuss strategy against the Soviets under the watchful eye of CIA and ISI handlers. That guest house was known to the mujaheddin as "al Qaeda" ("the Base") and it would later (and rather erroneously) lend its name to a group of Saudi-backed and influenced fanatics who would one day carry out the horrible terrorist attacks against the World Trade Center and the Pentagon. But perception management campaigns are a hallmark of the Bush cartel. One could not get a more believable Arab terrorist leader like bin Laden from Hollywood central casting. The stock footage of bin Laden firing an AK-47, coming out of a cave talking on a mobile satellite phone, listening to the Voice of America as his hijackers slammed into the Twin Towers on 9/11, the imagery of the towers resembling an "11" on 9/11 (the emergency telephone number), the quick passage of the Patriot Act, questioning John Kerry's Vietnam War record, bogus documents on Bush's Air National Guard service being fed to CBS News by a White House disinformation machine and bogus intelligence on Iraq being fed to the UN Security Council and Congress — it's all perception management — a grand attempt to deceive and mislead. It is all the imagery and political skullduggery required for an impending "Clash of Civilizations," a New Crusade, a Christian evangelist Great Apocalypse, a Resurgent Jihad, a Jewish Rebuilding of the Temple — and more. The perception management results have been a blessing for the Bush/Saudi/Carlyle cartel that now controls Washington, Houston, Riyadh, Baghdad, Kabul, and most of the world. As Russia continues to bury and identify its dead children from Beslan, Vladimir Putin says he will strike anytime and anywhere against the terrorist supporters. SPETSNAZ teams "operating" in Saudi Arabia, the gated communities and country clubs of Houston, and the Saudi's shill law offices on K Street should not be ruled out by Moscow.

It must be stressed that bin Laden and his associates never used the name al Qaeda to describe themselves — that was something the U.S. government and corporate news media created as a moniker for them. Ever since 1985, bin Laden's group has been known to themselves and their allies as the Islamic Salvation Foundation, a group that financed its operations through Saudi,

Pakistani, and Sudanese-based Islamic charities and the sale of Afghan opium. In 1998, bin Laden created an international Islamist coalition called the "Islamic Struggle Front" with allies in Bangladesh, Egypt, and Pakistan that issued a fatwa declaring it legitimate to kill Americans everywhere, civilians or military. That year, the U.S. embassies in Nairobi and Dar es Salaam in East Africa were bombed by bin Laden loyalists. All the while, the head of Saudi intelligence, Prince Turki bin Faisal (who remains the de facto head of Saudi intelligence while moonlighting as Saudi Arabia's ambassador to Great Britain), maintained his friendship with bin Laden, who he had known since the "al Qaeda" leader was an economic and marketing student at the University of Jeddah.

Even after the Soviets withdrew from Afghanistan in 1989, the CIA and Saudis pumped one-half billion dollars into mujaheddin coffers, a good portion going to bin Laden and his allied groups. This was at a time some within the mujaheddin began setting their sights on new targets, especially the United States, after U.S. troops began arriving the next year in Saudi Arabia in the prelude to Desert Storm and the first U.S.-led invasion of Iraq.

According to a Washington Justice Department insider, a few years after Desert Storm and bin Laden's new antipathy toward the United States, Richard Perle, Douglas Feith and Feith's Israeli-American partner Marc Zell, were involved in setting up the Bosnia Defense Fund using an account at Riggs Bank in Washington. Millions of dollars in contributions for Bosnia to buy weapons and military training from companies like Military Professional Resources Inc. (MPRI) flowed into the account from countries like Egypt, Malaysia, Saudi Arabia, the United Arab Emirates, Brunei, Jordan, and Kuwait. From Washington the money was wired to Sarajevo where some of the weapons "bled" from the armories of the Bosnian forces and into the hands of radical Islamists sent to the Balkans by bin Laden to begin a jihad against the West in Bosnia, Macedonia, Kosovo, and Albania. It was the very same type of banking network that propped bin Laden up in Afghanistan during the anti-Soviet jihad. Using the facilities of the Bank of Credit and Commerce International (BCCI), Saudi charities from princes, mosques, and wealthy private contributors were funneled into the coffers of bin Laden and his allies.

Compare this to the involvement of Perle, Feith, and other neoconservatives in the Bush administration with the likes of Ahmad Chalabi and his nephew Salem Chalabi (the latter the Baghdad law partner of Marc Zell) and one begins to see a pattern hearkening back to the halcyon days of the Reagan Iran-Contra scandal and Afghan mujaheddin escapade. That the same individuals continue to be linked to war profiteering and espionage at the top echelons of government is reportedly at the heart of the current FBI investigation of the role of the neoconservatives in the current investigation of the American Israel Public Affairs Committee (AIPAC), Office of Special Plans personnel, the leak of highly-classified and compartmented communications intelligence (COMINT) information by Ahmad Chalabi to Iran, the use by the White House of bogus Niger documents regarding procurement of uranium from that country by Iraq, and the illegal outing of Ambassador Joseph Wilson's CIA wife to columnist Robert Novak.

There is also the curious role of Turkey in the current U.S. spy scandals. Former FBI translator Sibel Edmonds has spoken of a non-governmental foreign intelligence operation within the FBI office where she worked centered around the Turkish American Council. Both Turkey and Israel were intimately involved with the Afghan mujaheddin, including the forces that later coalesced around bin Laden. Some 60,000 rifles and 100 million rounds of ammunition were withdrawn from Turkish army stocks for delivery to the mujaheddin, although some of the weapons found their way into the hands of the Iranians, according to Middle East expert and veteran former ABC news correspondent John Cooley in his thought-provoking and well-researched book *Unholy Wars: Afghanistan, America and International Terrorism*, a book the CIA for years attempted to suppress. According to Ahmad Rashid in his excellent book, *Taliban*, "Israel saw the Taliban as an anti-Iranian force which could be used to undermine Iranian influence in Afghanistan and Central Asia." Rashid also states that later, "Turkey also played a role in turning around Israel's policy in Afghanistan" because "the Israelis and more significantly some Jewish lobbies in the USA were not initially critical of the Taliban." That Israel and Turkey may have been cooperating in an espionage ring inside the FBI should not be a surprise — their intelligence agencies had been cooperating for a number of years, especially in Afghanistan.

Similarly, according to George Crile's most revealing book about the U.S. support for the mujaheddin, *Charlie Wilson's War*, Israel and Pakistan, although lacking diplomatic relations, cooperated in secretly upgrading Pakistan's Chinese-made T-55 tanks and providing support to the mujaheddin. It is noteworthy to point out that bin Laden's vitriol against Israel has been a relatively recent development. Long before he denounced Israel's treatment of the Palestinians, bin Laden remained focused on the expulsion of "infidel" U.S. troops from the Arabian Peninsula, especially Saudi Arabia.

Support for the embryonic "al Qaeda" and its Wahhabi/Saudi/Salafist/ISI-affiliated mujaheddin allies was largely the work of big business-owned and operated Texas politicians like former Representative Charlie Wilson. The bin Laden family had a long association with Texas. Osama's older brother Salem was a financier of George W. Bush's oil businesses. The bin Laden family and their Saudi financial colleagues owned Texas airlines, airports, and real estate.

Because of the intensive lobbying efforts (all documented in Crile's book) carried out with the help of Texans like Houston socialite and TV personality Joanne Herring, Baron and Baroness di Portanova, and Vice President George H.W. Bush, in concert with Richard Perle, former New Hampshire Senator Gordon Humphrey, the Congressional Jewish Caucus, and the ever-enigmatic shady operator Richard Armitage, radicals like bin Laden and his associates, Dr. Ayman al Zawahiri and Professor Abdul Rasul Sayyaf (the founder of a Saudi-financed and ISI-organized "Terrorist University," which spawned the Philippine terrorist "Abu Sayyaf Group"), were able to cobble together an impressive jihadist army armed with stockpiles of Soviet-made weapons from Egypt, captured Soviet weapons from Israel, and tons of cash from billionaire Saudi benefactors. George H.W. Bush and George W. Bush's Florida election "fixer" and newly-named Bush debate coach James Baker III have both been honored guests, according to the *Wall Street Journal*, at the bin Laden family's palatial headquarters in Jeddah. With the active support of Pakistan's military dictator Mohammed Zia Ul-Haq (who was killed along with the U.S. ambassador, Pakistan's ISI chief Akhtar Abdul Rahman, and others in a mysterious 1988 plane crash determined by an unpublished Pakistani court of inquiry report to have been caused by the pilot being knocked out by gas in the cockpit), the Afghan mujaheddin became increasingly radicalized in the Wahhabi traditions. Out of Saudi-nurtured and Pakistani-organized madrasas would come future Taliban leaders like Mullah Mohammed Omar.

Senator Ted Kennedy was in the Senate in the late 1970s and 1980s, and he must have experienced déjà vu as some of these same Texas interests championed the war against Iraq and the demarche to the Taliban to deal with the United States on the proposed UNOCAL trans-Afghan CentGas pipeline or face a "carpet of bombs." Kennedy correctly stated that the Iraq war was cooked up in Texas to benefit a Bush in the White House. So was America's support for the mujaheddin and bin Laden in Afghanistan although the main beneficiary was a previous Bush in the White House.

Notwithstanding page 56 of the 9/11 Commission Report, which states "… bin Ladin and his comrades had their own sources of support and training, and they received little or no assistance from the United States," the United States and its Saudi allies funneled millions of dollars to bin Laden and his mujaheddin forces through Pakistani interlocutors. Of bin Laden, Cooley writes, "Through his own personal reputation as a pious Muslim who favored the cause of Wahhabi Islamism … he seemed to both Saudi intelligence and the CIA an ideal choice for the leading role he began to play [in the jihad against the Soviets in Afghanistan]."

The decision to groom bin Laden as an American agent of influence among the mujaheddin came at the same time William Casey, an elderly and drooling version of Austin Powers' "Dr. Evil," headed the CIA. Cooley adds, "Delighted by his impeccable Saudi credentials, the CIA gave Osama free rein in Afghanistan, as did Pakistan's intelligence generals." Cooley posits that the CIA was more than happy to see a buildup of Wahhabi Sunni power in Afghanistan to serve as a counterweight to Iranian Shi'ism being advocated by the Ayatollah Khomeini. This is the very same motivation that Ahmad Rashid reasoned was behind Israel's support for the Taliban. And when bin Laden was victorious with his fifty Arab mujaeddin over 200 Soviet troops in the Battle of Jaji, he became an instant hero: "Bin Laden, the Hero of the Battle of Jaji," a folk hero the United States and Israel could use to their advantage. Support for the mujaheddin and bin Laden was a decision that Langley and Tel Aviv would come to regret. (The Israelis have experienced two such "blowbacks." They also created Hamas as a counter-weight to Yasir Arafat's Fatah movement).

Perle, according to Crile's book, actually wanted to use Afghanistan as a playground for all sorts of fantastic schemes, including a campaign by the mujaheddin to entice Soviet soldiers to defect to their side. One CIA clandestine services officer, Gust Avrakotos, called Oliver North and Perle "cuckoos of the Far Right" and called them idiots to their faces.

Fast forward to today and we see Perle and North both involved as cheerleaders for the U.S. invasion of Iraq. These "cuckoos of the Far Right" convinced the world that American troops would be welcomed by undulating Iraqis throwing flowers and sweets at American jeeps and tanks. Instead, Iraq has now become a welcome haven for followers of bin Laden just as parts of Afghanistan remain in the hands of his supporters. Bin Laden may whisper every day the same thing he said of Reagan, "I like Bush. He believes in God. He's helping us. He's better than the others." Others like Bill Clinton, who launched a cruise missile attack against bin Laden in Afghanistan but only after the ISI tipped off the Saudi exile that the missiles were on their way. Others like John Kerry, who investigated how bin Laden and his cronies received their funding through BCCI and Saudi interlocutors in networks that reached right into the offices of Vice President George H.W. Bush and William Casey's CIA. This, of course, should come as no shock to those who have followed and continue to follow the dastardly deeds of the Bush/Saudi/Pakistani/bin Laden/Carlyle Group cartel and their international machinations.

And it should come as no shock that the only people who suffered as a result of the 9/11 attack three years ago have been Americans, who have seen their basic civil liberties trashed and burned and their best and brightest military men and women sacrificed in a senseless war in Iraq; Afghans, who have seen their country ravaged by continuous death and destruction from a resurgent Taliban and al Qaeda and U.S. "collateral damage" and "friendly fire"; and Iraqis, who have been subjected to death, turmoil, and even torture and sexual molestation by a coalition of the coerced and mercenary soldiers of fortune and lawless brigands acting on behalf of the Bush White House political apparatchiks. Counterterrorism expert and journalist Peter Bergen commented at the Cato conclave, "the Iraq war was a Christmas present for Osama bin Laden." Yes, one can hear bin Laden murmuring over and over again from his own secret undisclosed location, "I like Bush even more than I liked Reagan."

On July 20, 2005, I wrote the following about the Bush-Saud-bin Laden relationship on *WMR*:

Saudi King Fahd has officially accepted the resignation of Saudi ambassador to the United States Prince Bandar bin Sultan (affectionately nicknamed "Bandar Bush" by members of the

Bush family). But his replacement should shock every American citizen, especially those who lost loved ones in repeated "al Qaeda" terrorist attacks on U.S. soil and abroad.

The Saudis have shot a hypocritical blast at the United States by naming Prince Turki al Faisal, the former head of Saudi intelligence and current ambassador to London, as their next ambassador to Washington. During his 27-year stint as head of Saudi intelligence, Turki met on several occasions (at least five times) with Osama bin Laden and his lieutenants. Turki was originally named in a $1 trillion lawsuit filed by families of the victims of 9/11. The lawsuit claimed Turki helped fund bin Laden.

A Federal judge ruled that Turki had immunity from such a suit and, after an article in *Paris Match* alleged that Turki helped fund al Qaeda, Turki sued the magazine for libel and won a large settlement and apology. In 2002, Turki told CNN, "I met bin Laden five times during the jihad against the Soviets in Afghanistan."

However, by his own admission, Turki had an additional meeting with bin Laden and his allies in 1991, some two years before the radical terrorist leader helped engineer the 1993 World Trade Center bombing. One was a coordination meeting held in Saudi Arabia to help overthrow the Marxist government of South Yemen. The defeat of the South Yemeni government took place in 1994, well over a year after the WTC van bombing in New York, a period of time when bin Laden was living in Khartoum, benefiting from the largesse of wealthy Saudi businessmen and Royal family members. According to the London *Sunday Times*, Turki also met with bin Laden representatives at a Paris hotel in 1996 and in 1998 with Taliban leader Mullah Mohammed Omar and Osama bin Laden in Kandahar, Afghanistan, while bin Laden was virtually running the country. Turki took over the Saudi Istakhbarat al Amiyyah intelligence service from his uncle Kamal Adham. Although Turki was removed as head of Saudi intelligence as a result of U.S. pressure after 9/11, he will now represent his nation in Washington, DC.

Anthrax: A biological warfare attack on the Senate Democratic leadership

Often overlooked in the 9/11 attack scenario is the biological warfare attack on the U.S. Congress in the weeks following

9/11. Two U.S. Postal Service employees, as well as other Americans, died in the attack and the business of the Congress was disrupted, but not so much that it was not able to pass the Bush administration's Patriot Act. Although the Bush administration maintained it did not foresee the anthrax attack on Congress, documents obtained from the U.S. Postal Service proved otherwise. I wrote about the anthrax attack in August 2003:

This reporter has obtained a U.S. Postal Service "Management Instruction" that warned of the potential for anthrax being sent through the postal system. The instruction, authored by Yvonne D. Maguire, Vice President for Human Resources, was issued on October 4, 1999, almost two years to the day before anthrax sent through the mail killed photojournalist Bob Stevens in Boca Raton, Florida. Stevens died on October 5, 2001.

The instruction, titled "Emergency Response to Mail Allegedly Containing Anthrax," states, "In 1998 and 1999 there have been several instances where Postal customers have reported receiving letters or parcels that allegedly contained a specific biologically hazardous material, anthrax." The instruction declares the mailings were considered to be hoaxes. The instruction outlines emergency steps to be taken in the event of an anthrax mailing. These include mechanical shutdown of equipment (including air handling equipment), isolation, evacuation, and notification of proper authorities. In the case of the Washington, DC Brentwood postal center, these steps were not immediately taken when anthrax was mailed to the Senate offices of Tom Daschle and Pat Leahy. The Centers for Disease Control (CDC) in Atlanta said that Brentwood was not immediately shut down because it said the small anthrax spores could not escape from a sealed envelope.

Dr. Ken Alibek (born Kanatjan Alibekov), formerly the deputy director of the Soviet bio-war laboratory Biopreparat until he defected to the United States in 1992, said the FBI told Postmaster General John Potter that the mail sent through Brentwood had not broken open. Alibek, speaking to an April 25 meeting of former Brentwood employees, many of whom are now suffering from possible anthrax-related ailments, said the CDC was engaging in "perception management" when it told the FBI and Postal Service that the anthrax letters were well sealed. Alibek said the CDC had "no expertise" to say that. He also criticized the CDC for suggesting that Stevens' death from anthrax in Florida was the result of a hunting trip. Alibek emphatically stated, "you cannot catch anthrax on the street or in the forest ... the CDC was stupid about the hunting story, they knew it was terrorism."

Two postal workers subsequently died from inhaling finely-milled weapons-grade anthrax later discovered to have been derived from the Ames strain held at the U.S. Army Medical Research Institute for Infectious Diseases (USAMRIID) at Fort Detrick, Maryland. Alibek said whoever mailed the anthrax was very clever because the mail sorting machines additionally milled the anthrax spores and further aerosolized them permitting the spores to be spread more effectively.

In 1988, the Foundation on Economic Trends warned that Fort Detrick and the CDC in Atlanta were shipping through the U.S. postal system the "deadliest diseases known to man." One such shipment in 1987 from the CDC to Fort Detrick contained the Crimea-Congo virus, a deadly pathogen carried by ticks. The shipment was "lost" somewhere in the main Philadelphia post office. Later in 1988, Postmaster General Anthony Frank banned Army bio-toxin shipments through the mail after the Army said it would step up such shipments to its new bio-war laboratory at Utah's Dugway Proving Grounds, a facility that has the only aerosolized anthrax laboratory in the United States. The Army wanted to ship anthrax, botulism, Q fever, and dengue fever through the mail. After the anthrax mailing, it was discovered that Fort Detrick was not only missing specimens of the Ames strain of anthrax but also cultures of Ebola, simian AIDS, hanta virus and two "classified" agents. Russian bio-war experts claim that the severe acute respiratory syndrome (SARS) that has killed over 100 people worldwide is a man-made virus, a mixture of mumps and measles that cannot occur in nature.

On August 8, 2006, *WMR* had a follow-up story on the all-but-forgotten anthrax attack:

U.S. Postal Service employees of the Brentwood postal facility (now called the Curseen-Morris Mail Processing and Distribution Center, named for the two postal workers killed in the anthrax attack) in Washington, DC, victims of the first biological weapons attack in the United States in 2001, now face additional attacks — by the senior management of the U.S. Postal Service, including GOP political hack Postmaster General John Potter. According to Brentwood sources, the jobs of the current

73

Brentwood employees are being threatened by an administration bent on privatizing the U.S. Postal Service.

Clerk jobs at Brentwood are being transferred to postal facilities as far away as Richmond and Philadelphia, a hardship for longtime residents of the Washington, DC area. Postal service drivers are finding their jobs being outsourced to contract drivers and maintenance workers are being downsized. Postal service management is also dragging its feet on implementing safety measures at Brentwood designed to prevent a repeat of the deaths resulting from the 2001 anthrax mailings.

Brentwood postal employees are also on the receiving end of "aggressive discipline" for speaking out about the changes that are affecting their employment and personal safety. Meanwhile, this coming November will represent the fifth anniversary of the anthrax attacks and resulting postal employee deaths at Brentwood. Plans for a memorial have received no support from either the Postal Service or the Bush administration. Evidence points to the U.S. Army's illegal biological weapons laboratory at Fort Detrick, Maryland as the source for the anthrax used in the attacks.

The Bush administration had broken so many treaties and laws, the possibility that it engaged in the type of bio-warfare that even Adolf Hitler ruled off the table was, in fact, a real one. The SARS outbreak in Asia occurred as China's economy was booming and America's was settling into a lethargic recession. I wrote about SARS in August 2003:

E vidence is mounting that the Bush administration may be engaging in a new form of warfare: bio-economic attacks against countries that either opposed the U.S. war on Iraq or were showing signs of surpassing the United States in economic vitality and growth. Revelations that the Severe Acute Respiratory Syndrome (SARS) does not occur naturally and that anthrax may have been introduced onto an Egyptian merchant vessel bound for Canada from Brazil has raised eyebrows among biological warfare experts.

The use of bio-economic warfare as a weapon of mass destruction was first suggested by Dr. Edgar J. DaSilva, the Director for the Division of Life Sciences of the UN Educational, Scientific, and Cultural Organization (UNESCO). Da Silva stated in a 1999 article in the Electronic Journal of Biotechnology that bio-economic warfare — "the undermining and destruction of economic progress and stability" — can be traced to "the development and use of biological agents against economic targets such as crops, livestock and ecosystems." DaSilva also noted that such warfare can often be perceived by the public as naturally-occurring because "such warfare can always be carried out under the pretexts that such traumatic occurrences are the result of natural circumstances that lead to outbreaks of diseases and disasters of either endemic or epidemic proportions."

The United States, particularly the Central Intelligence Agency — through its joint efforts with the U.S. Army's biological warfare laboratory at Fort Detrick, Maryland — has pioneered in the field of bio-economic warfare. In the 1970s, the CIA directed a bio-economic warfare campaign against Cuba. In his book, *Biological Warfare in the 21st Century,* author Malcolm Dando describes the Cuba campaign as involving the use of blue mold against the nation's tobacco crop, cane smut against the sugar crop, African swine fever against the livestock population, and a hemorrhagic strain of dengue fever against the human population. These attacks were designed to destabilize Cuba's agricultural based economy. The Cuba operations were conducted after President Richard Nixon, in a 1969 Executive Order, banned the use of biological warfare agents. Nixon's order and his 1972 signing of the Biological and Toxin Weapons Convention with Britain and the Soviet Union outlawing bio-weapons were systematically ignored by the CIA and Pentagon.

Almost at the same time that Western financial institutions were forecasting a record growth in China's gross domestic product — estimates ranged from 7.5 to 7.6 percent — the country's southern Guangdong Province experienced its first outbreak of SARS. After the disease began spreading and Chinese officials scurried to deal with the virus, the economic cost to mainland China was devastating — $2.2 billion according to the Far Eastern Economic Review. In addition, SARS cost Hong Kong $1.7 billion. For the Bush administration, which was experiencing America's worst economic downturn in ten years and was spending billions on the war against Iraq, the idea of a booming Chinese economy did not sit well. In addition, China was in the final stages of planning its first manned space launch at a time when the United States lost its second space shuttle due to incompetence. The Contrasts between an economically vitalized China and a United States caught in the malaise of recession, war, and technological failure could not have been more stark. Then we heard about the first outbreak of SARS....

There is definitely a right-wing element involving scientists, military, intelligence, and government contractor personnel in the study, production, and distribution of biological weapons, including anthrax, gas gangrene, Dengue fever, and other pathogens. As the right-wing in the United States calls for retaliation against countries that failed to support America's war on Iraq, it may be more than coincidental that SARS has broken out in China and the virus has been transmitted to Canada via the busy travel routes existing between China, Hong Kong, and major Canadian cities like Toronto and Vancouver due to Canada's large Asian population. Not only has China's economy drastically suffered, but Toronto, Canada's most populous city, is facing an economic disaster. After the SARS outbreak in Canada, it was discovered that an Egyptian vessel carrying bauxite from Brazil to an Alcan aluminum plant in Saguenay, Quebec suffered the death of its first mate from anthrax just prior to departing Brazil for Canada. Fortunately, Canadian authorities were alerted before the ship docked in Quebec, whose majority French-speaking population has been just as outspoken against America's war policies as their kinfolk in France.

Considering Dr. DaSilva's warnings about bio-economic warfare, the world should be on guard against a deliberate policy by the right-wing elements that populate the Bush administration to use bio-weapons to punish countries for failure to cooperate with the United States. Considering that the CIA and Pentagon considered buying genetically-fused bacteria and viruses from South African freelance bio-war scientists and that Russian scientists now claim that SARS is a similarly genetically-fused mumps and measles pathogen, an immediate investigation of Fort Detrick's stockpiles and their points of origin should be initiated by the Congress, which has shown an amazing lack of oversight for all the questionable activities of the Bush administration, including 9/11, Enron, and even the anthrax mailings that targeted two of the Senate's top leaders.

Although the Bush administration contends that the anthrax mailings, like the hijacking of commercial planes and turning them into virtual cruise missiles, were unprecedented and a surprise, history refutes such claims. In 1988, the Foundation on Economic Trends warned that Fort Detrick and the Centers for Disease Control in Atlanta were shipping some of the "deadliest diseases known to man" through the U.S. postal system. One such shipment in 1987 from the CDC to Fort Detrick contained the Crimea-Congo virus, a deadly pathogen carried by ticks. The shipment was "lost" somewhere in the main Philadelphia post office. In 1988, Postmaster General Anthony Frank banned U.S. government bio-toxin shipments through the mail after the U.S. Army said it would increase its postal shipments to its new bio-war laboratory at Utah's Dugway Proving Grounds, a facility that has the only aerosolized anthrax laboratory in the United States. The Army also wanted to ship anthrax, botulism, Q fever, and dengue fever through the mail, a frightening idea considering the reports that Fort Detrick was missing several pathogenic strains after the commencement of the anthrax mailings.

Unless Congress begins asking the tough questions, we will never know what went missing from Fort Detrick. Could the missing "bugs" have been West Nile virus, AIDS, bubonic plague (there have been several recent "mysterious" outbreaks of this disease in India, Kazakhstan, Libya, Congo, and Brazil), or even SARS? Why can't the American people expect a full investigation of and accounting for America's supposedly "banned" bio-weapons program?

The U.S. Congress, which is now in the hands of some of the most right-wing and venal ideologues in its history, will probably not want to delve into America's secret labyrinth of bio-weapons progenitors and dispensers, especially since it involves a number of their ideological soul mates. The vitriol spewing from the mouths of the Congressional leadership is strictly reserved for gays, African-Americans, the French, Hollywood liberals, the drug addicted, and abortion rights advocates. As far as the right-wing leadership is concerned, there is no questioning the military, Justice Department, or the intelligence agencies. Those who dared are no longer in a position to do so. Senators Bob Graham and Richard Shelby are off the Senate Intelligence Committee. They have been replaced by dupes and yes-men for Langley and Detrick.

China and Canada are now suffering from the SARS virus. Quebec almost received a possible deadly blow from ship-born anthrax spores. The Bush administration is now deciding how best to punish France, Germany, Russia, and other countries for their lack of support. Nothing, including the use of bio-economic warfare, should be put past the Bush administration. In the absence of an independent U.S. Congress, the world should demand that UN inspectors be given access to all U.S. bio-weapons laboratories. There is still no evidence that Saddam Hussein used bio-weapons but there is a lot of actual and circumstantial evidence that the United States has and continues to do so with possibly disastrous consequences for the entire world.

Afghanistan: The forgotten war

L ittle did the American public know that it was Iraq that was planned as the target for a massive U.S. military attack after 9/11. The Bush administration even negotiated with the Taliban for the handover of Osama bin Laden to the United States before launching Operation Enduring Freedom on October 7, 2001. Although the Unites States and its allies, which included the Afghan Northern Alliance, managed to unseat the Taliban from Kabul and Kandahar, it never caught Osama bin Laden or his number two, Dr. Ayman Zawahiri, although it had ample opportunities to do so.

As the Bush administration turned its attention to attacking Iraq, the Taliban hunkered down for a long war in Afghanistan. I wrote about this almost forgotten war in 2004:

C onsider the following highly-classified report about the situation on the Afghan front:
"Judging by the most recent communications that we have received from Afghanistan in the form of encrypted cables, as well as by telephone conferences with our chief military adviser ... the situation in Afghanistan has deteriorated sharply ... Bands of saboteurs and terrorists, having infiltrated from the territory of Pakistan ... are committing atrocities ..."
This dispatch could have come in the last two weeks from the U.S. Central Command, which is facing a renewed surge in Taliban and al Qaeda activity in Afghanistan. It is now estimated that the Taliban and their al Qaeda allies now control one-third of the battle-torn nation. The battlefield killing in Afghanistan by al Qaeda units of former National Football League player Pat Tillman, who volunteered for the U.S. Army Rangers in the aftermath of 9/11, points to the precarious position of the United States in Afghanistan. [It later turned out that Tillman was killed by his own

U.S. Army colleagues in a case of "friendly fire" and that the Army covered up the incident. Tillman's family's suspicions were aroused by the official cover-up.[1] The Taliban and al Qaeda are far from out of commission. And to make matters worse, President Bush secretly diverted a $750 million budget supplemental appropriated by Congress for the Afghan operation in order to build up for his pre-9/11-planned war against Iraq.

The above classified report, however, did not emanate from the U.S. Central Command or the Pentagon. It is a declassified Top Secret (Only Copy) Working Transcript of a meeting of the Politburo of the Central Committee of the Communist Party of the Soviet Union, dated March 17, 1979. The words are those of Soviet Foreign Minister Andrei Gromyko to his colleagues, who included General Secretary Leonid Brezhnev, his eventual successors Konstantin Chernenko and Yuri Andropov, Soviet Defense Minister Dmitri Ustinov, and a junior Politburo member named Mikhail Gorbachev.

In many respects, the Soviet Union's attempt to suppress an Islamic insurgency in Afghanistan led to the downfall of the world's "second superpower." The Soviet occupation of Afghanistan helped to trigger anti-Soviet restlessness in its own Central Asian Soviet Republics, which are now all independent of Moscow. What goes around eventually comes around. The United States, which built up the Islamic guerrilla groups in Afghanistan, eventually was attacked by some of their more radical offshoots. It now faces an Islamic rebellion not only in Afghanistan but also in Iraq. Eventually, if Israel does pull out of the Gaza Strip, Hamas will likely emerge as the governing power in that territory. [That eventually did occur in 2007]. Hamas has now declared war on the United States for supporting Ariel Sharon's intention to annex parts of the West Bank in violation of international law.

Other passages from the Soviet archives are almost a carbon copy of what the United States not only faces in Afghanistan but also Iraq. The words of the Soviet military, political, and intelligence leadership are as important for the Bush administration today as

---

1. In July 2007, it was revealed that Tillman had been shot three times in the forehead by an M-16 from 10 yards away. Far from friendly fire, Tillman, who is quoted as saying about the Iraq war, "This war is so fucking illegal," appeared to have been targeted for elimination in "the fog of war." The Bush White House fought off efforts to deny Representative Henry Waxman's House Committee on Oversight and Government Reform access to Tillman documents until July 2007.

they were for the Kremlin political elite in 1979 and throughout the 1980s.

We are constantly told by the Bush administration and its ambassador to Kabul, the Afghan-American neoconservative Zalmay Khalilzad, that the regime of Hamid Karzai is firmly in control of much of Afghanistan. That is as laughable as the Soviets being told by their clients in Kabul that they, also, were firmly in control. From the March 17, 1979, transcript, the words of Central Committee Secretary Andrei Kirilenko, who saw potential problems for the Red Army in Afghanistan, could easily be applied to U.S. forces in Afghanistan and Iraq today:

"The question arises, whom will our troops be fighting against if we send them there? Against the insurgents? Or have they been joined by a large number of religious fundamentalists, that is, Muslims, and among them large numbers of ordinary people? Thus, we will be required to wage war in significant part against the people."

Kirilenko also raised the problem of Soviet support for its client in Kabul, Nur Mohammed Taraki, who was committing major human rights violations against Islamic religious leaders:

"… Taraki must be instructed to change his tactics. Executions, torture, and so forth cannot be applied on a massive scale. Religious questions, the relationship with religious communities, with religion generally and with religious leaders take on special meaning for them. This is a major policy issue. And here Taraki must ensure, with all decisiveness, that no illicit measures whatsoever are undertaken by them."

Alexei Kosygin, the Soviet Premier, also raised misgivings about going into Afghanistan. He said about sending Soviet arms to the Afghan army,

"If [the Afghan army] collapses, then it follows that those arms will be claimed by the insurgents."

The next day, March 18, 1979, Kosygin reported an amazing revelation from his phone conversation with Taraki: "Almost without realizing it, Comrade Taraki responded that almost nobody supports the government." According to a formerly Top Secret phone transcript, Taraki told Kosygin, "there is no active support on the part of the population [in Herat]. It is almost wholly under the influence of Shi'ite slogans — follow not the heathens, but follow us. The propaganda is underpinned by this."

Kirilenko then reported that the 17th Afghan Army Division in Herat, numbering 9000 men, had gone over to the side of the insurgents. Kosygin added that an anti-aircraft battalion had also joined the rebels. Compare what the Soviets discussed with what George W. Bush must be hearing from his Iraqi viceroy, Paul Bremer, about Iraqi support for the U.S. occupation, what the Iraqi people think about the neoconservative stooge Ahmad Chalabi, the Shi'ite uprising in southern and central Iraq, the U.S. winning the "hearts and minds" of the Iraqi people, and mass defections by U.S.-trained Iraqi army and police personnel to the insurgents. The old Soviet Politburo members must be laughing up their sleeves about the U.S. predicament in both Iraq and Afghanistan.

The head of the Soviet KGB, Yuri Andropov, presented a stark warning to his colleagues about what the Soviets would encounter in their Afghan occupation:

"Comrades, I have considered all the these issues in depth and arrived at the conclusion that we must consider very, very seriously, the question of whose cause we will be supporting if we deploy forces into Afghanistan. It's completely clear to us that Afghanistan is not ready at this time to resolve all the issues it faces through socialism. The economy is backward, the Islamic religion predominates, and nearly all the rural population is illiterate. We know Lenin's teachings about a revolutionary situation. Whatever situation we are talking about in Afghanistan, it is not that type of situation. Therefore, I believe that we can suppress a revolution in Afghanistan only with the aid of our bayonets, and that is entirely inadmissible. We cannot take such a risk."

Gromyko supported Andropov:

"I completely support Comrade Andropov's proposal to rule out such a measure as the deployment of our troops into Afghanistan. The army there is unreliable. Thus our army, when it arrives, will be the aggressor. Against whom will it fight? Against the Afghan people first of all, and it will have to shoot at them … we must keep in mind that from a legal point of view too we would not be justified in sending troops. According to the UN Charter a country can appeal for assistance, and we could send troops, in case it is subject to external aggression. Afghanistan has not been subject to any aggression. This is its internal affair … a battle of one group of the population against another."

Kirilenko added, "… there is no basis whatsoever for the deployment of troops."

The following day, March 19, Gromyko laid on the table, with Brezhnev present, what the Soviets would lose by an invasion of Afghanistan: "We would be throwing away everything we achieved with such difficulty, particularly détente, the SALT-II negotiations would fly by the wayside, there would be no signing of an agreement (and however you look at it that is for us the greatest political priority), there would be no meeting between Leonid Ilyich with Carter, and it would be very doubtful that Giscard d'Estaing would come to visit us, and our relations with Western countries, particularly the Federal Republic of Germany, would be spoiled."

After Taraki was killed by his deputy, Hafizullah Amin, in October 1979, Brezhnev pushed for his doctrine that no socialist country could revert to capitalism. The Soviet military prevailed and a decision was made to launch an invasion of Afghanistan in December 1979. All the protestations of some of the leading members of the Soviet old guard were swept aside. The Soviets faced a 10-year costly battle in terms of lives and money and were eventually forced to withdraw, leaving Afghanistan in the hands of radicals who would one day launch and nurture the Taliban and al Qaeda.

It is noteworthy what an October 2, 1980 formerly Secret Soviet Communist Party report said about U.S. support for the mujaheddin, "American instructors are taking an active part in the training of the rebels on the territory of Pakistan. These instructors have come mainly from the Washington-based 'International Police Academy' and the Texas-based school of subversion." And in what would help lay the groundwork for the establishment of the Taliban and al Qaeda, the Soviet leadership was warned, "The American CIA has devised special recommendations for the use of religious movements and groups in the struggle against the spread of Communist influence. In accordance with these recommendations, agents from the American special services in Pakistan are carrying out various work among the Pashtun and Baluchi tribes ..."

By 1986, it was clear to the new Soviet leader, Gorbachev, that the occupation of Afghanistan was a disaster. In talking about the Soviet client in Kabul, Babrak Karmal, Gorbachev stated in a Top Secret Draft transcript, "B. Karmal is very much down in terms of health and in terms of psychological disposition. He began to pit leaders against each other." (Take note of what Ahmad Chalabi is now doing in Iraq now that Bremer has given a green light to restoring former Baathist leaders to power. Chalabi is talking about conspiracies by Iraqi Sunnis and Lakhdar Brahimi, the UN chief envoy. Chalabi refers to Brahimi being in league with Arab nationalists and socialists because he is an Algerian and a Sunni). In 1986, Babrak Karmal was replaced by the Soviets with Mohammed Najibullah. Karmal fled to Moscow where he remained in exile until his death in 1996 (take note Mr. Chalabi). Eventually, after the Taliban government captured Kabul, they grabbed Najibullah and tortured and hanged him. (An event that Chalabi and Karzai should both take note of. In fact, Karzai has announced his willingness to allow middle and low-ranking Taliban members back into the government — Baathists back in power in Iraq and Taliban back in government in Afghanistan! What the hell was the purpose of these wars anyway?)

From the Soviet archives we may see the future for the United States. Like Brezhnev and the hard-line Soviet military leaders, Bush ignored his Secretary of State, geographical area experts, and Republican "graybeards" and launched an invasion of Iraq. Bush also failed to understand that no invader has ever been able to make Afghanistan into a version of itself. Alexander the Great failed (even though the Afghan city of Kandahar is named for him in a phonetically corrupt fashion); the Russians and their successors, the Soviets, failed; Britain failed; and most assuredly, the United States will never be able to turn Afghanistan into a democracy.

The Soviet Union believed it could transform Afghanistan into a secular-oriented socialist state (not a bad goal when considering the alternative: that Afghanistan instead became a radical Islamist breeding ground for the people who would fly airliners into the World Trade Center and Pentagon).

The Soviet defeat in Afghanistan eventually helped create the climate for its ultimate collapse. We now read Top Secret transcripts and cables from the Soviet archives. Most members of the old Soviet Politburo, many of whom warned against the Afghan adventure, are now dead. Nothing remains of the Soviet Union, which once boasted the largest nuclear Navy in the world, a huge Army, a huge space program, and a worldwide political ideology for which it was the nominal head.

As the neoconservatives lead the United States into deeper involvement in Iraq and Afghanistan, possible future military forays into Iran, Gaza, Syria, and North Korea, withdrawal of the United States from the United Nations system, and a policy of ruthless assassination of its enemies, how long will it take for future historians to be scanning documents from the CIA, National Security Council, and the Republican Party documenting the in-fighting within the last American presidency — a second term — of George W. Bush? The Soviet Union collapsed practically overnight. The Roman Empire took a number of years to fall, but it was inevitable. Nazi Germany's fate became known in a matter of a few years. The United States will not last forever, but the Bush administration may be speeding up the process for its ultimate fall. How long will it be before U.S. twenty and fifty dollar bills are sold as cheap souvenirs at street bazaars in the former United States like Soviet ruble notes are sold today on the streets of Moscow? The Soviet leaders were unable to stop their country's march to war in Afghanistan. Recent revelations from Bush administration officials show that several key players were unable to stop Bush and Cheney's determined march to war in Iraq. One world superpower went down in flames in 1990. Will the other last until 2010?

Chapter 4

The War of Lies
and the Lies of War

There clearly was a relationship. It's been testified to. The evidence is overwhelming.... It goes back to the early '90s. It involves a whole series of contacts, high-level contacts with Osama bin Laden and Iraqi intelligence officials.

— Vice President Dick Cheney, June 17, 2004

The march to war in Iraq was rife with disinformation, propaganda, and forgeries. The neocon approach is to do anything to achieve their political ends regardless of illegality.

The world witnessed this perfidy in the various intelligence documents "produced" to justify the invasion of Iraq. Almost all of these documents had been outright forgeries or had been altered. I wrote about this subject for *CounterPunch* on April 29, 2003:

After the United States and Britain were shown to be providing bogus and plagiarized "intelligence" documents to the UN Security Council that supposedly "proved" Saddam Hussein's weapons of mass destruction program, the world's media is now being fed a steady stream of captured Iraqi "intelligence" documents from the rubble of Iraq's Mukhabarat intelligence headquarters.

The problem with these documents is that they are being provided by the U.S. military to a few reporters working for a very suspect newspaper, London's *Daily Telegraph* (affectionately known as the "Daily Torygraph" by those who understand the paper's right-wing slant). The *Telegraph's* April 27 Sunday edition reported that its correspondent in Baghdad, Inigo Gilmore, had been invited into the intelligence headquarters by U.S. troops and miraculously "found" amid the rubble a document indicating that Iraq invited Osama bin Laden to visit in March 1998. Gilmore also reported that the CIA been through the building several times before he found the document. Gilmore added that the CIA must have "missed" the document in their prior searches, an astounding claim since the CIA must have been intimately familiar with the building from their previous intelligence links with the Mukhabarat dating from the Iran-Iraq war of the 1980s. Moreover, the CIA and other intelligence agencies, including Britain's MI-6, have refuted claims of a link between bin Laden and Iraq.

Gilmore also made it a point to declare he was not providing propaganda for the United States, a strange statement by someone who claims to be a seasoned Middle East correspondent. However, it is highly possible he was providing the propaganda for the benefit of a non-government actor, the neoconservative movement, which uses the Pentagon as a base of operations, and employs deception and perception management tactics to push its sinister agenda.

The U.S. has been quite active in inviting *Telegraph* reporters into the Iraqi intelligence headquarters. Other documents "found" by the paper's reporters "revealed" Russian intelligence had passed intercepts of Tony Blair's phone conversations to Iraqi intelligence, that German intelligence offered to assist Iraqi intelligence in the lead-up to the war, that France provided Iraq with the contents of US-French diplomatic exchanges, and that anti-war and anti-Bush Labor Party Member of Parliament George Galloway had solicited hundreds of thousands of dollars from Iraq, which were skimmed from the country's oil-for-food program.

Galloway immediately smelled the rat of a disinformation campaign when he responded to the *Telegraph* about the "found" document. "Maybe it's the product of the same forgers who forged so many other things in this whole Iraq picture... It would not be the Iraqi regime that was forging it. It would be people like you [*Telegraph* journalists] and the Government whose policies you have supported," Galloway said.

It is amazing that the U.S. military would be so open about letting favored journalists walk freely about the Mukhabarat building when the Pentagon has clamped tight security on the Iraqi Oil Ministry. The reason for this is obvious. While the Mukhabarat building can be salted with phony intelligence documents, the Oil Ministry is likely rife with documents showing the links between Saddam Hussein and Dick Cheney's old firm, Halliburton. The company signed more than $73 million in contracts with Saddam's government when Cheney was its Chief Executive Officer. The contracts, negotiated with two Halliburton subsidiaries — Dresser-Rand and Ingersoll Dresser Pump Co. — were part of the UN oil-for-food program, ironically the same program which figures prominently in the charges against Galloway. But unlike the charges against Galloway, the reports about Cheney's links to Saddam Hussein's oil industry originated with relatively more main stream media sources, including ABC News, the *Washington Post*, and the *Texas Observer*.

Gilmore told the BBC that he noticed that on the Mukhabarat documents he discovered, some information was "erased." The erasures were apparently made with a combination of black marker ink and correction fluid. He said he scraped away at the paper with a razor and miraculously found the name bin Laden in three places. The standard procedure for redacting a classified document is to only use a black indelible marker to mask classified information. However, the proper procedure for trying to read through such markings is not to scrape away the ink as if the document were an instant lottery ticket. Toner print often bleeds through the indelible marker ink. If one holds up such a sheet of paper at a 45 degree angle and under a bright phosphorescent light, the lettering under the ink can be "read" because the lettering almost appears to be "raised." If a razor blade were used to scrape away the markings, the indelible ink and the toner ink would be obliterated. Gilmore's claims appear to be spurious.

It was not long before the Iraqi-al Qaeda "smoking gun" document was reported around the world. America's right-wing propaganda channel, Fox News, featured the "found" document on its lead story on its *Fox Sunday News* program. Fox anchorman Tony Snow asked the ethically-tainted Iraqi National Congress leader Ahmed Chalabi about the document. Chalabi responded, saying the document provided enough information that Saddam Hussein was knowledgeable about the September 11 attacks on the United States, a canard that has been rejected by intelligence agencies around the world. However, for those who forged or doctored the document, it was mission accomplished.

To understand the process in disseminating such propaganda masked as news, it is important to understand the relationship between the *Daily Telegraph* and its parent company, the Hollinger Corporation, which is owned by British citizen and former Canadian, Conrad Black. Hollinger, like Rupert Murdoch's News Corporation, is a mega-media company that spins right-wing propaganda around the world through 379 newspapers, including the *Jerusalem Post*. Tom Rose, the publisher of the *Jerusalem Post*, is a major supporter of Ariel Sharon's Likud Party and is a favorite guest on the right-wing talk shows on Clear Channel radio stations, including that of G. Gordon Liddy of Watergate infamy. Clear Channel, headquartered in Dallas, is owned by close Bush supporters and one-time business partners. To add to the spider's web, one of Rose's *Jerusalem Post* directors is Richard Perle, a member of Donald Rumsfeld's advisory board.

The "smoking gun" document on Galloway was further played up on Fox News Sunday. William Kristol, an ally of Perle and a dean of the neoconservatives, and Fox's Brit Hume, a right-wing ideologue who masquerades as a reporter, said the documents implicating Galloway in accepting money from Saddam Hussein was the "tip of the iceberg." They then suggested that French President Jacques Chirac, other Western politicians, and Arab journalists working for such networks as Al Jazeera, would soon be "outed" by further Iraqi intelligence documents. For good measure, Fox also announced that Galloway may have given classified satellite imagery to al Qaeda. As is so often the case, the Fox News panelists provided no evidence for their slanderous claims.

Welcome to the new digital and satellite age McCarthyism. Phony documents are "dropped" into the hands of a right-wing London newspaper owned by Conrad Black. They are amplified by Black's other holdings, including the *Jerusalem Post* and *Chicago Sun-Times*. The story is then picked up by the worldwide television outlets of News Corporation, Time Warner, Disney, and General Electric and echoed on the right-wing radio talk shows of Clear Channel and Viacom. Political careers are damaged or destroyed. There is no right of rebuttal for the accused. They are guilty as charged by a whipped-up public that gets its information from the Orwellian telescreens of the corporate media.

The media operating in concert with political vermin to whip up popular opinion to stamp out criticism is nothing new. It was practiced by Joseph Goebbels quite effectively in Nazi Germany. It was a British-born actor named Peter Finch who so eloquently and prophetically warned us about the sorry state of today's media. In Paddy Chayefsky's excellent movie, *Network*, Finch plays UBS

TV news anchormen Howard Beale. When UBS's entertainment division decides to fire Beale because of low ratings, he begins to rant and rave on the air. He is then given his own television entertainment show, "The Mad Prophet of the Airwaves." The most famous scene in the movie is when Beale exhorts his viewers to go their windows and yell, "I'm mad as hell, and I'm not going to take it anymore." We should all be mad as hell about the propaganda in the newspapers and on the airwaves; George Bush and Tony Blair; Rupert Murdoch and Conrad Black; Clear Channel and Viacom; the neoconservative think-tank bottom feeders; Rumsfeld and his circle of Pentagon ghouls such as Perle, Paul Wolfowitz, and Newt Gingrich; and the religious fundamentalists who give aid and succor to America's war machine. To paraphrase Howard Beale, "We should not take them anymore!"

Another lie leading up to the Iraq war was the bogus intelligence that suggested Saddam Hussein had attempted to buy yellowcake uranium from Niger in West Africa. This scam was engineered through Rome and the government of Italian Prime Minister Silvio Berlusconi, who governed with the support of Italy's neo-fascist party.

On October 26, 2005, I wrote the following in *WMR* about the Italian connection to the fraudulent documents on which Bush based his 2003 State of the Union "revelations" about Iraq and Niger:

More details are emerging from the Italian newspaper *La Repubblica* concerning the backdooring of forged Niger documents into the White House and the Pentagon's Office of Special Plans by a special cell operating inside the Italian intelligence agency SISMI. The essential element of the Italian revelations is that Nicolo Pollari, the head of SISMI, went around CIA Director George Tenet and the CIA Rome station chief Jeff Castelli to establish a personal liaison with then-National Security Adviser Condoleezza Rice, Deputy Defense Secretary Paul Wolfowitz, Deputy Undersecretary of Defense for Policy and Plans Douglas Feith, Pentagon and National Security Council consultant Michael Ledeen, and Deputy National Security Adviser Stephen Hadley.

Pollari bypassed his own SISMI chief in Washington, Admiral Giuseppe Grignolo, an expert on WMD proliferation, to ensure forged Niger documents and other tainted intelligence on Iraqi weapons went directly to Rice and Ledeen through the Italian ambassador to Washington, Gianni Castellaneta, a Pollari loyalist. During the summer of 2002, Castellaneta set up a meeting between Pollari and Rice, a meeting at which phony intelligence on Iraqi WMDs was allegedly transmitted by the Italian official.

Grignolo had excellent relations with the CIA's Deputy Director for Operations James Pavitt (who was Valerie Plame Wilson's ultimate boss). The outing of Plame, Brewster Jennings & Associates, and the emaciation of the CIA's Counter Proliferation Division by Porter Goss loyalists is seen by intelligence officials in Washington and Rome as a blatant attempt to expose and ruin an untainted source of intelligence on WMD proliferation, thereby setting the stage for more phony WMD intelligence "finds" and a possible nuclear terrorism event.

There was another interesting connection between the Bush administration, the Italian government, and the use of Italy as a base for distributing phony intelligence. I wrote about it on *WMR* on July 18, 2005:

Mel Sembler, a rich Florida developer of shopping malls and playgrounds for the rich and famous, was awarded the coveted U.S. ambassadorship to Italy as a result of the hundreds of thousands of dollars he pumped into GOP coffers, particularly the campaigns of George W., George H.W., and Jeb Bush. The first President Bush awarded Sembler the ambassadorship to Australia. During the 2000 presidential campaign, Sembler's wife, Betty, was a member of the Republican Jewish Caucus. She also co-chaired Jeb Bush's gubernatorial campaign. In 2000, Mel served as National Finance Chairman for the Republican National Committee. After taking office, Bush quickly named Sembler a member of the Export-Import Bank, an entity that had guaranteed loans for a number of multi-million projects, including oil pipeline construction, in which Halliburton had a major stake.

Now, Sembler serves as George W. Bush's liaison to the neo-Fascists and pro-Iraq War politicians in Prime Minister Silvio Berlusconi's government, particularly neo-Fascist leader and Deputy Prime Minister Giancarlo Fini, who is considered Ariel Sharon's "man" inside the Berlusconi government.

The result of Sembler's reign in Rome has been the sinking of U.S.-Italian relations to the lowest point since Benito Mussolini ruled Italy. U.S. troops shot and killed the deputy chief of Italian intelligence (SISMI) in Baghdad and wounded a freed Italian hostage, journalist Giuliana Sgrena.

Thirteen U.S. intelligence agents are wanted by Milan authorities for the illegal kidnapping of an exiled Egyptian Imam from a Milan street in early 2003. A secret unofficial parallel Italian intelligence network, DSSA, tied to extreme right-wing groups, is being linked to forged Niger documents central to the Rovegate scandal. And now, according to the *Los Angeles Times*, Sembler is pressuring Sardinia's center-left regional president Renato Soru to lift a moratorium on coastal development on his pristine Mediterranean island.

Sembler has not merely been suggesting a lifting of the moratorium but actively lobbying Soru to permit development. It is obvious that Sembler is misusing his position as ambassador to help enrich himself and his wealthy mega-construction business friends. Soru is also pressuring the United States to vacate its Naval Support Activity nuclear submarine base on La Maddalena island off Sardinia's north coast, an issue that has earned him the wrath of the neocons in the Bush administration.

European countries that were skeptical of claims of an Iraqi nuclear weapons program were pilloried by people like Defense Secretary Donald Rumsfeld as "Old Europe."

***

Having traveled to Europe over a hundred times, I understood how the Europeans were reacting to the onset of a fascist regime in Washington. The ugliness of right-wing American nationalism also crept into the pages of the once esteemed *Washington Post*. I wrote about the phenomenon of renewed American jingoism for the *Online Journal* on May 19, 2005:

America has become an ugly place. It is anti-foreign in almost every aspect. There is no time for any religion other than a fundamentalist and uniquely American-created notion of Judeo-Christianity rooted in the belief that a white-bearded European God sent a fair haired and blue-eyed Aryan named Jesus

Christ (not a brown-skinned, black-curly haired, Aramaic- and, probably, Greek-speaking Essene Jew, who may have been exposed to Buddhist teachings during thirteen unaccounted years of travel, and whose name was Yeshua ben Yosef haDavid) to Earth to die for the sins of a chosen few Southern white bigots, rich Republicans, and Christian crusaders wearing American military uniforms and private-contractor fatigues.

This religious belief would be comical if it had not already reaped dire consequences of death, despair, and destruction—in Iraq, in Afghanistan, in Palestine, in Africa, in Southeast Asia, and around the world.

Make no mistake about it, America is a hated nation bent on world domination in a modern-day religious crusade. Not all nations share our beliefs. The United Nations does not share our beliefs.

Europe has come in for particular abuse from the American religious neofascists. The neocon-occupied U.S. Senate accuses politicians in France, Britain, and Russia who do not share American "values" of accepting petrodollar bribes from Saddam Hussein. American firms like Halliburton and its subsidiaries, which reaped millions in profits from trading with Saddam, go unmentioned.

A senior White House staff member, later identified to this author as Karl Rove, told a colleague that since the United States dominates the world it can create its own reality. The staffer added that if the Bush regime does not like the reality they've created, in 30 minutes they can change it. What awesome power almost total control of the international media and popular culture can bestow on Imperial America!

It is a hallmark of ideologically-driven dictatorships that their social control mechanisms extend to every facet of people's lives: what they read in the press, what they watch on TV and hear on the radio, what they hear from the pulpit, and what they're told to do at work (wear American flag pins, contribute to the Republican Party, discriminate against gays and women and Latinos and African-Americans and Native Americans and Muslims and atheists).

You say things aren't that bad yet? There probably isn't any activity more innocuous than a crossword puzzle. It's a non-political, uncontroversial pastime, right? Guess again. The *Washington Post*'s crossword puzzle is likely the most widely done by those in political power. Whether they work as a desk officer at the State Department, an FBI agent, a Secret Service guard at the White House, chances are that if they use Washington's mass transit systems, they do the *Post*'s crossword puzzle. And this obviously has not been lost on the opinion manipulators in the White House and the Temple of Doom known as the Republican Party political machine.

In May 16's edition of the *Post*, the following clue was found for 57 Down: Prefix with dollar or trash. "Euro" is the answer.

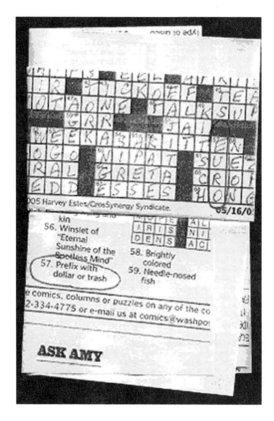

Although "Eurotrash" has been used to describe European campy pop culture, like all code words it has another, more cutting and hurtful meaning. Various neocons have used this term to describe Europe in general, France, Germany, Scandinavia, Iberia, and other countries that reject American neocon imperialism and global designs. The neocons accentuate the term Eurotrash to include degenerate behavior, avant-garde chic, kitschy nightclubs, homoerotic exhibitionism, post-modernism, egotism, laziness, drug legalization, poor hygiene, social democracy, labor rights, and internationalism.

The *Post*'s puzzle answer came one day before British anti-war Member of Parliament George Galloway was due to testify in a Joe McCarthy-like Senate hearing chaired by arch-neocon Norm Coleman of Minnesota. Coleman's kangaroo committee issued a dubious report about several European politicians receiving UN "Oil-for-Food" money from Saddam. The source of the information was Iraq's Oil Ministry, led by congenital liar and con man Ahmad Chalabi, and interviews with former Saddam officials incarcerated in U.S. military prisons.

A November 8, 2003, screed by Harvard professor Alan Dershowitz in the *New York Daily News* (owned by leading neocon Mort Zuckerman) referred to Europeans who criticize Israel as "Euro Trash." In the run-up to the U.S. invasion of Iraq, a former Republican congressman from New York named Dan Frisa wrote an article for the neocon NewsMax.com titled "Anti-U.S. Euro Trash-Talk." And the jingoist term "Eurotrash" continues to spring forth from the mouths of America's bigots of the radio airwaves and cable news networks.

Americans continue to be conditioned by the neocon perception managers and spinmeisters. Will America ever wake up from this seeming hypnotic state and realize who and what have been allowed to take over our nation?

Perhaps one of the most dangerous developments in Bush's "war on terror," presumably aimed at Islamic terrorists, was the proselytization of the U.S. military by Christian "Dominionist" elements dedicated to a world Christian empire. In January 2007, I wrote an article for *Hustler* titled "Praise the Lord and Bless the Ammunition":

A group of military officers and evangelical Christian leaders are attempting to transform the U.S. military into a cadre of zealous fundamentalist Christian warriors poised to engage the United States in a modern-day Crusade.

The "Christian Embassy," an entity that claims Washington, DC as its headquarters, facilitates the infiltration of the military officer and enlisted ranks by fundamentalist Christians bent on turning the U.S. military into a vanguard of Christian soldiers ready to march to war for Jesus Christ.

The Pentagon makes no secret of its support for the Christian Embassy. The Pentagon's Chaplain's Office proudly proclaims on its Web site that it sponsors the Christian Embassy Bible Study Groups and provides a link to the Christian Embassy Web site so interested parties can check out the latest Christian Embassy Bible Study schedule.

All this may sound quite innocent until the Christian Embassy is examined in more detail. The "embassy," a 501 (c) (3) nonprofit organization, lists its address as Suite 730, 2000 14th Street North, Arlington, VA 22201, located in an office building amid the high-rise labyrinth of military and intelligence contractors that marks the region north and west of Arlington National Cemetery.

The Christian Embassy's Web site also provides a link for on-line direct contributions. Clicking on the contributions link takes one to the Web site for the Campus Crusade for Christ International, an organization that for decades has sought to evangelize college campuses around the United States and abroad. In fact, the Christian Embassy is an affiliate of the Campus Crusade for Christ.

If this all sounds like an interconnecting web of nonprofits, it is, and it is designed to be that way. Just like Enron's offshore entities and the pass-through "brass plate" firms used by defense and intelligence contractors to cover their tracks, the Christian fundamentalists use a series of nonprofits to mask what is, in effect, a large multinational enterprise of tax-exempt organizations that seeks to create a "Christian Dominion" on Earth in anticipation of the return of the "Messiah."

The Christian Embassy, founded in 1975, proclaims its mission as reaching out to "leaders at the White House, Capitol Hill, the Pentagon, and foreign embassies located in Washington, D.C." But the Christian Embassy has a darker past, according to John Edward Hurley, a longtime Washington observer of politics and colleague of the late White House correspondent Sarah McClendon. Hurley said the same right-wing elements that are behind the Christian Embassy attempted to create such a fundamentalist warrior caste in 1987, when they tried to seize control over Confederate Memorial Hall, a historic museum dedicated to the history of the District of Columbia area during the Civil War.

"They first wanted a 'Confederate Embassy,' which they would then convert into a 'Christian Embassy,'" said Hurley who fought off attempts by Council of Conservative Citizens-affiliated individuals and organizations, including the infamous Oliver North, to use Confederate Memorial Hall for anti-Communist "Freedom Fighter" receptions honoring the Afghan *Mujaheddin*, Nicaraguan Contras, and the Angolan anti-communist guerrillas of UNITA. Hurley says some of the same individuals, including those involved with private military companies, small arms manufacturers, and current major players in the Christian Embassy movement were part and parcel of the attempt to create a tax-exempt Confederate Embassy at the Confederate Memorial Hall in Washington in the late 1980s. Hurley has spent two decades fighting this network of "Christian Identity" right-wingers in a series of retaliatory lawsuits brought by the right-wing network against Hurley, McClendon, and other colleagues. Furthermore, some of these notorious right-wingers can be found today in mid-level positions in the George W. Bush administration, says Hurley.

Perhaps no place in the U.S. military establishment has seen the power of the dominionist/fundamentalist modern-day crusaders more then the U.S. Air Force Academy in Colorado Springs, which also happens to be the headquarters for such Christian Right activities as James Dobson's Focus on the Family; Rev. Ted Haggard's New Life mega-church, painted in the blue and silver colors of the Air Force; and the Navigators, a group also having close connections to the military, particularly the Navy. Haggard is no longer at the helm of the church he founded, resigning in November 2006 because of allegations of homosexuality and drug use.

Mike "Mikey" Weinstein, a former Reagan White House Counsel, an Air Force academy graduate, and the father of two Air Force Academy cadets — one is now a commissioned Air Force officer — became so alarmed at the proselytizing at the academy, he founded an organization — the Military Religious Freedom Foundation — to alert the public to the dangers posed by the modern-day Crusaders. Weinstein also sued the Air Force for its blatant evangelization activities, including the bullying of non-evangelicals by cadets. Weinstein's suit sought to prohibit Air Force personnel — including chaplains — from attempting to "involuntarily convert, pressure, exhort or persuade a fellow member of the USAF to accept their own religious beliefs while on duty." In essence, the suit "asked the Air Force to treat all religions neutrally," according to Weinstein. The suit was dismissed on a technicality by U.S. Federal Judge James Parker in Albuquerque.

Weinstein's sons, who are Jewish as is their father, experienced the anti-Semitic-laden bullying first hand. The most prominent recent evangelizer was Brig. Gen. Johnny Weida, the Air Force Academy's third-in-command when Weinstein brought his suit. Weida was later promoted to Major General and is now stationed at Wright-Patterson Air Force Base in Ohio.

Weinstein told *Hustler* that while his Christian daughter-in-law was a cadet, Weida personally asked her to attend an Easter Passion Play at disgraced Colorado Springs evangelist Ted Haggard's church. Haggard resigned from his New Life Church after it was discovered he had engaged the services of a male prostitute.

The Air Force responded to Weinstein's suit by issuing new guidelines to its chaplains and the academy, but pressure from Colorado Springs' Focus on the Family and the Christian fundamentalist pressure network, including fundamentalist GOP members of Congress, soon resulted in these guidelines being significantly weakened.

Weida's promotion was not the first for a neo-Crusading general. Army Lt. Gen. William "Jerry" Boykin, while appearing in uniform before evangelical Christian congregations, lambasted Muslims for worshipping idols, suggested that God put George W. Bush in the White House, called the U.S. Army the "house of God," and referred to Islamic insurgents as "agents of Satan." In 2003, Boykin, in a speech to the First Baptist Church in Daytona Beach, Florida, referred to the United States as a "Christian nation" and, in reference to a Somali warlord, he stated, "I knew that my God was bigger than his. I knew that my God was a real God and his was an idol." After his comments, Boykin was rewarded with the post of Deputy Undersecretary of Defense for Intelligence under Defense Secretary Donald Rumsfeld.

At the onset of the Iraqi insurgency, the U.S. Marines were also subjected to evangelizing conniving. Marines in Iraq were handed a pamphlet called "A Christian's Duty." The Marines were exhorted to pray for George W. Bush, his family, and his staff and then mail in a pledge form to Bush to prove that such prayers were rendered.

Weinstein calls attention to the Officer's Christian Fellowship (OCF), an organization with close connections to the powerful Christian "Fellowship Foundation" in Arlington, Virginia. The Fellowship is a politically powerful force in both political parties and counts Hillary Clinton as one of its major supporters. The Fellowship Foundation is a group of right-wing Christian businessmen, politicians, and defense contractors with roots in America's fascist "America First" pre-World War II movement, which is headed by Douglas Coe, whom Mrs. Clinton calls "Doug" and refers to in her "autobiography" as her spiritual mentor. Mrs. Clinton's relationship with a right-wing evangelical group that idolizes Rev. Billy Graham but also has links to Pat Robertson, Sun Myung Moon, Gary Bauer, James Dobson, and other fringe fundamentalists may be the subject of a number of her First Lady papers.

In her "autobiography," *Living History*, Mrs. Clinton writes about a lunch she attended on February 14, 1993 at the Cedars, the headquarters of the rather mysterious and cult-like Fellowship, also known as "The Family":

"The lunch … was held at the Cedars, an estate on the Potomac that serves as the headquarters of the National Prayer Breakfast and the prayer groups it has spawned around the world. Doug Coe, the longtime National Prayer Breakfast organizer, is a unique presence in Washington: a genuinely loving spiritual mentor and guide to anyone … Doug became a source of strength and friendship, and he, too, also often sent me notes of support."

Mrs. Clinton's "prayer partners" at the Cedars included Susan Baker, wife of Bush family consigliere James Baker and Joanne Kemp, wife of Jack Kemp who ran with Mrs. Clinton's 1996 opponent Bob Dole as vice presidential candidate. Other Fellowship core members include GOP presidential candidate Senator Sam Brownback of Kansas, who is also a member of the secretive Opus Dei Catholic sect; former Attorney General John Ashcroft; and former GOP House Majority Leader Tom DeLay.

The OCF's stated goal is "a spiritually transformed military, with ambassadors for Christ in uniform, empowered by the Holy Spirit." The OCF is complemented by the Christian Military Fellowship for enlisted personnel. Weinstein has pointed out that at the 702 U.S. military installations in 132 countries these two organizations are represented.

The Christian Embassy also states that it seeks out foreign defense attachés at 174 foreign embassies and the Organization of American States in its outreach efforts. The Christian Embassy "desires that these attachés, as well as ambassadors, return [home] with a personal relationship with the King of Kings, Jesus Christ." The ambassadors of Benin and Ethiopia and the wives of the Romanian and Peruvian ambassadors have publicly endorsed the Christian Embassy.

The evangelization of the military shows no signs of abatement. Weinstein told *Hustler* that he has received complaints from soldiers, sailors, and Marines about attempts by the evangelicals to force them to convert. "We've had contact 24/7 from people around the world," said Weinstein, adding, "96 percent of the complaints are from Christians, with three-quarters of them traditional Protestants and one-quarter Catholics, the other four percent are Jewish, Islam, Buddhist, agnostics, atheists, and Wiccans."

The influence of the Christian Embassy on the military was highlighted by a post-9/11 video released by the organization that featured uniformed top brass in the Pentagon praising the embassy's evangelization of the military and its Pentagon prayer meetings. Among the flag-rank officers appearing in the video are Army Brig. Gen. Vince Brooks, Air Force Maj. Gen. Jack Catton, Jr., Air Force Maj. Gen. Pete Sutton, and Army Brig. Gen. Bob Caslen.

Two top Cabinet civilians, Undersecretary of the Army Pete Geren and Undersecretary for Veterans Affairs Dan Cooper, also appear in the promotional video. The film states that Cooper makes time in his schedule for a weekly bible study. Pentagon Senior Executive Service employee Judy Guenther calls her relationship with the Christian Embassy "very exciting." Guenther serves the Army Secretariat as the Director of Investment for the Deputy Assistant Secretary of the Army for Budget.

Catton got into hot water in May 2006 when he sent an e-mail, through the military telecommunications system, urging his military and civilian peers and subordinates to donate to a Republican congressional campaign fund. He stated, "we are in need of Christian men with integrity and military experience in Congress." Although Catton was investigated, he now serves as the Director of Requirements for the Headquarters Air Combat Command, Langley Air Force Base, Virginia.

In language that could only be fully understood by *Dr. Strangelove*'s General Jack Ripper, General Caslen states that when he is among other generals and admirals in the Flag Officers' Fellowship, "we are the aroma of Jesus Christ." Air Force Colonel Cynthia Islin appears on the video stating she went to Ethiopia on a trip sponsored by the Christian Embassy. Islin, as do all the other officers, appears in uniform.

Representatives Robert Aderholt (R-Alabama), John Carter (R-Texas), Vern Ehlers (R-Michigan), and Gresham Barrett (R-S. Carolina), and former Representatives Tom DeLay (R-Texas) and

J. D. Hayworth (R-Arizona) also laud the work of the Christian Embassy.

The Christian Embassy took down a link to the video and threatened YouTube.com with legal action if they did not remove the video after groups like the Military Religious Freedom Foundation brought attention to it. However, *Hustler* has obtained a copy of the video and its featured statements of support for the Christian Embassy by Pentagon officers and members of Congress.

The narrator proclaims, "There are over 25,000 Department of Defense leaders working in the rings and corridors of the Pentagon. Through bible studies, 'discipleship,' prayer breakfasts, and outreach events, Christian Embassy is mustering these men and women into a intentional relationship with Jesus Christ."

Enterprising journalist Jeff Sharlet has been on the Christian Dominionist beat for some time, having written two revealing exposés on the Fellowship and the Christian Embassy for *Harper's*. He discovered the existence of the Christian Embassy's Pentagon video after delving into the importance of Confederate General Stonewall Jackson — referred to as the "Soldier of the Cross" in Christian home-schooling textbooks — in the panoply of America's fundamentalist trappings. The links to Stonewall Jackson substantiate Hurley's contention that there is collusion between the Christian Dominionists and the neoconfederates.

Pentagon Chaplain Col. Ralph Benson of the U.S. Army sums up the goals of the Christian Embassy and the entire Dominionist movement at the end of the video. He concludes that the Christian Embassy is a "blessing to the Washington area … a blessing to our country … when our world is in a worldwide war on terrorism what more do we need than Christian people leading us … in this hour of need?" Christian people leading us, indeed … just like the travesty called the Crusades.

Although the so-called "Christian Zionists" espoused their support for Israel, their support was very conditional. Everything the Christian Dominionists did was through the prism of Biblical prophecy as they interpreted it. The anti-Semitic underpinnings of the fundamentalist right were nowhere more apparent than at military academies like the U.S. Air Force Academy deep within the Rocky Mountains "Bible Belt." I wrote about the proselytizing of the Colorado Springs academy in January 2007:

Mikey Weinstein, the director of the Military Religious Freedom Foundation who has been battling against the takeover of the Air Force Academy and other military commands and units by right-wing proselytizing fundamentalist Christians, has received his share of anti-Semitic comments from the Christian Right.

However, nothing summarizes the agenda of the Christian Right (which is holding its annual National Prayer Breakfast tomorrow at the Washington Hilton) more than the following screed from a retired Navy Senior Chief Petty Officer:

"In this day of turmoil worldwide, with the adherents of Islam threatening the annihilation of Israel and America, I was flabbergasted that this small group of liberal American-born Jews are so determined to tear apart the very fabric that produces those detested evangelical Christians to stand shoulder to shoulder with the nation of Israel ... I came to two conclusions: 1) that the Jews of Israel should be grateful to the greatest degree that you and your kind were born and/or living in America rather than in Israel. Had it been otherwise, Israel would have been lost long before now ... ; you and yours are the present day version of the Sons of Korah, Joseph's brothers, the crowd demanding the golden calf at the foot of Sinai, the mob at Kadesh-Barnea ... For you liberal, ungodly Jews, nothing has changed down through the centuries. You and your ilk are Jews in name only and have no concept of what God had prepared for you ... Personally I believe there should be a campaign to swap you and your liberal Jewish ilk for citizens of Israel who at least put their existence on the line every day, while you, and your ilk, live off of the freedoms which have been secured for you by those awful Christian forefathers ... You, sir, are a disgrace to America, a disgrace to Yahweh, a disgrace to Jesus Christ and a disgrace to Israel. May I sum it up for you, Mikey — you are a disgrace."

To put things in perspective, Mikey Weinstein is a former Air Force officer who once served as Deputy White House Counsel for Ronald Reagan. He has warned about the takeover of the U.S. military by a group of fundamentalist "end times" Christians.

**

The push by a number of Republicans (and one-time nominal Democrats like Connecticut Senator Joe Lieberman) and senior officers of the U.S. military for a Holy War between Judaism and Christianity on one side and Islam on the other, was the subject of an op-ed I wrote in 2006:

In an era of increasing religious fundamentalism of all stripes, it is hypocritical to single out one faith for failing to curb a minority of adherents who preach religious war and hatred of others. Islam certainly has no monopoly in the United States on preaching volatile messages intended to whip up followers to commit acts of violence.

It is a careful First Amendment balance to control what is preached from pulpits in mosques, churches, synagogues, and other places of worship across the country and not potentially infringe on freedom of speech and freedom of religion. While preaching violence and calling for terrorism are akin to yelling "fire" in a crowded movie theater, an act that is illegal, there is a slippery slope involved in controlling speech, particularly that which is of a religious nature.

While there is strong evidence that Wahhabism, one of the more extreme branches of Islam, has funded — through the largesse of Saudi benefactors — extremist tracts and textbooks found in mosques and religious schools in the United States, an overwhelming majority of mosques do not preach violent Jihad against the West. Moreover, a vast number of Muslim leaders of all Islamic denominations and sects — Sunni, Sh'ia, Sufi, Qadiyani, Yazidi, Druze, Zaydi, Alawi, and Dawoodi Bohra — have condemned violence in the name of any religion, including Islam. An overwhelming majority of Muslims practice ijtihad — personal introspection about their faith and how to translate their faith into daily actions.

Jihad, or holy war, is a last resort in Islam. For the radicals, however, it is the only choice. In an era of tabloid television, a small minority of radical Islamists receives all the attention; however, the majority of Muslims are unfairly tainted by the Jihadist extremism of a minority.

Nevertheless, the notion of cracking down on hotheads who preach violence could easily be extended to other faiths, as well as Islam. Christian televangelist Pat Robertson has called for the democratically elected President of Venezuela, a fellow Christian, to be assassinated.

Jerry Falwell blamed the 9/11 terrorist attacks on gays and pro-choice supporters. Falwell also called the Prophet Mohammed a "terrorist." Billy Graham's heir, Franklin, called Islam an "evil and wicked religion." Evangelist Jimmy Swaggert, not one to talk, referred to Mohammed as a "sex deviant."

Similarly, some Jewish commentators and Representative Tom Tancredo (R-CO) have called on the United States to bomb Islam's holiest city, Mecca. Jewish Defense League Chairman Irv Rubin was charged with trying to bomb a Southern California mosque, and the congressional office of an Arab-American Republican congressman.

With so much religious vitriol running as narrow streams within the three Abrahamic tradition religions (Judaism, Christianity, and Islam), it is hypocritical to lay blame for preaching terrorism merely on Islam.

If there is to be a debate and interfaith dialogue on religion and terrorism, it must address the terrorism called for against women's health clinics by people like Christian fundamentalist Randall Terry; it should cast light on the taking over of Christian congregations by the extremely dangerous dominionist and reconstructionist movements that have been likened to the Taliban; it should be directed against the Jewish Defense League and their incendiary speech and activities concerning Arab Americans and Palestinians; and it should speak to the Wahhabi, Muslim Brotherhood, and associated Jihadist infiltration of Islamic mosques and schools in America and elsewhere.

A Holy man from the East once addressed extremism and hatred. He said, "Hatred never ceases through hatred in this world; through nonviolence it comes to an end." Those were the words of the Buddha. They are words that the leaders of the religions of the Abrahamic traditions should heed and embrace.

Perhaps nothing from America's Iraq debacle was more disgraceful than the torture by U.S. military and contractor personnel of innocent Iraqis, including the sexual molestation of women and children. The sick minds that perpetrated these atrocities and crimes against humanity were the subject of a May 2004 article I wrote for *CounterPunch*:

With mounting evidence that a shadowy group of former Israeli Defense Force and General Security Service (Shin Bet) Arabic-speaking interrogators were hired by the Pentagon under a classified "carve out" sub-contract to brutally interrogate

Iraqi prisoners at Baghdad's Abu Ghraib prison, one only needs to examine the record of abuse of Palestinian and Lebanese prisoners in Israel to understand what Secretary of Defense Donald Rumsfeld meant, when referring to new, yet to be released photos and videos: "If these images are released to the public, obviously its going to make matters worse."

According to a political appointee within the Bush administration and U.S. intelligence sources, the interrogators at Abu Ghraib included a number of Arabic-speaking Israelis who also helped U.S. interrogators develop the "R2I" (Resistance to Interrogation) techniques. Many of the torture methods were developed by the Israelis over many years of interrogating Arab prisoners on the occupied West Bank and in Israel itself.

Clues about worse photos and videos of abuse may be found in Israeli files about similar abuse of Palestinian and other Arab prisoners. In March 2000, a lawyer for a Lebanese prisoner kidnapped in 1994 by the Israelis in Lebanon claimed that his client had been subjected to torture, including rape. The type of compensation offered by Rumsfeld in his testimony has its roots in cases of Israeli torture of Arabs. In the case of the Lebanese man, said to have been raped by his Israeli captors, his lawyer demanded compensation of $1.47 million. The Public Committee Against Torture in Israel documented the types of torture meted out on Arab prisoners. Many of the tactics coincide with those contained in the Taguba report: beatings and prolonged periods handcuffed to furniture. In an article in the December 1998 issue of *The Progressive*, Rabbi Lynn Gottlieb reported on the treatment given to a 23-year old Palestinian held on "administrative detention." The prisoner was "cuffed behind a chair 17 hours a day for 120 days … [he] had his head covered with a sack, which was often dipped in urine or feces. Guards played loud music right next to his ears and frequently taunted him with threats of physical and sexual violence." If additional photos and videos document such practices, the Bush administration and the American people have, indeed, "seen nothing yet."

Although it is still largely undocumented if any of the contractors named in the report of General Antonio Taguba were associated with the Israeli military or intelligence services, it is noteworthy that one, John Israel, who was identified in the report as being employed by both CACI International of Arlington, Virginia, and Titan, Inc., of San Diego, may not have even been a U.S. citizen. The Taguba report states that Israel did not have a security clearance, a requirement for employment as an interrogator for CACI. According to CACI's Web site, "a Top Secret Clearance (TS) that is current and U.S. citizenship" are required for CACI interrogators working in Iraq. In addition, CACI requires that its interrogators "have at least two years experience as a military policeman or similar type of law enforcement/intelligence agency whereby the individual utilized interviewing techniques."

Speculation that "John Israel" may be an intelligence cover name has fueled speculation whether this individual could have been one of a number of Israeli interrogators hired under a classified contract. Because U.S. citizenship and documentation thereof are requirements for a U.S. security clearance, Israeli citizens would not be permitted to hold a Top Secret clearance. However, dual U.S.-Israeli citizens could have satisfied Pentagon requirements that interrogators hold U.S. citizenship and a Top Secret clearance. Although the Taguba report refers twice to Israel as an employee of Titan, the company claims he is one of their sub-contractors. CACI stated that one of the men listed in the report "is not and never has been a CACI employee" without providing more detail. A U.S. intelligence source revealed that in the world of intelligence "carve out" subcontracts, such confusion is often the case with "plausible deniability" being a foremost concern.

In fact, the Taguba report does reference the presence of non-U.S. and non-Iraqi interrogators at Abu Ghraib. The report states, "In general, US civilian contract personnel (Titan Corporation, CACI, etc...), third country nationals, and local contractors do not appear to be properly supervised within the detention facility at Abu Ghraib."

The Pentagon is clearly concerned about the outing of the Taguba report and its references to CACI, Titan, etc., which could permanently damage U.S. relations with Arab and Islamic nations. This may explain why the Taguba report is classified Secret No Foreign Dissemination. The reference to "third-country nationals" in a report that restricts its dissemination to U.S. coalition partners (Great Britain, Poland, Italy, etc.) is another indication of the possible involvement of Israelis in the interrogation of Iraqi prisoners. Knowledge that the U.S. may have been using Israeli interrogators could have severely fractured the Bush administration's tenuous "coalition of the willing" in Iraq. General Taguba's findings were transmitted to the Coalition Forces Land Component Command on March 9, 2004, just six days before the Spanish general election, one that the opposition anti-Iraq war

Socialists won. The Spanish ultimately withdrew their forces from Iraq.

During his testimony before the Senate Armed Service Committee, Rumsfeld was pressed by Senator John McCain about the role of the private contractors in the interrogations and abuse. McCain asked Rumsfeld four pertinent questions, "...who was in charge? What agency or private contractor was in charge of the interrogations? Did they have authority over the guards? And what were the instructions that they gave to the guards?"

When Rumsfeld had problems answering McCain's question, Lt. Gen. Lance Smith, the Deputy Commander of the U.S. Central Command, said there were 37 contract interrogators used in Abu Ghraib. The two named contractors, CACI and Titan, have close ties to the Israeli military and technology communities. Last January 14, after Provost Marshal General of the Army, Major General Donald Ryder, had already uncovered abuse at Abu Ghraib, CACI's President and CEO, Dr. J.P. (Jack) London was receiving the Jerusalem Fund of Aish HaTorah's Albert Einstein Technology award at the Jerusalem City Hall, with right-wing Likud politician Israeli Defense Minister Shaul Mofaz and ultra-Orthodox United Torah Judaism party Jerusalem Mayor Uri Lupolianski in attendance. Oddly, CACI waited until February 2 to publicly announce the award in a press release. CACI has also received grants from U.S.-Israeli bi-national foundations.

Titan also has had close connections to Israeli interests. After his stint as CIA Director, James Woolsey served as a Titan director. Woolsey is an architect of America's Iraq policy and the chief proponent of and lobbyist for Ahmad Chalabi of the Iraqi National Congress. An adviser to the neoconservative Foundation for the Defense of Democracies, Jewish Institute of National Security Affairs, Project for the New American Century, Center for Security Policy, Freedom House, and Committee for the Liberation of Iraq, Woolsey is close to Stephen Cambone, the Undersecretary of Defense for Intelligence, a key person in the chain of command who would have not only known about the torture tactics used by U.S. and Israeli interrogators in Iraq, but who would have also approved them. Cambone was associated with the Project for the New American Century and is viewed as a member of Rumsfeld's neoconservative "cabal" within the Pentagon.

Another person considered by Pentagon insiders to have been knowledgeable about the treatment of Iraqi prisoners is U.S. Army Col. Steven Bucci, a Green Beret and Rumsfeld's military assistant and chief traffic cop for the information flow to the Defense Secretary. According to Pentagon insiders, Bucci was involved in the direction of a special covert operations unit composed of former U.S. special operations personnel who answered to the Pentagon rather than the CIA's Special Activities Division, the agency's own paramilitary group. The Pentagon group included Arabic linguists and former members of the Green Berets and Delta Force who operated covertly in Iraq, Afghanistan, Iran, Pakistan, and Uzbekistan. Titan also uses linguists trained in the languages (Arabic, Dari, Farsi, Pashto, Urdu, and Tajik) of those same countries. It is not known if a link exists between Rumsfeld's covert operations unit and Titan's covert operations linguists.

Another Titan employee named in the Taguba report is Adel L. Nakhla. Nakhla is a name common among Egypt's Coptic Christian community, however, it is not known if Adel Nakhla is either an Egyptian-American or a national of Egypt. A CACI employee identified in the report, Steven Stephanowicz, is referred to as "Stefanowicz" in a number of articles on the prison abuse. Stefanowicz is the spelling used by Joe Ryan, another CACI employee assigned with Stefanowicz to Abu Ghraib. Ryan is a radio personality on KSTP, a conservative radio station in Minneapolis, who maintained a daily log of his activities in Iraq on the radio's Web site before it was taken down. Ryan indicated that Stefanowicz (or Stephanowicz) continued to hold his interrogation job in Iraq even though General Taguba recommended he lose his security clearance and be terminated for the abuses at Abu Ghraib.

In an even more bizarre twist, the *Philadelphia Daily News* identified a former expatriate public relations specialist for the government of South Australia in Adelaide named Steve Stefanowicz as possibly being the same person identified in the Taguba report. In 2000, Stefanowicz, who grew up in the Philadelphia and Allentown areas, left for Australia. On September 16, 2001, he was quoted by the *Sunday Mail* of Adelaide on the 9/11 attacks. He said of the attacks, "It was one of the most incredible and most devastating things I have ever seen. I have been in constant contact with my family and friends in the U.S. and the mood was very solemn and quiet. But this is progressing into anger." Stefanowicz returned to the United States and volunteered for the Navy in a reserve status. His mother told the *Allentown Morning Call* in April 2002 that Stefanowicz was stationed somewhere in the Middle East, but she did not know where because of what Stefanowicz said was "security concerns." His mother told the *Philadelphia Daily News* that her son was in Iraq but she knew nothing about his current status.

As a postscript to the aforementioned article, I received a warning e-mail from CACI's Washington, DC law firm, Steptoe & Johnson. I had tangled with these mouthpieces before when they were shilling for the NSA on behalf of the Clipper Chip, the NSA's Trojan horse encryption computer chip that would permit the government to eavesdrop on encoded communications. The company that we in the privacy community referred to as "Step on your toes and grab your Johnson" was as off-base about defending its client's torture and sexual molestation of innocent Iraqis, including children, as it was in defending the Clipper Chip.

Perhaps no other place felt the brunt of the "War of Lies and the Lies of War" than the Pentagon. I had a unique view into the inner workings of the Pentagon in the days after 9/11. What I reported was the presence of a neocon cabal within the Pentagon's top policymaking organs, as in this report from October 2003:

The recent leak of a memo from Secretary of Defense Donald Rumsfeld to his four top advisers is emblematic of continued deep divisions within the Bush administration over Iraq policy. Rumsfeld states in the memo that Americans did not sign up to a "long, hard slog" in Iraq. Pentagon insiders believe that a group of top military officers leaked the memo to *USA Today* in order to embarrass Rumsfeld and his neoconservative allies, including his deputy Paul Wolfowitz and aide William Luti, who both are accused of manufacturing intelligence to justify the war against Iraq.

This reporter has obtained a memo for the record from a former top official within Luti's organization in the Pentagon, the Deputy Under Secretariat of Defense for Special Plans (Office of Special Plans-OSP) and Near Eastern and South Asian Affairs (NESA). OSP was subsequently renamed the Office of Northern Gulf Affairs. The memo indicates that Luti and a group of his advisers "produced propaganda for the Iraq war drive." The memo also indicates that although Undersecretary of Defense for Policy Douglas Feith was a close collaborator of Wolfowitz and Rumsfeld, it was Luti who ran the show. Luti is quoted as saying, "Feith can't wipe his ass without me."

The neocon self-described "cabal" within the Pentagon set out to disparage their opponents in the State Department from the very beginning of the plan to attack Iraq. In addition, Luti took direct assignments from Lewis "Scooter" Libby, Vice President Dick Cheney's chief of staff. Luti, who while a Navy Captain, served as a congressional fellow within House Speaker Newt Gingrich's office, came to the Pentagon directly from Cheney's White House office. Luti and his advisers also worked closely with the National Security Council's Middle East director, Iran-Contra felon Elliott Abrams, to formulate the Iraq war plans. Other neocons who wielded influence over NESA/OSP included David Wurmser, formerly of the State Department's counter-proliferation bureau and now on Cheney's staff as Middle East adviser; his wife, Meyrav Wurmser, of the right-wing Hudson Institute; and John Bolton, the Undersecretary of State for Arms Control and a leading war hawk on Iraq, Syria, Iran, Cuba, and North Korea.

Luti, in particular, was a harsh critic of the moderates in the Bush administration. He referred to retired General Anthony Zinni, the former envoy to Israel and the Palestinian Authority, as a "traitor" and the State Department as "bastards."

Luti also fired a number of NESA officers who were considered outside the neocon ranks. These included Larry Hanauer, a retired military officer and career civil servant who served as the head of the Israel-Syria-Lebanon desk. He was replaced by David Schenker, a former official at the Washington Institute for Near East Policy (WINEP), a pro-Likud think tank. Also replaced or reduced in influence were Paul Hulley, the OSP/NESA deputy director who, while reportedly still in his job has lost any influence over policy-making and Joe McMillan, the NESA office director who was transferred to the National Defense University. One anti-Luti staff member stated that what was going on in NESA/OSP "made Iran-Contra look like child's play by comparison."

After Luti arrived at the Pentagon, the OSP was established under Luti so that he could bypass International Security Affairs Deputy Undersecretary Peter Rodman, who although a Henry Kissinger disciple, was not considered an ally of the neocons. Luti's other close advisers included Harold Rhode, a close confidant of Iraqi National Congress leader Ahmad Chalabi; Michael Makovsky (the brother of WINEP official David Makovsky); Abram Shulsky; Chris Lehman, brother of former Navy Secretary and current 9/11

Commission member John Lehman; Michael Rubin; Reuel Marc Gerecht (a former CIA officer); Lt. Col. Bill Bruner (the former military aide to Gingrich); Larry Franklin (who carried out a series of meetings with Iran-Contra figure Manucher Ghorbanifar on the second phase of the OSP's plans to go into Iran); Navy Lieut. Commander Youssef Abou-Enein, an Egyptian-American medical intelligence officer on loan from the Armed Forces Medical Intelligence Center at Fort Detrick, Maryland.

Abou-Enein was responsible for checking the translation into English of CIA Foreign Broadcast Information Service Arabic language reports, and reporting any mistranslations or failure to include "proof" of Saddam's terrorist ties. It is noteworthy that Fort Detrick was the source of the Ames strain of aerosolized anthrax used in the postal attack on the Democratic leadership of the U.S. Senate. In 2002, anonymous letters purported received by the FBI accused Fort Detrick's Egyptian-born scientist Dr. Ayaad Assaad of threatening a bio-war against the United States. The FBI never released the letters, and Assaad claimed that the bureau was trying to protect the person who actually sent them. Suspicion about the author of letters centered on Lt. Col. Philip Zack, described as a "Mr. Z" by *New York Times* reporter Nicholas Kristoff. Although Zack left employment at Fort Detrick after his harassment convinced Dr. Assaad to quit his job at the U.S. Army Medical Research Institute for Infectious Diseases (USAMRIID), Zack continued to visit the medical research facility. Zack was known for his strong pro-Israel and anti-Arab views, a stance shared by Luti's organization in the Pentagon whose link to Fort Detrick was Abou-Enein.

Luti's advisers also included John Trigilio, a Defense Intelligence Agency (DIA) liaison officer who was charged with interviewing Chalabi's Iraqi sources. Although Trigilio has publicly supported Luti, he is not counted as a core member of the inner circle and the memo states that he may be used as a scapegoat by the neocons, particularly by his supervisor Shulsky, in the event of any congressional investigations into possible illegal activities of the OSP.

The DIA intelligence officer at NESA was Bruce Hardcastle, a Middle East expert and a person who became one of Luti's biggest foes. Luti constantly prevented Hardcastle from giving briefings to defense intelligence officers from other countries at bilateral "bilat" meetings. Hardcastle earned the enmity of Luti when he insisted that any intelligence coming from Chalabi associates had to be cross-checked for validity and veracity before it was reported as fact.

In addition, in December 2002, a group of six Israelis, mostly generals, were permitted to enter Feith's office without signing the guest log, a mandatory requirement for visitors to Pentagon offices.

The memo also states that although Richard Perle resigned as Chairman of the Defense Policy Board he continues to maintain the same office at the Pentagon. His replacement as chairman, former Republican Representative Tillie Fowler of Florida, rarely involves herself in Board activities, opting to tend to her law practice in Florida.

Journalist Seymour Hersh reports in *The New Yorker* that a similar organization to NESA/OSP was set up by Bolton in the State Department. Bolton routinely bypassed his Bureau of Intelligence and Research disarmament expert, Greg Thielmann, going so far as shutting him out of morning staff meetings.

By August 2004, it was clear that the neocons had profited handsomely from the Iraq War. The key players in dragging the United States into the Iraq quagmire and their networks of influence peddling began to be written about, and the disinfectant of sunshine sent many of the neocon vermin running into the shadows and under their rocks. In August 2004, I wrote the following article about the neocons and the beginning of their downfall:

2004 may be remembered in history books as the year that saw the beginning of the end for the grip of the neoconservatives (and their Christian fundamentalist allies) on U.S. foreign and defense policy. The strong showing of Democrats John Kerry and John Edwards in the race to unseat the most right-wing and reactionary administration in our nation's history is just one part of the political dynamic that may soon see neoconservatism go the way of past dangerous ideologies, including McCarthyism, Nazism, and Stalinism, in addition to fascism and Trotskyism — the latter two serving as the political underpinnings of neoconservatism.

Thanks to the unity of the Democratic Party and the desire of some "Old Guard" Republicans to see their party pulled out from under the influence of the neocon global dominators and evangelical end timers, we are now seeing the unraveling of the neocon web of control over the United States, particularly the Defense Department. A number of the GOP old guard are willing to concede the upcoming presidential election to the Democrats so that they may cleanse themselves of the neocons and evangelicals.

Soviet government experts always spoke and wrote about what it took for a Soviet leader to be unseated: when any two of the three bastions of political power in the U.S.S.R. — the military, the KGB, and the Communist Party — united to turn against the party boss, he was gone. George W. Bush and Dick Cheney failed to realize that in turning their administration into a closed and totalitarian force for hidden agendas favoring the neocon ideology, they invited upon themselves a united front of opposition virtually unmatched in American history.

In their case, the Democrats united as they have never united in the recent past to oust Bush and Cheney. Moreover, the old guard Republicans (including the president's own father and his chief aides and long-time colleagues) decided the neocon/evangelical stranglehold over the GOP had to come to an end. Secretary of Defense Donald Rumsfeld's cabal of neocons within the Pentagon alienated both the flag-rank officers and career civil service personnel who eventually teamed up with officials of the U.S. intelligence community to ensure the neocons would soon meet their Waterloo. Add the State Department's Foreign Service cadres, the United Nations bureaucracy, and the governments of traditional U.S. allies to the mix, and the fate of the neocon/evangelical political alliance was sealed. It appears clear from recent criminal investigations that they will all soon be gone and for America's national security, their departure from power will not come too soon.

There have been many straws that broke many a camel's back in the unfolding story of the undoing of the neocons but none has perhaps served as more of a catalyst than the trashing of Ambassador Joseph Wilson and the exposure of his wife Valerie as a CIA undercover operative by the neocon element operating from the White House office of Dick Cheney. With special prosecutor Patrick J. Fitzgerald in the process of dotting the I's and crossing the T's in his investigation of who in the White House (and possibly the Pentagon) leaked the name of Plame to conservative columnist Robert Novak, there will soon be high-level indictments of Cheney's Chief of Staff Lewis I. ("Scooter") Libby and his foreign policy adviser David Wurmser. [In the end, only Libby was indicted, Wurmser skated, and Libby's prison sentence was commuted by George W. Bush.] Justice Department insiders report that Fitzgerald successfully "flipped" one of the targets of his investigation, Cheney's deputy Chief of Staff John Hannah, to the prosecution side. The indictments may range from perjury before the grand jury to violating a law against purposefully revealing the name of a U.S. intelligence agent. Eventually, indictments for fraud and espionage could be added to the rap sheets of key Bush administration officials.

Make no mistake about it, the violation of the Intelligence Identities Protection Act of 1982 by the disclosure of Plame's identity and that of her non-official cover corporate umbrella organization, Brewster Jennings & Associates, and its official counterpart, the CIA's Nonproliferation Center, had a disastrous impact on the ability of the United States to track the proliferation of weapons of mass destruction around the world. At least one anonymous star — representing a covert U.S. agent killed while working abroad — placed on the CIA's Wall of Honor during the past year was a direct result of the disastrous disclosures from Cheney's office. The political vendettas of the neocons in exposing Plame's dangerous work and retaliating against Wilson's exposure of Bush's use of bogus Niger government documents regarding a fanciful Iraqi uranium shopping spree in West Africa ensured a negative reaction by America's military-intelligence complex.

The attack on Wilson and Plame resulted in other doors being opened that shined a long-sought light on the nefarious political and financial activities of the neocons. One involved Libby and his connections to the international arms trafficker, organized crime syndicate head, and American fugitive Marc Rich, who was once a lucrative client of Libby's. Rich, Libby, former Defense Policy Board chair Richard Perle, Deputy Defense Secretary Paul Wolfowitz, Undersecretary of Defense for Policy and Plans Douglas Feith, and National Security Council and Pentagon consultant Michael Ledeen represent a sinewy network of those who, along with their ideological and financial compatriots in the Likud Party in Israel, have profited from the war against Iraq. Adding insult to injury, neither the CIA nor FBI were happy that Israeli spies operating under the cover of Israeli "art students" and moving van operators, picked up by federal agents and local "first responder" law enforcement officers before and after 9/11, were quickly deported by immigration officers before they could be fully interrogated.

The penetrations of FBI and other federal law enforcement data networks by Israeli software and telecommunications companies with the active approval of Attorney General John Ashcroft and FBI Director Robert Mueller have left a bitter taste in the mouths of federal law enforcement and intelligence personnel.

But the winds that have favored the neocons and their political and financial masters may now be turning against them. There is a reason why Perle and his American Enterprise Institute (AEI) friends, including "Second Lady" Lynne Cheney and former Reagan National Security Council staffer Michael Ledeen, were uncomfortable when Iraq con man and Iraqi Governing Council member Ahmed Chalabi's offices in Baghdad were raided this past May by Iraqi police, FBI and CIA officers. Any links between the neocons and the Likud are particularly troubling for Mrs. Cheney, who reportedly sits upon a $125,000 AEI fellowship funded by Likud Party interests. [After their fall from leadership positions at the United Nations and World Bank, respectively, John Bolton and Paul Wolfowitz would join their neocon chums at AEI.]

The Chalabi files recovered by U.S. intelligence and law enforcement provided enough information to begin a criminal investigation of a Baghdad-Jerusalem-Washington syndicate that was profiteering from America's misguided invasion and occupation of Iraq. The investigation led to shadowy Israeli-owned firms registered in Delaware and Panama that were fraudulently obtaining contracts and sub-contracts to provide everything from cellular phones and VIP security to the interrogation of Iraqi prisoners using seconded members of Israel's feared Unit 1391 "special techniques" interrogation center. Not only were these firms operating in Iraq with the concurrence of the neocons in the Pentagon, but some of the later were personally benefiting from the contracts.

Peeling apart the Chalabi files demonstrated that the neocon agenda for Iraq extended far beyond political ideology and into a realm where law enforcement can be most effective: fraud.

According to Pentagon and Justice Department sources, U.S. investigators discovered that Chalabi and his business partners were involved in fraudulently obtaining cellular phone licenses in Iraq. The Pentagon's Undersecretary of Defense for International Technology Security John (Jack) Shaw smelled a neocon rat when the Iraqi Coalition Provisional Authority (CPA), in late 2003, awarded cellular phone contracts to three companies — Orascom, Atheer, and Asia-Cell — with ties to Ahmed Chalabi. As with all those who challenge the impropriety and illegal activities of the neocons, Shaw was, in turn, charged with improperly steering Iraq cell phone contracts to Qualcomm and Lucent. However, it is Shaw, reported by his longtime colleagues to be a solid and trustworthy civil servant, who has the confidence of law enforcement, Pentagon investigators, and the military brass. Anything with Ahmed Chalabi's fingerprints on it also bears the fingerprints of his nephew Salem Chalabi. Salem, named as the chief prosecutor in Saddam Hussein's trial, is a law partner of L. Marc Zell, a Jerusalem-based attorney who was the law partner of Feith — the head of the Pentagon's Office of Special Plans that concocted phony intelligence on Iraq's weapons of mass destruction and ties to al Qaeda, with the assistance of Likud operatives seconded by Ariel Sharon's government.

The neocons' attack on Shaw was predictable considering their previous attacks on Wilson, Plame, former U.S. Central Command chief General Anthony Zinni, former counter-terrorism coordinator Richard Clarke, former Treasury Secretary Paul O'Neill, CIA counter-terrorism agent Michael Scheuer (the "anonymous" author of *Imperial Hubris*), fired FBI translator Sibel Edmonds (who likely discovered a penetration by Israeli and other intelligence assets using the false flag of the Turkish American Council), and all those who took on the global domination cabalists. But Shaw showed incredible moxie. When he decided to investigate Pentagon Inspector General reports that firms tied to Perle and Wolfowitz were benefiting from windfall profit contracts in Iraq, Shaw decided to go to Iraq himself to find out what was going on. When Shaw was denied entry into Iraq by U.S. military officers (yes, a top level official of the Defense Department was denied access to Iraq by U.S. military personnel!), he decided to sneak into the country disguised as a Halliburton contractor. Using the cover of Cheney's old company to get the goods on Cheney's friends' illegal activities was another masterful stroke of genius by Shaw. But it also earned him the wrath of the neocons. They soon leaked a jaded story to the *Los Angeles Times* that Shaw actually snuck into Iraq to ensure that Qualcomm (on whose board sat a friend of Shaw's) was awarded a cell phone contract.

But nothing could be further from the truth. Shaw, who worked for Ronald Reagan and George H.W. Bush, represented the Old Guard Republican entity that in August 2003 set up shop in the Pentagon right under the noses of Rumsfeld, Wolfowitz, and Feith to investigate the neocon cabal and their illegal contract deals.

The entity, known as the International Armament and Technology Trade Directorate, was soon shut down as a result of neocon pressure. Not to be deterred, Shaw continued his investigation of the neocons. Although the neocons told the *Los Angeles Times* that the FBI was investigating Shaw, the reverse was the case: the FBI was investigating the neocons, particularly Perle and Wolfowitz, for fraudulent activities involving Iraqi contracts. And in worse news for the neocons, Rumsfeld was giving the IG's and Shaw's investigations a "wink and a nod" of approval.

The financial stakes for the Pentagon are high — the Iraqi CPA's Inspector General recently revealed that over $1 billion of Iraqi money was missing from the audit books on Iraqi contracts. For Shaw and the FBI, it was a matter of what they suspected for many years — that Perle, Wolfowitz, and their comrades were running entities that ensured favorable treatment for Israeli activities — whether they were business opportunities in a U.S.-occupied Arab country or protecting Israeli spies operating within the U.S. defense and intelligence establishments.

Shaw certainly must have recalled how, during the Reagan administration, an Israeli spy named Jonathan Pollard was able to steal massive amounts of sensitive U.S. intelligence over a long period of time and hand it over to his Israeli control officer, a dangerous and deadly agent provocateur named Rafel "Rafi" Eitan. He must have also recalled that when a young National Security Council staffer named Douglas Feith was suspected of being an Israeli agent of influence, he was stripped of his job and security clearance by then-National Security Adviser Bill Clark, but soon managed to find another job (and another top level clearance) under then Deputy Defense Secretary Richard Perle. And it was certainly known that during Pollard's subsequent appeal of his life sentence for spying for Israel that one of his attorneys was none other than right-wing stalwart and neocon friend, Ted Olsen, the former Solicitor General of the United States under Ashcroft and the person in charge of all U.S. attorneys. It was from Olsen's cadre of U.S. Attorneys that Fitzgerald was selected to investigate the Plame leak and ultimately other high crimes by neocon officials of the Bush administration.

Fitzgerald continues to expand his case against the leakers of Plame's identity. But he may be getting more than he originally bargained for. As his investigation expanded into the bowels of the Pentagon, he was bound to discover that the treachery of the neocons was not merely confined to the leaking of the name of a covert CIA officer — disastrous in itself — but coupled with other activities that call into question the loyalties and financial dealings of those who swore an oath to the U.S. Constitution. With Ashcroft's deputy, James Comey, the person who appointed Fitzgerald, increasingly finding himself frozen out of Ashcroft inner sanctum deliberations, it is clear that the neocons are worried about what Fitzgerald is discovering and how far his investigation will go. Also unusual was the fact that as Fitzgerald's case began to gain steam — with George W. Bush and Dick Cheney both retaining criminal defense attorneys — FBI Director Robert Mueller transferred the lead FBI agent on the Plame case, John C. Eckenrode, a well-seasoned 29-year veteran of the bureau, to head up the FBI's Philadelphia office. An FBI spokesman in Philadelphia said that such transfers just "happen."

The recent arrest warrants issued by the Iraqi government for Ahmed and Salem Chalabi (Ahmed's for counterfeiting Iraqi dinars and Salem's for murdering an Iraqi Finance Ministry official) indicates that Shaw's instincts about the fraud engaged in by them and their neocon friends in the Pentagon were right on the money. The recent decision by the chief judge in the Plame case to order NBC's Tim Russert to testify about who from the White House contacted him about Plame's identity, while troubling for First Amendment freedom of the press protections, is an indication that time is growing short for the leakers — and it is three months before a U.S. presidential election that could be crucial and a windfall for Kerry and the Democratic Party.

Instead of Saddam Hussein's trial being the focus of the election campaign — something the neocons hoped for — it may be the trials of the Chalabis and potentially other members of the Iraqi National Congress, the entity that was nurtured by Perle, Wolfowitz, Feith, former CIA Director James Woolsey — that may be the focus of the campaign. However, the Chalabis escaped from Iraq before they could be arrested. If they turn up in the United States or a member of the laughable "coalition of the willing," the Bush administration and the neocons will be caught between a rock and a hard place. If they refuse to hand over the Chalabis, their true motives will be on display for the entire world to see. If they help to turn over the Chalabis, the Iraqis will be in a position to rat out their neocon friends on the fraud already discovered by Shaw, the IGs of the Pentagon and CPA, the FBI, and the CIA. The CIA should have never been underestimated by the neocons. When the agency came under attack, they were able to marshal all their impressive resources, including Bush 41 confidants C. Boyden Gray, Brent Scowcroft, James Baker III and even George H.W. Bush himself.

In addition, the penetration of the Pentagon over the past three years by those with close connections to Likud interests cannot sit well with either former Reagan Defense Secretary Caspar Weinberger or former National Security Agency (NSA) Director and CIA Deputy Director Bobby Ray Inman, who ordered a severing of U.S. intelligence sharing with Israel after the Pollard affair and other Israeli penetrations of NSA signals intelligence programs through joint Israeli-NSA contracts known as DINDI and PIEREX. Those contracts were eventually canceled after Israeli engineers used friendly U.S. contractors to obtain Sensitive Compartmented Information (SCI) intelligence on NSA operations in the Middle East and around the world. The fact that Ahmed Chalabi, an ally of Pollard's old friends in the Pentagon, was caught passing on NSA cryptologic intelligence to Iran on the agency's ability to crack Iranian diplomatic and military codes must have served as a painful reminder to Weinberger and Inman. It also ensured that the Republican Old Guard would continue to coalesce to ensure the routing of the neocons.

There may yet be a silver lining in the mess brought about by the neocons. In addition to possible indictments of Libby, Wolfowitz, and others for everything ranging from contract fraud, to disseminating, via an Italian con man named Rocco Martino, Niger government documents known to be false, and leaking the name of a covert CIA agent and her proprietary firm, there may be a settling of accounts with Israel over the involvement of it and its agents of influence in the various scams that prodded the U.S. into a war in Iraq.

Every recent Israeli Prime Minister — Yitzhak Shamir, Yitzhak Rabin, Shimon Peres, Benjamin Netanyahu, Ehud Barak, and Ariel Sharon — has demanded that Pollard be released by the United States and allowed to go to Israel. And every American administration — that of Reagan, Bush 41, Clinton, and up to now Bush 43 — has refused. But it may be time for a deal with the Israelis — a deal that would, for once, favor U.S. national security interests. As the influence of the neocons drastically falls, the idea of a Cold War-style agent swap is gaining momentum. If Israel would release the formerly jailed Israeli nuclear technician Mordechai Vanunu from a virtual house arrest in Jerusalem, the United States would release Pollard. One caveat — since when it comes to intelligence matters, Israel cannot be trusted to deal in good faith, Vanunu would be released and given a medical examination by independent American medical personnel before Pollard is turned over to the Israelis. The U.N. checkpoint in divided Nicosia, Cyprus might serve as the "Checkpoint Charlie" for such a swap. Vanunu would be turned over to the Americans from the Greek side and into the relatively Israeli-Russian Mafia-free Turkish Northern Cyprus, while Pollard would be subsequently handed over to the Israelis from the Turkish side.

The United States, after suffering major losses in its ability to track the proliferation of nuclear weapons because of the neocon leaks and disinformation, would have a new intelligence asset in Vanunu — someone who had inside information about Israel's illegal acquisition of nuclear technology. Even though he was jailed in 1986, some of the illegal international nuclear trade networks operating out of the former U.S.S.R. and eastern bloc — which Israel used to its own advantage and as a supply pipeline to its Dimona nuclear weapons plant — may yet yield important intelligence for the CIA's Nonproliferation Center. Let Valerie Plame, whose more recent expertise in international nuclear proliferation would complement Vanunu's prior knowledge, serve as his debriefing officer. Vanunu may even be useful in the continuing criminal investigations of Israeli intelligence activities in the early 1980s — activities that continue to implicate senior members of the current Bush administration. In all, such a deal would be a major win for the national security of the United States. For this writer and U.S. intelligence and Navy veteran, that is the only national security for any country that truly matters in the long run.

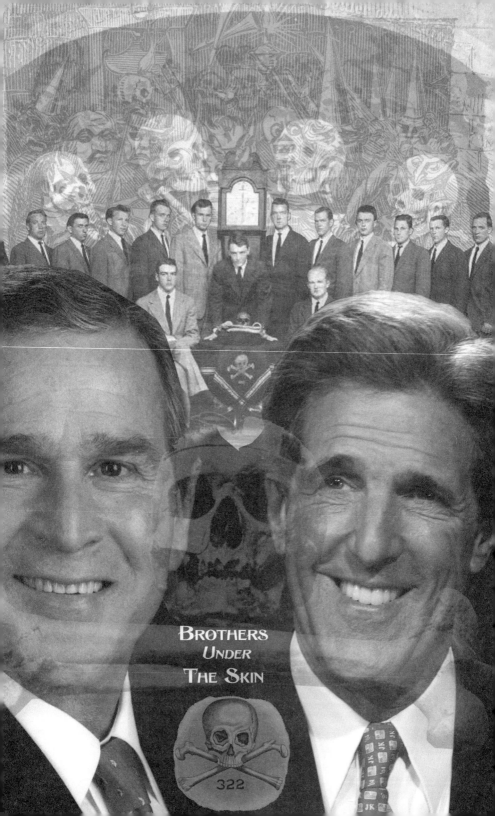

BROTHERS
UNDER
THE SKIN

322

Chapter 5

The 2004 Election

Of course, we're after Saddam Hussein — I mean, bin Laden. He's isolated.
Seventy-five percent of his people have been brought to justice.
— George W. Bush, debate with John Kerry, October 1, 2004
Coral Gables, Florida

November 2, 2004 capped off a watershed political year
in America. Although I had supported the Howard
Dean campaign, seeing him as the only candidate
who understood the damage that had been done to the United
States by the Bush administration, and had even toyed with the
idea of challenging northern Virginia's unlikable Democratic
Congressman Jim Moran in the Democratic primary, what really
mattered to me in the end was the possibility that Senators John
Kerry and John Edwards could oust the corrupt Bush-Cheney
regime. Kerry was not a very stirring candidate, and seemed
tone-deaf in handling the swift boat attacks shot across his bow
by Karl Rove's deep-pocketed mud-throwing machine, but that
did not matter as much as seeing Bush and Cheney run out of
Washington.

The corporate media had almost totally prostituted themselves
to the Bush administration and the neocon war machine in
promoting the Iraq war, and then allowed well-funded 527
political action committees to "swiftboat" John Kerry. Earlier,
they had jumped all over Howard Dean's speech after his Iowa
caucus loss as the "I-have-a-scream-speech." No one bothered
to report on the fact that the corporate media has used a noise

cancelling microphone to isolate Dean's voice from the hundreds of others at his campaign headquarters. This was a new form of psychological-perception warfare. And the Democrats were woefully unprepared to ensure countermeasures for themselves and to counterattack the Republicans at the same time.

There were concerns about Kerry from the beginning. After all, he and Bush were both members of a secret society at Yale called the "Order of Skull & Bones." I wrote about this disturbing facet of the 2004 election in June 2004:

Having just hit the half-century mark age-wise, I can't remember a time when Americans were more apprehensive and frustrated than they are today. Sure, there was Watergate. But thanks to our then-working system of checks and balances, the American political system righted itself and did not capsize as some doomsayers predicted. After Richard Nixon's resignation, the newly-sworn-in President, Gerald Ford, said America's national nightmare was over. Unlike 1974, 2004's nightmare — called the George W. Bush administration — shows no signs of abatement. And for that reason, a majority of Americans with IQs representing a semblance of education are growing increasingly restless. How and when this simmering boil among Americans will overflow is anyone's guess, but the consequences may shock advertising-sponsored political pundits, corporate newspaper editors, and bought-and-paid for pollsters.

From the halls of the Pentagon to the State Department, the offices of constitutional lawyers to political insiders, and the analytical shops of the Central Intelligence Agency to the Defense Intelligence Agency, people have had it with the ideologues (neoconservatives, evangelical dominionists, Christian Zionists, reactionary Catholics, expansionist Israel-Firsters, creative destructionists, Moonies, apocalyptic fundamentalists, and plain old fascists and assorted other kooks) who have nested and reproduced within the three branches of our Federal government. The growing restlessness in America now crosses political party lines, age, racial, and ethnic groups, religious affiliations, and income brackets.

Every day brings a new outrage to those of us who realize that the future of America hangs in the balance. John Kerry should be reaping a whirlwind of support from those angered and disgusted at every syllabic-challenged utterance from the current occupant of the White House. But Kerry's support is lukewarm, even among committed Democrats. The reason is simple — all those who have ranted and raved over the years about the influence of special interests in controlling American foreign and domestic policy have been right on the money all along. The fact that Kerry is part of the nexus of filthy-rich special interests and policy making results in many of his prospective voters saying they will be voting against Bush and not necessarily for Kerry.

Kerry's reluctance to besmirch or even talk about Yale's Skull and Bones crypto-Masonic and jingoistic fraternity (of which he is a member) adds to the apprehension of many Americans. But Bush still stirs an angry bile across the land. Recent news that he has one of Saddam Hussein's favorite pistols in a room adjacent to the Oval Office should be no surprise. Bush likes to show the gun off to his visitors. After all, the Skull and Bonesmen regale themselves in objects looted from battlefields and graves. In their fraternity house at Yale, affectionately called "The Tomb," the Bonesmen are surrounded by Hitler's silverware, Nazi war booty (including swastika iconography), Apache Chief Geronimo's skull (allegedly grave robbed from Fort Sill, Oklahoma, by George Dubya's grandfather, Bonesman Senator Prescott Bush of Connecticut), and the skulls of Pancho Villa, President Martin van Buren (what did he ever do to piss off the Bushes?) and abolitionist leader John Brown. And it should come as no surprise that nine members of a wealthy New England blue blood family, the Cheneys, who made their wealth in the Chinese silk trade, were Bonesmen. One branch of that family made its way to Nebraska with one of their progeny, Richard Brice Cheney, eventually moving to Wyoming where he launched the Cheney family's move back into political power.

If Kerry wants to reassure us that his administration will be radically different from the Bush-Cheney junta, he should immediately resign from Skull and Bones, denounce their sordid agenda and rituals, and demand that human remains robbed from graves be returned to their proper burial places. We can understand why George W. Bush likes the death cult aspects of this gruesome and morose society of wealthy snot-nosed rich kids, but there is no reason for Kerry to honor whatever goofy pledges he made to these ghouls when he was initiated by them.

Between the Yalie death cultists, Christian evangelical end timers, neoconservative global hegemonists, and those with IQs lower than George W. Bush (91), the rest of us (the good news is that we are still a majority), including a number with one or more stars on their military uniforms, are becoming irritated to the point where something is going to break. Some quotes recently picked up from two and three-star generals and bird colonels: "I took an oath to the Constitution, not Bush, Cheney, or Rumsfeld"; "If the Pentagon were being overrun by the enemy and I had one bullet left, I'd use it on Stephen Cambone" (the Undersecretary of Defense for Intelligence); "Too bad they missed Wolfowitz!" (a reference to the October 2003 Iraqi insurgent bombing of the Al Rashid hotel in Baghdad where Wolfowitz was staying). And this from a National Guard Colonel: "The Governors are ready to revolt if any more of their Guardsmen are sent to Iraq."

If Bush, Cheney, and Rove interfere with the election process, either by postponing the November 2 election because of an unspecified "terrorist" threat or other concocted reason, many in the senior levels of the military are prepared to honor their oath to the Constitution and protect our nation from enemies "domestic." That includes presidents and their staff who want to overturn the Constitutional process for their own nefarious purposes.

A longtime colleague, a well-known constitutional lawyer, told me that he would support the military taking such unprecedented action against an out-of-control executive branch. A seasoned Washington political observer, well known to television audiences, echoed the lawyer's sentiment — he even called for military trials of Bush, Cheney, and their henchmen after their ouster. Yes, the outrage factor is at an all-time fever pitch. In my lifetime, I've seen nothing like it. Yet, it is wholly understandable. Every day the Bush regime outrages us and the world, the gulf widens between the reasoned masses and the perception managers and ideologues who surround the pathetic one in the White House.

Al Gore (the man who should rightly be President) has certainly had enough. He let Bush have it in a recent speech in New York City. The whining right-wingers who back Bush cried foul. To those who think Kerry is "Bush-Lite," Gore's words were a health tonic. Gore said Bush, like Faustus, sold his soul in return for global domination. It's not known if Gore, a Harvard man, has read up on Yale's Skull and Bones, but such a comparison has much merit. Gore wowed the audience with a call for the resignation of Bush's national security and defense team: the whole shebang of neocons and incompetents: Rumsfeld, Wolfowitz, Douglas Feith, Cambone, Condoleezza Rice. As Howard Dean would say, "Yee Haw!"

If the military does have to purge the Executive Branch of nut cases and *les démagogues très dangereux*, they will find support

124

from Gore, who somehow wound up on a "check baggage" alert list at Reagan National Airport when he was boarding a flight to Wisconsin. Candidates for the Green Party and the Libertarian Party's presidential candidate have been similarly placed on passenger watch lists in what has become a Soviet-style system of internal travel controls and checkpoints. Across the political spectrum, people want their Constitution protected and if the military steps up to the plate, they will have widespread support.

So enough of this regime of fascists and suicidal Christian cultists. If the Bush junta and their pantywaist supporters want to take this battle into the streets they will find patriotic constitutionalist Americans up to the task. We have most of the military brass on our side and the real military veterans who have faced diminishing benefits under Bush (not that flotsam and jetsam of society that ride into Washington on Harleys every Memorial Day weekend and claim they have some God-given right to speak for veterans even if they do get a guided tour of the White House from the moron-in-chief in return for their meaningless political endorsement).

The neocons appear to be sensing that the tide is turning against them. Their archangel, Richard Perle, recently complained that a gaggle of former intelligence officers helped bring down his friend, the Iraqi con man Ahmad Chalabi, by publishing defamatory stories about him. Hey, Richard, I plead guilty! But we won't stop with Chalabi. Former and current intelligence officers, retired and active duty military officers, and all those who want to see sanity return to American foreign policy won't stop until we see you and your duplicitous friends — Michael Ledeen, Elliot Abrams, Manucher Ghorbanifar, and the other Iran-Contra alumni — similarly exposed as agents of influence who gladly walk the line between the Israelis and Iranians and eke as much out of both as possible. Dan Senor, the Coalition Provisional Authority spokesman, not only worked for the criminal Carlyle Group, but his association with a company that seeks to accelerate Israeli technology infusion into the U.S. defense and homeland security markets, deserves special condemnation and continued scrutiny once he folds up his Baghdad tent and moves back to the United States.

The frustration of Americans is matched by that of the people of Iraq, Britain, Haiti, Italy, Australia, and other nations that have come under the control of Bush's minions. The recent elections that threw out right-wing allies of Bush in Spain, South Korea, and India should serve as a stark warning to the neocons. Your time is also coming. Some members of the recently-dissolved Iraqi Governing Council, like the U.S. military, are in open revolt against the neocons. Tony Blair and Australia's John Howard are on the political ropes. Italy's neo-fascist Prime Minister Silvio Berlusconi digs himself deeper into political and legal troubles.

The neocons, the swaggering Bush hegemonists, and their off-base "End Times" religious allies must be ejected from the American body politic. They did more to destroy this country's constitutional fabric than any recent past conspiratorial group — including the Communist Party, Weathermen, Freemen, or Ku Klux Klan. None of them ever gained control of the White House and Pentagon.

Let John Kerry begin the process of cleansing America of this ilk by resigning from and denouncing Skull and Bones. Pass a Federal law requiring them to return human remains to proper burial places and stolen war booty to their rightful owners (in the case of Hitler's silverware, that would be the U.S. Government). The moron-in-chief should turn Saddam's pistol over to the new Iraqi government's archives.

If our military leaders decide to honor their oath to the Constitution, let those of us who would normally find abhorrent a *Seven Days in May* scenario, welcome their action. If retired Generals Anthony Zinni and Joseph Hoar are any indication, our military leaders have more of an appreciation for our way of life and traditions than the "selected" occupants of the Executive Branch. Our military leadership may be the only power in the land that can challenge those who seek to destroy the United States, if not the entire world.

During the 2004 summer presidential campaign, the American people were frustrated by the lack of a strong-willed campaign by the Democratic ticket of John Kerry and John Edwards. Howard Dean had shown real guts. but a noise-canceling microphone and a waiting corporate media did him in after his defeat in the Iowa caucuses.

Kerry would not bring up Bush's introduction of fascism in the United States: the "f"-word was strictly forbidden in those days. On July 4, 2004, Independence Day, using the "free speech zone" of the Web, I wrote about the drift of the United States to fascism:

On June 28, no less than the U.S. Supreme Court voiced its own clear majority opinion that the Bush administration vastly exceeded its constitutional powers by throwing into military prisons, without a right to counsel or a trial, U.S. citizens and foreigners suspected of terrorist activities. This Independence Day serves as an important watershed date — never before in the history of our nation has an administration thumbed its nose so willfully at our scarred founding documents — the Declaration of Independence and the Constitution of the United States.

Under the tutelage of the most extremist Attorney General we have ever witnessed [that was until Alberto Gonzales succeeded him] — the singing John Ashcroft — innocent citizen after innocent citizen has been subjected to politically-motivated prosecutions; unfair surveillance and harassment; and racial, religious, and ethnic profiling. Hundreds of thousands of people abroad have scrapped travel plans to the United States because of new requirements for bureaucratic visas, fingerprinting, and photographing. In fact, travel by Americans to the Soviet Union and Warsaw Pact countries was far easier than it now is for Eastern European and other friendly nationals to visit the United States.

At a whim and without a shred of logical reasoning, the Homeland Security Department can raise and lower its banal terrorist alert system colors. When the alert status is raised, uniformed military personnel and police SWAT teams appear on the cable news networks standing guard at the Golden Gate Bridge, Holland Tunnel, Liberty Bell, Gateway Arch, and the Seattle Space Needle. Independence Day has become a particularly favorite day for Tom Ridge to play around with his terrorist-alert crayon box.

During the past year, Americans have been warned about people carrying almanacs and road atlases, floating land mines in marinas, poisoned prescription drugs from Canada, terrorist scuba divers, bombs in Ohio shopping malls, kids' model rockets, and men with beards. While recently clearing security at Reagan National Airport in Washington, I witnessed one passenger being forced to play his harmonica to prove that it wasn't some sort of bomb. Fortunately, he played some very good blues and received a round of applause from the other bewildered passengers.

Instead of respecting the wishes of states, cities, counties, towns, and college campuses across the land — from Maine and New Jersey to Alaska and Hawaii, which have passed anti-Patriot Act resolutions — the Bush administration wants to scrap the sunset provisions of portions of the act. The Justice Department wants to make permanent and expand further its surveillance and other draconian powers through a Patriot II Act.

Because the ranking member of the Senate Judiciary Committee stood in the way of President Bush's attempt to pack the Federal bench with more right-wing ideologues, Vice President Dick Cheney used the opportunity of a chance encounter on the Senate floor to tell Senator Patrick Leahy of Vermont to profanely do something to himself. That sort of conduct would not even have been tolerated in the Roman Senate over two thousand years ago.

In a past era, which was not that long ago, Americans were free to protest their leaders and their policies. Now, those who exercise their First Amendment rights are herded like cattle into "Free Speech Zones." Our liberties, so valued by our Founding Fathers and Mothers, are in such a pitiful state that they would turn aside in horror if they could see what has become of the nation for which they toiled, fought, and died.

Messrs. Bush, Cheney, Ashcroft, and their colleagues should be ashamed of themselves and "We the People" ashamed of them.

In March 2004, I had the opportunity to debate Fox News' Sean Hannity after I wrote an article comparing the policies of George W. Bush to those of Adolf Hitler. The neocon spin machine was not amused. I wrote an article in March 2004 on the visceral neocon reaction to the comparison:

In a number of columns written after George W. Bush's extra-constitutional seizure of powers post 9/11, I pointed out a number of similarities between Bush's GOP and Hitler's Nazi Party.

The bombast from the usual suspect circles was swift and predictable. Writing in the neoconservative *National Review*, Byron York bemoaned the fact that "Wayne Madsen wrote that Bush is 'borrowing liberally from Hitler's play book.'" Following the same line, the *New York Post*'s editorial page editor, arch-neocon propagandist John Podhoretz, in his new book, *Bush Country*, whined that when I wrote about Hitler's oratory skills being light years ahead of Bush's, I was somehow praising Hitler. This is so typical of the right-wing attack dogs: ignore the main point and fire off a broadside of false innuendo. No reasonable historian would deny that Hitler's speechmaking abilities were far ahead of the syllable-challenged Bush's. Contrasting the policies of Bush and Hitler following terrorist attacks in their countries is a legitimate area for historical comparative analysis. Although Hitler was certainly behind the burning of the Reichstag, he and Bush both virtually tore up their respective constitutions and began viciously denouncing their political enemies. Both Bush and Hitler failed in every business venture they started, until, of course, they became leaders of their countries in questionable elections.

The neocon spin machine continues to defend Bush against charges that he practices the same sort of reactionary political politics as embraced by Hitler. On Fox News' *Hannity & Colmes*, I was asked to defend my comparison.

Guest Co-host Michael Wolff: "But you don't see a legitimate distinction between Adolf Hitler and George Bush?"

Madsen: "Well, look, if you look at some of the policies, preemptive warfare, we know that Hitler did that against Poland. He did it against France; he did it against the Soviet Union. Trashing the United Nations, that's what Hitler did to the League of Nations."

Sean Hannity: "Don't you see how you're alienating the majority of the American people with your rhetoric?"

Madsen: "I don't think so. The way to combat terrorism isn't to take the United States Constitution and the Bill of Rights and shred it like Mr. Hitler did [to his constitution] after the Reichstag fire."

The exchange on Fox was prompted by two television advertisements likening Bush to Hitler that were submitted in a contest sponsored by MoveOn.org. Cathy Young, writing an op-ed on behalf of *Reason*, a so-called libertarian magazine whose motto is Free Minds and Free Markets, said comparisons between Bush and Hitler should be retired. It is interesting that a magazine like *Reason* would use the phrase Free Minds and Free Markets. Considering that *Reason* champions the so-called rights of companies over the Lilliputians of the working class, that motto is not much different from the sign over the main gate of the Auschwitz concentration camp: "Arbeit Macht Frei" — "Work Brings Freedom."

Recently, radio shock jock Howard Stern said the real reason why the pro-Bush and Dallas-based Clear Channel dropped his nationally-syndicated morning program from its stations was not because the company was trying to placate the Federal Communications Commission over offensive material on the airwaves but was in response to his attacking the Nazi- and Taliban-

129

like policies of Bush. Stern also suggested that the fundamentalist right-wingers supporting Bush were organized into Nazi-like cells. Stern is just one more in a long list of people who have disagreed with Bush and have faced the wrath of the Bush storm troopers. Let us not forget what the creepy management of Clear Channel did when the Dixie Chicks spoke out against Bush. They banned their songs from their radio stations and sponsored compact disc smashing events in the same manner that Hitler's minions banned books and burned them in huge bonfires around Germany.

John Ashcroft's Gestapo-like Justice Department has engaged in definite selective prosecutions of those who have openly opposed Bush's policies or have contributed money to the Democratic Party's coffers. Take former Illinois Republican Governor George Ryan: Ashcroft's right-wing prosecutors indicted him after he commuted the death sentences of Illinois's death row population. Ryan cited police and prosecutorial misconduct in Chicago and the state capital of Springfield as a major reason for his decision. Ashcroft and Bush, both self-anointed born-again Christians, are in love with the death penalty and championed executions while serving as governors of their states of Missouri and Texas, respectively. In 2002, a Purim sermon at a Washington, DC synagogue suggested Ashcroft was like Haman, the evil vizier of the Persian King Ahasuerus. Haman, like Hitler, plotted to annihilate the Jews and the two are often compared in Jewish liturgies.

And then there is Martha Stewart, a past generous contributor to Democratic candidates and causes. She was indicted by Ashcroft's New York feds after she lied about dumping her Imclone stock in an insider trading deal. Never mind the fact that Enron's former chairman, Kenneth Lay (affectionately called "Kenny Boy" by Bush) still walks free despite the fact that he ripped off billions of dollars from stockholders and employees. [Lay is now deceased.] It was a hallmark of the Hitler regime to accuse political opponents of the Nazis of committing economic crimes against the state. The Nazis charged a number of non-Nazi business leaders with contributing to Germany's hyper-inflation following World War I. Many were later arrested and had their property seized. The Nazis allowed only a few large corporations to flourish, particularly those that generously contributed to the Nazi cause. Arms manufacturer Gustav Krupp was won over to the Nazi cause in 1933 when the Nazis told him that they would increase defense spending to record levels. For his part, Krupp led an industrial fund called the Adolf Hitler Spende. The fund collected money for

Hitler's election coffers in return for special treatment for German industries. Ken Lay, meet Gustav Krupp.

On the subject of Enron, it was Lay and his buddies in Houston who financially raped California in 2001 by conspiring to raise the state's electric utility rates to a usurious degree. Who paid the price when California was plunged into financial ruin? Democratic Governor Gray Davis, who was recalled in a right-wing financed election after having served less than a year of his second term. And who replaced Davis? Self-described Hitler, Nazi, and Kurt Waldheim admirer Arnold Schwarzenegger, the new Republican Governor of California whose congressional soul mate, Senator Orrin Hatch of Utah, wants to amend the US Constitution to allow an Austrian émigré like Schwarzenegger to run for President. Where before have we seen national laws changed to allow a right-wing Austrian to run for political office in an adopted homeland?

But the neocons still continue to attack those who draw comparisons between Bush and Hitler. Shamefully, the neocons keep silent as Mel Gibson releases a big screen version of the Passion plays that were historically used throughout Europe to fan the flames of anti-Semitism. Many religious experts have pointed out that Gibson's *The Passion of the Christ* will only further exacerbate tense relations between Christians and non-Christians. Not so, say the evangelical Christians and their neocon allies — especially those affiliated with the Catholic right-wing secret society Opus Dei and the New American Century/American Enterprise Institute crowd. Shamefully, they mimic the kapos of Nazi Germany's concentration camps and keep silent as Gibson's movie fans the flames of religious intolerance. Worse, the hallelujah chorus for the extreme right failed to urge Gibson to condemn his father Hutton's historical revisionist comments that Germany could not have killed 6 million Jews. "Do you know what it takes to get rid of a dead body? To cremate it? It takes a liter of petrol and 20 minutes. Now, six million of them? They [the Germans] did not have the gas to do it. That's why they lost the war," the elder Gibson told a New York radio show. He then suggested that many Jewish victims of the Holocaust had actually emigrated to the United States and Australia.

Yet, GOP radio and television mouthpieces like Sean Hannity, Laura Ingraham, and Rush Limbaugh defend Mel Gibson's movie while, at the same time, deride those who would compare what is happening in the United States now to what occurred in Germany in the early and mid 1930s. They feel we should just ignore Arnold Schwarzenegger, Hutton and Mel Gibson, and the foaming-at-the-mouth racists and xenophobes of evangelical Christendom and right-wing Catholicism. I, for one, will not ignore what are indisputable signs that the right wing in the United States has made a sharp turn into the netherworld of fascism and racial and religious xenophobia.

"Mixing with Blacks was out of the question ... The Negro problem, indeed the racial problem in general, is viewed differently in the industrialized North than in the more agricultural South, which had drawn a sharp line for centuries between the colored and Whites." That passage could have been written by any number of racist Republicans, from Strom Thurmond, to his number one fan Trent Lott, to Haley Barbour and Sonny Perdue, the neoconfederate GOP Governors of Mississippi and Georgia, respectively. However, this interpretation of race relations in the United States was prepared in 1942 by Hitler's *Reichsorganisationsleitung*, a Nazi Party propaganda mill headed by Robert Ley. Haley Barbour, meet Robert Ley.

The GOP is also engaged in a national campaign of gay bashing. Using gay marriage as a *casus belli*, the GOP, fronting for the evangelical Christian Taliban of Ashcroft, Pat Robertson, Bob Jones, and Jerry Falwell, wants to turn the clock back on the civil liberties and equal treatment for gays and lesbians. But the GOP, like the Nazis, is hiding a dark secret. The Nazi youth movement (*Wandervogel*) was led by a number of homosexuals, including the sadistic Gerhard Rossbach, who would lay the groundwork for the Nazi Brown Shirts as a result of his creation of the post-World War I *Freikorps* (Free Corps). Rossbach recruited German Army Captain Ernst Roehm, another homosexual, into his movement. Roehm would eventually become the leader of the SA Storm Troopers of the Nazi Party. Many of the early Nazi leaders in Munich were, in fact, gay. Heinrich Himmler began to see Roehm and his associates as dangerous to the party. Even Hitler was suspected of having a homosexual past, especially when he was living the life of an itinerant on the streets of Vienna. Some of Hitler's followers formed a secret occult order called the Ordo Novi Templi (Order of the New Temple).

But even as Roehm and his homosexual colleagues helped extend Nazi rule in Germany, Hitler, after his ascension to power in 1933, banned pornography, homosexual bars and bathhouses, and homosexual rights groups. The Nazi anti-gay laws were only directed against homosexuals who were opposed to the Nazis, not against those who supported Hitler. In June 1934, Hitler and his allies ordered the extermination of Roehm and his SA associates, as well as other political enemies, in the Night of the Long Knives. One of the chief executioners was Reinhard Heydrich, one of Hitler's top advisers, who was also a homosexual.

Fast forward to today. Although Bush and his evangelical allies condemn homosexuality, the ranks of the Bush's brain trust are rife with gays who support the gay bashing agenda of the GOP. It should be pointed out that these ranks do not include the Log Cabin Republicans, a moderate Republican gay advocacy group. From Bush's fraternity Skull & Bones, to Bush "best friend" and fellow Bonesman Victor Ashe, the former Mayor of Knoxville, Tennessee; to Karl Rove; to Bush's successor as Governor of Texas, Rick Perry; to other Republican politicians in Texas; to some of Bush's top ideological advisers and media cheerleaders, rumors are swirling about homoerotic fraternity initiations, secretive trysts, sudden divorce filings, and tropical island getaways. Skull & Bones, meet the Order of the New Temple.

Germany's Foreign Minister Joachim von Ribbentrop was often said to be the friendly face of Nazism. A frequent guest at Europe's high society dinner parties, Ribbentrop would brush aside fears about Germany's ambitions, including its imperial designs on its European neighbors. Colin Powell, who has been called the "good cop" in the Bush administration's crowd of "bad cops," permitted his right-wing Latin America assistant, Roger Noriega, a former chief of staff to Sen. Jesse Helms, to strong-arm and hoodwink Haitian President Jean-Bertrand Aristide into accepting a peace agreement that the brutish Haitian opposition, armed and supported by the Bush administration, had no intention of signing. Noriega's machination was supported by his predecessor, Otto Reich, who serves as Condoleezza Rice's National Security Council point man for Latin America. After Aristide was kidnapped at his home at gunpoint by U.S. troops accompanied by U.S. Deputy Chief of Mission Luis Moreno and flown on an American plane to house arrest in the Central African Republic, the democratically-elected Haitian President proclaimed that his removal was unconstitutional and had been forced by Washington. In 1936, a beleaguered and exiled Ethiopian Emperor Haile Selassie appeared before the League of Nations in Switzerland to condemn its inaction over the Italian Fascist invasion of his country. "God and history will remember your judgment," Selassie told the League. Colin Powell, meet Joachim von Ribbentrop.

Yes, there certainly are many comparisons between the policies of Bush and Hitler. More astounding is the fact that Bush's grandfather, Senator Prescott Bush of Connecticut, was an investor in Nazi businesses and industries during World War II. No wonder his son, George H.W. Bush was urged to sign up as the youngest Navy pilot to fight the Japanese in the Pacific. Pursuant to the Trading With the Enemy Act, Prescott Bush had his assets seized during World War II. They included interests in Union Banking Corporation, Holland American Trading Corporation, Seamless Steel Equipment Corporation, and the Silesian-American Corporation (a joint operation between Prescott and his father-in-law George Herbert Walker). Silesian-American would press-gang slave laborers from the Polish town of Oswiecim, the future home of the Auschwitz concentration camp. After the war, Prescott received his "properties" back and sold them, laying a major foundation of the Bush family fortune.

The similarities between the Bush and Nazi gangs are unmistakable. The list of those who see the similarities grows every day. The latest on the list is Howard Stern. He joins former German Justice Minister Herta Daubler-Gmelin, CBS's *Hitler: The Rise of Evil* miniseries' director Ed Gernon, financier George Soros, filmmaker Michael Moore, actress and comedienne Janeane Garofolo, German author and TV moderator Franz Alt, playwright Harold Pinter, Cuban President Fidel Castro, former South African President Nelson Mandela, "Boondocks" cartoonist Aaron McGruder, retired Western Michigan University English professor Edward Jayne, columnist Nicholas von Hoffman, author John Pilger, and Mexican writer Carlos Fuentes in comparing Bush's policies and antics to those of Hitler. I am proud to have my views associated with those of such visionary luminaries.

During the 1930s, the famous writer H.G. Wells was rebuked by the conservatives of his day for comparing Hitler to Caesar and suggesting that Hitler was a "certifiable lunatic." Wells turned out to be right on the money. Those of us who see a creeping fascism with Bush and his cronies will, one day, be vindicated by the annals of history.

***

During the morning of November 2, 2004, I spoke to friends and colleagues around the country about voter turnout. The news was good. There was heavy turnout in African-American urban, Hispanic rural, and Democratic-leaning suburbs and exurbs around the country. During the mid-afternoon, I was at the National Press Club in Washington and began seeing exit polling data. The news was good for the Democratic ticket. Kerry was leading in exit polls in Pennsylvania, Ohio, Florida, Michigan, and Illinois. If the trends held, we would have a new President.

At 6:00 P.M., I attended an election watch party at the United Press International bureau on H Street, around the corner from the White House. As the first bottles of wine were being cracked, a few of us, having seen the exit polls, toasted the new President of the United States, John Kerry.

The first returns were encouraging. Although Bush won Kentucky and Indiana, which was no surprise, Kerry began racking up electoral votes in the northeast. The interesting thing was the fact that the networks, between 7 and 8 P.M, could not call Virginia or South Carolina. Things looked good. The African-American turnout in South Carolina had been reported at record levels with similar record turnouts being reported in the Washington suburbs in northern Virginia.

However, a bit after 8:00 P.M, something seemed wrong, very wrong. In a case of déjà vu from the 2000 election, Ohio was too close to call. As the night wore on, Ohio appeared to be the new Florida. However, exit polls indicated that Kerry was ahead in Ohio by 3 percentage points.

The original excitement over the prospects of a new administration tapered off to a nervousness and then the realization that another election had been stolen.

The day after the election debacle, it was clear that there were major election problems in Ohio, Florida, and other states. The hand of Karl Rove could, once again, be seen in "election engineering," or just plain, "election fraud." With enough over votes, under votes, caged votes, provisional votes, spoiled votes, flipped votes, and rejected votes, Bush and Cheney were able to eke out an electoral vote victory, as well as pile up a 3 million vote and very dubious popular vote majority. On November 5, I wrote the following for *Online Journal*:

Karl Rove, the political sorcerer who is called "Turd Blossom" by his political master, George W. Bush, has his nasty fingerprints all over the 2004 Election in a scam that can best be called "Grand Theft Election."

There was something very wrong in Ohio, which Bush claims he won handily. Not only had the head of computer voting machine maker Diebold and Ohio's Republican establishment of Governor Bob Taft and Secretary of State Kenneth Blackwell conspired to suppress registration and voter turnout in heavily Democratic precincts, but the Ohio Secretary of State's Web site was only reporting results from nine counties as of 11:30 A.M. on November 3, just three hours before John Kerry conceded the election to Bush. Totaling the results from the nine counties (Fayette, Fairfield, Geauga, Jefferson, Portage, Mahoning, Trumbull, Richland, and Washington), John Kerry was clearly ahead. A tenth county, Columbiana, suspiciously showed up as "NO RESULTS."

The totals from the 8 Ohio counties reported on the Secretary of State Web site were: BUSH 267,771, KERRY 294,648.

There has to be a way for those of us who voted for Kerry and Edwards to sue Diebold Chief Executive Walden O'Dell and Diebold board member W.R. Timken for conspiring to deliver Ohio's electoral votes to Bush. O'Dell and Timken are also top fundraisers for Bush, so-called "Pioneers." O'Dell told the *Cleveland Plain Dealer* in 2003 that he was "committed to helping Ohio deliver its electoral votes to the president next year."

The fact that Diebold machines were used in the Ohio rip-off should make O'Dell and Timken the subjects of criminal investigations. Of course, that will not happen in a GOP vassal state like Ohio. But why not a civil suit by those of us nationwide who voted for Kerry and had our presidency stolen from us as a result of racketeering and corrupt practices by a cabal of Republicans and fat cat corporate types? In a civil suit, through the process of discovery, O'Dell's and Timken's e-mails, letters, and other records could be ordered open by a judge. They could also be deposed as witnesses before plaintiffs' attorneys.

Then there were the strange hiccups with the official election Web sites reporting results in states and counties across the nation.

During the morning of November 3, attempts to access the Pinellas County, Florida, election Web site were met with the following:

The page cannot be found.

The page you are looking for might have been removed, had its name changed, or is temporarily unavailable.

At 11:52 A.M. on November 3, the St. Lucie County, Florida election Web site showed no returns, long after the polls closed:

Welcome To St. Lucie County Live Election Returns
Election results will appear shortly.

Attempts to access Miami-Dade County's [a major scene of the 2000 election crime] election Web site during the morning of November 3 were similarly unsuccessful.

On the Florida Secretary of State Web site there appeared some verbiage about a link to the Marion County election Web site. But there was no link. Ditto the same for Nassau County, a county that saw widespread voter intimidation and suppression of African-American votes in 2000.

Indian River County, Florida election results were also of interest and indicated fraud:

Registered voters as of October 4, 2004 included Republican: 41,866; Democratic: 24,515; Independent: 15,262. Votes on Nov 2 were Bush: 36,744; Kerry: 23,850.

Democrats had almost complete turnout if you match turnout to their registered voters. Republicans were down some 4000, but what happened to the Independents' votes? There were less than 1 percent for the third party candidates. We were told Independents were breaking for Kerry. Even if 23,850 for Kerry included a majority of the Independents and even a few moderate Republicans, the results from Indian River don't indicate that.

In pivotal New Mexico, by mid morning on November 3, the state election Web site was missing several returns from areas with large Native American populations. Cibola and San Miguel Counties were missing in addition to one precinct in Dona Ana County with the following close returns listed: Bush: 26,072; Kerry: 25,608.

One precinct in McKinley County with the following returns listed: Bush 7,132; Kerry: 12,725

One precinct in Sandoval County with the following close returns listed: Bush: 22,482; Kerry: 21,215.

Fifteen precincts in Socorro County with the following close returns listed: Bush: 3,197; Kerry: 2,638.

New Mexico was eventually declared for Bush in a close election, even though it went for Gore in 2000.

There were also missing returns from a very close race in Nevada.

Clark County (Las Vegas) had 271,465 people vote early and 220,501 vote at polls on election day.

Kerry received 279,575 votes to Bush's 253,432 in Clark.

If, as we were told, early votes were breaking 60-70 percent for Kerry in areas he won, it looks like he should have had more like 300,000 votes in Clark County, which would have tipped the state to him. Kerry lost Nevada "officially" by only 21,000 votes. This does not include the 50,705 absentee votes in Clark County (which also likely broke for Kerry). There were also 10,000 undervotes and write-ins reported statewide, which seems very high for a small-population state like Nevada.

The turnout in Virginia was an all time high, especially in heavily Democratic counties and cities. Early on election night, NBC said it could not call Virginia because the returns were close. Yet, an examination of the vote count as compared to 2000 reveals that the massive 2004 turnout, especially with African Americans, young people, and Hispanics was not reflected in the final vote counts and percentages.

I personally witnessed two-hour-plus waiting lines at polling places in Arlington and Fairfax Counties. This was unprecedented, but it is not reflected in the vote count. This could be the result of both tampering with computer machines and voter suppression.

Kerry's vote totals in Virginia did not not make any sense considering the massive numbers of newly registered voters and the huge turnout in northern Virginia, Tidewater, and the economically-depressed southwest part of the state.

When Diebold machines were forced on Prince George's County, Maryland, the country's election administrator, Robert J. Antonetti, bitterly complained about them. He told the *Baltimore Sun* in 2003, "I feel very uneasy about it. There are too many loose ends."

On November 2, Prince George's County election officials reported a number of problems with Diebold encoders. The *Prince George's Gazette* reported that a number of polling places opened up to 45 minutes late because the wrong Diebold encoder had been delivered to polling places and voters could not vote until a new encoder arrived. It is not known how many records the Prince George's County maintained on problems with Diebold, but it is very interesting that early in the morning of November 3, the Associated Press reported,

"UPPER MARLBORO, Maryland (AP)—Fire broke out Wednesday at the Prince George's County courthouse, engulfing a large section of the ornate building. 'About 100 firefighters were at the scene,' fire and emergency medical service spokesman Chauncey Bowers said."

And Washington, DC News Channel 4 reported, "… pictures from Chopper 4 show that almost the entire building is completely ruined and a section could be in danger of partial collapse. Thick billowing black smoke can be seen for miles."

Early reports were sketchy on what records may have been destroyed by the flames in both the old courthouse building and an adjoining newer structure, but one report on Channel 4 stated that records had definitely been destroyed. Later reports claimed no records were stored in the burned out building.

But next time you see a Diebold employee, you may want to ask him, "Hey, pal, gotta match?"

Wayne Madsen New "Person of Interest" in Anthrax Probe ?

An OSI News Exclusive !

OSI : Information THEY don't want you to see …

Washington, June 4, 2006 : Federal investigators have refused to comment on rumors a mysterious 'W. MADSEN', who is said to have had ties to and dealings with the controversial NSA 'spy shop', is being 'looked at as a person of interest' in the nearly five-year-old Amerithrax investigation.

http://www.fbi.gov/anthrax/amerithraxlinks.htm

We have been able to confirm there is a Wayne Madsen: self-described as a Washington-based investigative reporter, who was employed by NSA during the Reagan Administration, and who is, to judge by his website : http://www.waynemadsenreport.com/ still privy to much top-secret government information.

Our informants point out that Washington, DC is not very far from Ft. Detrick, Maryland-home of the Army's Bio-research program-and a relatively short train ride away from Princeton, NJ , location of the deadly 'anthrax mailbox' .

This is what appeared on the Web site called PHXNews, with a link to the FBI's anthrax tip line.

Chapter 6

2005: The Momentum Builds and the Neocons Get Desperate

Wayne Madsen Report, which its publisher, Wayne Madsen, keeps refreshed with more news than any one reporter has a right to.

— OPEDNEWS.com

On May 25, 2005, I started a Web site designed to bring back the spirit of Drew Pearson's and Jack Anderson's famous syndicated newspaper column, "Washington Merry-Go-Round." Started by Pearson in 1932, and continued by Anderson after Pearson's death in 1969, the Merry-Go-Round was a much-feared Washington institution. If a politician came under the scrutiny of Pearson and later, Anderson, their careers were usually severely damaged or were ended altogether. Syndicated in almost one thousand newspapers and reaching some 40 million readers, the Washington Merry-Go-Round kept Americans informed of the tawdry affairs in Washington. Today's corporate media, fearful of alienating politicians and only interested in profits, has gutted investigative reporting.

With this in mind, the WayneMadsenReport.com was designed to bust through the din of the 24/7 cable news channels and all their fluff and propaganda disguised as news reports. On a shoestring budget and with the financial help of close friends, starting a new Web site was risky. How does one build a better mousetrap? There were already thousands of politically-oriented blogs, but none mirrored the spirit and intent of the Washington Merry-Go-Round. The *Drudge Report*, of the Republican talking points purveyor Matt Drudge, was closer to the right-wing muckraking of newspaper columnist Walter Winchell. Yet, it was enormously popular. Several progressive journalists admitted they read Drudge, but that is because there was not a liberal alternative nor was there anything on the Web even approaching the "inside Washington" flavor of Pearson's and Anderson's column.

Robert Sherrill of the *Chicago Tribune* described the impact that Pearson had on official Washington. He said Pearson was "the greatest muckraker of all time. Woodward and Bernstein may have toppled Richard Nixon, but as practitioners of muckraking they are drab apprentices compared to Pearson."

Pearson did not hesitate to mix his own opinion of Washington's powerful with his seemingly endless scoops. This is what he wrote on May 26, 1955, about former President Herbert Hoover, who was complaining about leaks to the media:

Hoover's Leaks

Herbert Hoover has been sore as blazes at this writer for publishing advance copies of some of his government reorganization reports.

Mr. Hoover has squawked about it vocally and vigorously, though privately. In fact, he's been so irked that he's given orders that all task-force reports on government reorganization be "classified" and he's threatened to prosecute anyone leaking information to Pearson.

It would appear that Mr. Hoover is not too familiar with the law, because his reports pertain not to military or defense secrets but only to problems of bureaucracy and red tape, and never in the entire history of the United States has it been against the law to publish information pertaining to efficiency in government.

Apparently Mr. Hoover hasn't changed much. When in the White House he also used to be riled over news-leaks, asked publishers to fire newsmen who published embarrassing stories.

So I hope he won't get too upset over today's leak about news leaks to Pearson.

A Web site dedicated to airing Washington's dirty laundry would clearly fill a void. With Microsoft Front Page, PhotoShop, and an Internet Service Provider, I was drawn into the world of "blogging." However, unlike many blogs, I attempted to report on stories that were not being chased after by the corporate-pack journalists.

Before launching WayneMadsenReport.com, I placed articles on a number of Web sites, including *CounterPunch*, *Online Journal*, *NewsInsider*, and others. Even placing articles on other Web sites was not without its problems, especially with the threats of lawsuits from a host of corporate shysters interested only in stifling debate and public discourse.

I wrote the following just prior to launching WayneMadsenReport.com in May 2005:

In the past year, I have been threatened with a libel suit in London from a rich Saudi billionaire whose Washington-based law firm just happens to have a former Bush-Cheney campaign finance chairman and one of George W. Bush's closest Texas pals as two of its major partners. I have earned the attention of an Orwellian Ministry of Truth-like "counter-propaganda" office at the U.S. Department of State, which maintains a Web site that criticizes my articles. It is against U.S. law for the International Public Diplomacy unit to directly respond to my counter-arguments; they can only legally respond to foreign queries, and not those from U.S. citizen journalists whom they cavalierly attack. I have now been threatened by the company CACI International, which, according to the Taguba Report, was involved in the prison torture at Abu Ghraib.

Unlike *Newsweek*, CBS News and *60 Minutes*, and the Public Broadcasting System and National Public Radio, I do not intend to allow the friends of Bush and the globally-despised U.S. military intelligence complex to stymie my right to report on the graft and corruption and the steady move toward fascism from my vantage point inside the Washington Beltway. To George W. Bush, Dick Cheney, Karl Rove, CACI (and its law firm Steptoe & Johnson), and Akin Gump Strauss Hauer & Feld and its Bush buddies and Saudi paymasters, I have one simple admonition: "Go to Hell!"

And to show that I mean business, I will soon establish a Web site called the Wayne Madsen Report that will expose the bottom-dwelling vermin now infesting our body politic. In the finest tradition of H.L. Mencken, Drew Pearson and Jack Anderson, Edward R. Murrow and other hard-hitting members of the Fourth Estate, I have a simple warning: if you hold political office or another responsible position in this three-degrees-of-separation town called Washington and you steal taxpayer's money, hypocritically proclaim born-again Christianity and then go out and beat up a female prostitute or call a gay male prostitute hot line, get busted for public urination on Capitol Hill, or engage in disloyal behavior against the United States, you can be sure your name and your activities will be featured on the Web site. You will be held accountable — it's as simple as that. You may not have to worry about the *Washington Post* or CNN, but you will have to contend with me.

And for Federal law enforcement officials who find it proper or exciting to subpoena journalists' notebooks and require testimony before grand juries, forget about me. I won't play your political games. I'll gladly go to prison rather than subject myself and my sources to interrogations from a neocon fascist regime.

Soon, there was an impact. A number of major media journalists began to regularly consult the Web site. And thanks to Air America and other progressive radio show hosts, including Randi Rhodes, Stephanie Miller, Mike Malloy, Rachel Maddow, Mike Papantonio, Robert F. Kennedy Jr., Peter B. Collins, Thom Hartmann, Peter Werbe, and a number of others, WayneMadsenReport's content began to be reported over the airwaves of America. And libertarian radio hosts like Alex Jones and others also began regularly reporting the site's contents.

Even Fox News offered up some publicity. In December 2006, I was on Bill O'Reilly's show debating him on his annual "war on Christmas" canard.

Through much of the Bush administration, it was nearly impossible to convince people in the Washington, DC area of the trouble our nation was in. Football, baseball, Final Four basketball, and the insatiable appetite of the American people for consumerism, best exemplified by the weekend sojourns to porcine palaces like CostCo and Sam's to stock up on goods that could supply army battalions, belied what was on most average Americans' minds. Forget about the fact that Bush, Cheney, and their ilk were systematically shredding the U.S. Constitution and plunging the country into an endless "global war against terrorism."

It is always nice to know that your enemies recognize that you are a pain in the ass. As *WayneMadsenReport* began to be quoted more extensively on the airwaves and in print, the right-wing started their predictable counter-attack. The following ploy that I wrote about in *WMR* on June 18, 2006 had all the makings of a Karl Rove-inspired dirty trick:

WMR has heard through the grapevine that Karl Rove and his pimply-faced minions at the Republican National Committee and right-wing boiler shops around the country are going to target this editor in the aftermath of his recent "pass" from the CIA "Leakgate" Special Prosecutor. If Rove and his boys think that trying to link me with the anthrax attacks is going to have any effect, they are in for a big disappointment. I won't even dignify their ridiculous insinuations with a response, but Mr. Rove might want to think twice about directing his particularly nasty venom at yours truly. A note appeared on a Reich-wing Web site called PHXNews, with a link to the FBI's anthrax tip line [see page 142].

An Internet WHOIS lookup shows that PHXNews is located at: 13952 Bora Bora Way, Marina del Rey, CA 90292. Typical of right-wing disinformation machines, they are well-funded to the point they can exist in a wealthy and chic place like Marina del Rey.

As if it were not bad enough to contend with the lies from the usual neocon and right-wing suspects, there was the odd situation of having a unit with the U.S. Department of State dedicated to attacking journalists, including taxpaying American journalists like yours truly. Although I raised hell with a number of State Department officials about the impropriety of using taxpayers' money to trash American citizens, and thus interfere with their

OVERTHROW A FASCIST REGIME ON $15 A DAY

ability to make a living, the usual response was just a shrug of the shoulders. After receiving a tip from a Finnish journalist for the respected Helsinki newspaper *Helsingin Sanomat*, I delved into the small "counter-misinformation" unit within the State Department and discovered that the main person in charge had some interesting past links to jailed GOP lobbyist Jack Abramoff. On April 18, 2005, a month before launching *WMR*, I wrote the following exposé of the State Department's "Ministry of Truth":

After revelations that the Bush White House cleared a gay male prostitute as a daily credentialed member of the White House press corps and that the administration was paying journalistic shills like Armstrong Williams, Maggie Gallagher, Michael McManus, and Karen Ryan to pump out pro-Bush propaganda to the media, nothing should come as any surprise when it comes to the Fourth Estate's buckling under to political pressure from the right-wing regime that rules America.

What is surprising is that, in addition to using the media to concoct favorable propaganda, the Bush administration maintains an office in the State Department that keeps an eye on American and other journalists and does not hesitate to attack them for straying from the party line.

To show how much censorship exists in America today, this journalist would have likely never known about the existence of a one-man office in the State Department that acts to debunk and attack anything the Bush administration deems is false. Thanks to a recent report by veteran America watcher and journalist Jyri Raivio in Finland's *Helsingin Sanomat* newspaper, it can now be reported in the United States that the State Department uses taxpayers' money to attack American journalists who refuse to parrot the Bush administration's disinformation and propaganda.

The head of the State Department's "Counter Mis-Information Team" is Todd Leventhal, a longtime neoconservative propaganda operative who once worked for the U.S. Information Agency's (USIA) Bureau of Information to counter Soviet and other disinformation with his own Brand X of American disinformation. Raivio reports that Leventhal was part of the Bush administration's effort to convince the world that Saddam Hussein had weapons of mass destruction (WMD). Leventhal also contends in the *Helsingin Sanomat* report that any suggestion that false WMD intelligence was cooked up by the Bush administration is merely a conspiracy

146

theory and that the faulty intelligence on Iraqi WMD was merely a huge "mistake."

It should not have come as any surprise that I was singled out by Leventhal for an attack over a story written for *Online Journal* about the assassination of former Lebanese Prime Minister Rafik Hariri and the involvement in the assassination's planning of two neoconservative Bush administration officials—namely, Deputy National Security Advisor Elliott Abrams and White House Deputy Chief of Staff Karl C. Rove—with whom Leventhal is ideologically aligned. Leventhal's operation is part of the State Department's International Information Programs Bureau, now headed by former Bush White House Communications Director and long-time Gerge W. Bush gal pal Karen Hughes.

Leventhal's barb appears at <http://usinfo.state.gov/media/Archive/2005/Apr/01-220547.html> and states, "*self-described* investigative journalist Wayne Madsen claimed that the Hariri assassination was 'authorized' by the United States because Mr. Hariri was known to adamantly oppose the construction of a major U.S. air base in the north of Lebanon."

Leventhal continues, "These claims are false. U.S. policy has expressly forbidden assassination since 1976, when President Ford signed Executive Order 11905. The prohibition against assassination was reaffirmed by President Carter and President Reagan, the latter in Executive Order 12333, which remains in force. Executive Order 12333 states, 'No person employed by or acting on behalf of the United States Government shall engage in, or conspire to engage in, assassination' ... Moreover, the U.S. military has confirmed that it has no plans for an air base in Lebanon.

"Mr. Madsen has made unreliable claims in the past. On October 20, 2004, he claimed that, in order to win reelection, the Bush administration 'has initiated plans to launch a military strike on Iran's top Islamic leadership, its nuclear reactor at Bushehr on the Persian Gulf, and key nuclear targets throughout the country.' Needless to say, no such events occurred."

Leventhal is obviously concerned that on numerous occasions this journalist's articles are picked up by media outlets around the world, including papers in Pakistan, Yemen, the United Arab Emirates, Turkey, and Egypt and serve to debunk the cacophony of propaganda emanating from Washington and its embassies abroad. Leventhal citing two Executive Orders that prohibit assassinations is laughable in light of recent well-documented disclosures that

U.S. interrogators killed at least one Iraqi general in custody. Since September 11, 2001, and adoption of George Tenet's Worldwide Attack Matrix—a carte blanche for political assassinations around the world—both Executive Orders cited by Leventhal are not worth the paper they are printed on.

Concerning my story about an "October Surprise" predicting a pre-election attack on Iran, even though it didn't happen, I stand by my sources — which, since the original article's appearance have multiplied in number, including crew aboard the USS *John F. Kennedy,* then on station in the Persian Gulf — against Leventhal's trite disinformation machine.

Similarly, the sources on the Hariri assassination and the plans for the U.S. air base are well-connected and trusted. The firm promised the air base construction contract by the Pentagon, Jacobs Engineering, is a major player in U.S. military and intelligence projects. The company was started by the late Dr. Joseph Jacobs, a Lebanese-American who served on the advisory board of the Rand Corporation's Center for Middle East Public Policy. The co-chair of that group during Jacobs' tenure was none other than Frank Carlucci, the chairman emeritus of The Carlyle Group — an organization that has criminal conspiracy written all over it.

Perhaps, if Leventhal and his neocon friends used such trusted sources as the many I have developed over some twenty years, rather than using deluded and alcoholic disinformation scoundrels like Iraq's "Curveball," this country would not be in the mess it is in today in Iraq and the entire Middle East. As a matter of fact, foreign ministries around the world could use their own Ministries of Truth for the sole purpose of wading through all the disinformation pumped out by the Bush administration: Iraq's WMD, Saddam's links to al Qaeda, Iraq's shopping for yellowcake uranium in Niger, and the many other lies and distortions.

First of all, some housekeeping is in order. Leventhal refers to this journalist as "self-described." True, I use the term "investigative journalist" in tag lines. However, it is not "self-described" that my articles have been cited by Project Censored, famed author Gore Vidal, keen investigative journalist Greg Palast, and newspapers from Austria to Zimbabwe. In addition, it was not self-aggrandizement that resulted in my investigative book on genocide in Africa being cited in a French government counter-terrorism judicial investigation, a UN War Crimes Tribunal, U.S. House of Representatives testimony, and respected periodicals in Africa and Europe.

Although he is basically a one-man show (he does have a full-time assistant and one part-timer), Leventhal does not seem to produce much for his work at the State Department. Leventhal was actually laid off by the State Department in 1996 after his Cold War-era counter-disinformation office was disestablished, but he was rehired in October 2003 after the White House decided to resurrect its propaganda effort under the rubric of "strategic influence operations." Leventhal's attacks are narrowly focused on particular stories, sources, and journalists. His Web site has an explanation of how to spot disinformation—Leventhal contends that most conspiracy theories are rarely true and that they are spread by ideological extremists, that is liberals, because right-wingers like Leventhal would never be willing to address right-wing extremism (such as Fox News, the *National Review,* and the *Wall Street Journal* editorial page) in the media. Leventhal's dismissing conspiracies as often untrue will, nevertheless, come as a great shock to the Criminal Division of the Justice Department, which has put away many a criminal based on violation of criminal conspiracy laws.

Another one of Leventhal's government-funded attack pieces flays ex-U.S. soldier Nadim Abou Rabeh, an Iraqi war veteran who had taken part in Saddam Hussein's capture. Leventhal pillories Rabeh for suggesting Saddam's capture in a "spider hole" was faked. Leventhal also calls "fanciful" reports that the United States used mustard gas in the siege of Fallujah, contends that the use of depleted uranium weapons by U.S. forces in Iraq is safe, and derides it as a "conspiracy theory" that the United States helped create Osama bin Laden and al Qaeda via its support of the Afghan mujaheddin through Saudi and Pakistani facilitators.

In addition, Leventhal criticizes reports that the United States could have done more to warn Indian Ocean nations of the tsunami event last December. Astonishingly, Leventhal claims that the Pacific Tsunami Warning Center in Hawaii did not possess the capability to figure out that the 9.0 magnitude earthquake would produce a devastating tsunami. Leventhal also criticized by name Canadian journalist Michel Chossudovsky, who first reported on the failure of America to adequately warn Asian and African nations of the impending disaster.

Having never heard of Mr. Leventhal, I decided to do a bit of checking on him as only a "self-described investigative journalist" can do.

First, there is Leventhal's association with apartheid South Africa's infamous "Project Babushka." According to a July 16,

1995 story in *Newsday*, during the 1980s, South Africa's military established a dummy front called the International Freedom Foundation (IFF). The IFF was an influence-peddling organization used to counter critics of the apartheid regime and buy right-wing American politicians to campaign against economic and military sanctions against the apartheid regime.

According to former South African top spy Craig Williamson, IFF and Project Babushka enrolled such right-wing Republicans as North Carolina Senator Jesse Helms, Henry Kissinger, California Republican Representative Robert Dornan, Indiana Republican Representative Dan Burton, Illinois Republican Representative Phil Crane, and right-wing GOP kook Alan Keyes. Helms even served as chairman of the editorial advisory board for the IFF's publication branch—a group that pumped out all sorts of propaganda claiming that the African National Congress and Nelson Mandela were Communists.

Helping to run the IFF's Washington, DC office at 200 G Street, SE (and next door to the right-wing Free Congress Foundation) was none other than Jack Abramoff, who is now embroiled in a series of kickback and payola allegations involving House Majority Leader Tom DeLay.

Abramoff, a former Hollywood movie producer, helped the IFF to produce the movie *Red Scorpion*, a film about an anti-Communist African guerrilla leader battling Marxist forces with the assistance of South African military advisers. Of course, the film was a propaganda piece aimed at extolling Angolan anti-Communist UNITA leader Jonas Savimbi, who was fighting Angola's Marxist government with the overt assistance of South Africa and the covert (and illegal) assistance of the Reagan-Bush administration. As late as 1990 and after Mandela's release from prison, the IFF was running anti-ANC and Mandela ads in American newspapers.

Abramoff's involvement in Reagan-era propaganda coincided with the appointment of longtime Reagan chum, Charles Z. Wick, as the head of the USIA. Wick, also a former movie producer, was most remembered for his famous Hollywood epic, *Snow White and the Three Stooges*.

One of the senior South African intelligence agents who used IFF cover was Wim Booyse. When Booyse visited Washington in1987 to attend IFF seminars, which were no more than covers for South African intelligence operations, he said he received specialized disinformation training from an expert at the U.S. Information Agency. And who was this expert on official government lying and distortion of the truth? Well, according to Booyse, it was none other than Todd Leventhal.

In a 1996 letter to the *Washington Post,* representing himself as an official of the USIA, Leventhal attacked former USIA official Alvin Snyder, who exposed U.S. government propaganda and lies in his excellent book on Reagan administration information warfare, *Warriors of Disinformation.* Leventhal dismisses Snyder's claims in a previous *Post* op-ed piece that the Reagan administration faked results of Star Wars tests, that the Soviets actually did mistake the downed Korean Air Lines 007 for a U.S. espionage aircraft, and that the U.S. engaged in blatant propaganda in Chile to support the Augusto Pinochet dictatorship.

In 1995, Leventhal attacked documentary producer Allan Francovich for his film, *The Maltese Double Cross,* which provided evidence that Iran and Syria, rather than Libya, were behind the downing of PanAm Flight 103 over Lockerbie, Scotland. Francovich, who later died while being questioned by U.S. customs and immigration agents at Houston's international airport, determined that the PanAm bombing was the result of a botched U.S. intelligence operation involving drugs and hostages in Lebanon. Leventhal's smears against Francovich resulted in the latter's May 12, 1995 letter to Britain's *Guardian* newspaper in which Leventhal's job as Program Officer for Countering Disinformation and Misinformation for the USIA is described as "Orwellian."

In 1994, Leventhal took on the *Los Angeles Times* over its story about the kidnapping of poor children from poverty-ravished Latin American barrios for the purpose of organ harvesting.

Leventhal's small propaganda operation at the State Department is remarkably similar to an aggressive media operation that scans newspapers, television, and radio for stories critical of Israel. CAMERA, or the Committee for Accuracy in Middle East Reporting in America, identifies and targets Israeli, American, and other journalists who question or provide alternatives to Israeli government propaganda.

In what is frightening and amusing at the same time, Leventhal makes an offer to those who have questions about the news stories they are reading: "If you wish, ask us. We can't respond to all requests for information, but if a request is reasonable and we have the time, we will do our best to provide accurate, authoritative information." The State Department's Web site provides Leventhal's phone number for those who wish to have him interpret the news for them: 202-203-7492. Just another friendly service from your taxpayer-funded Ministry of Truth!

Bev Conover, the editor of *Online Journal* and a colleague in the war against right-wing propaganda, wrote the following about the State Department operation:

We are flattered—flattered!—that the excellent work of investigative journalist Wayne Madsen and Online Journal have come to the attention of the State Department and are deemed worthy of attack by its Ministry of Truth (a.k.a. Counter Misinformation Team) honcho Todd Leventhal

While this is not quite as prestigious an honor as being included in Richard Nixon's Enemies List, especially since Mr. Leventhal's operation can barely be called a team—himself, a full-time assistant and one part-timer—and is part of the Karen Hughes-inspired International Propaganda ... Information Programs, we accept this honor as a start in getting the Bush administration's panties in a wad or, as our British cousins say, knickers in a twist.

Not all of us in the Fourth Estate will lie down to be trampled on by neocons, theocrats, Republicans and Democrats. To borrow the words of Dylan Thomas, we will "not go gentle into that good night," but we shall continue to "rage, rage against the dying of the light."

The apartheid-era South Africa connections to the neocons, especially Jack Abramoff, became very apparent after *WMR* was sent some unpublished transcripts from South African intelligence sources on the South African Truth and Reconciliation Commission hearings, which heard testimony from one-time South African super-spy Craig Williamson, who ran a group of right-wing Republicans in Washington, DC as agents of influence.

These transcripts were published by *WMR* on January 28, 2006:

WMR can reveal that according to government files obtained from South African sources, the South African apartheid military intelligence service, which supported Jack Abramoff's International Freedom Foundation (IFF) in Washington during the Reagan administration, held a number of secret operational meetings. The meetings, divided into senior level and junior-level sessions, were code-named "Sanhedrin."

In testimony before the South African Truth and Reconciliation Commission hearings in Johannesburg on September 11 and 23, 1998, former South African super-spy Craig Williamson, the person who ran Abramoff as an agent in Washington, testified on the secret meetings. In the second hearing, the Commission Chairperson studiously steered the commission away from the topic of "Sanhedrin," wheras the questioner in the first hearing kept inquiring why the term "Sanhedrin" was used by the intelligence services. [Transcripts in Appendix A.]

The choice of the term "Sanhedrin" to describe a parallel intelligence organization and secret "Star Chamber" court inside South Africa with links abroad, including the United States, is noteworthy. In ancient Israel, the Great Sanhedrin and lesser Sanhedrins in many cities sat as both the legislative and judical bodies of the land. Modern Israel has become a key hub for neocon intrigue, along with Washington and London (and briefly Rome, as will be described in the next chapter).

What can be gleaned from the South African transcripts is that a secret group of right-wingers in South Africa was determining who would live and who would die. The "Sanhedrin" sounded much like the "Cabal," which then-Deputy Defense Secretary Paul Wolfowitz used to describe the neocon cell operating inside the Bush administration, the cell that would determine the future of Iraq. In other words, who would live and who would die, as well as who would be hired and who would be fired.

***

WMR's stories on the Hariri assassination and the proposed U.S. airbase in northern Lebanon were later confirmed by other sources. On October 24, 2006, a report on Hariri was published on WMR:

A senior French DGSE — Direction générale de la sécurité extérieure — intelligence officer has told WMR that Lebanon's ex-Prime Minister Rafik Hariri was killed in a car bombing arranged by Israel's Mossad. The revelation from French intelligence is significant, as the French government of Jacques Chirac joined the Bush administration and the neocon policy establishments in Washington and Israel in blaming Syria for the attack. According to the DGSE officer, Israel and its American backers wanted to blame Syria for the assassination of the popular Lebanese leader, thus forcing the popular Lebanese revolt that saw the withdrawal of Syrian forces. That left Lebanon defenseless for the "Clean Break" attack launched by Israel, with U.S. support, against Hezbollah and Lebanon's infrastructure.

WMR was one of the first to report Israeli and American involvement in the assassination of Hariri, as well as those of Elie Hobeika, George Hawi, and other Lebanese politicians.

WMR published an additional report on the Lebanese airbase on April 16, 2007:

WMR was the first to report on the establishment of a major U.S. airbase in northern Lebanon to facilitate logistics for America's planned long-term stay in the Middle East, including the occupation of Iraq. On July 21, 2006, we reported, "With the carrying out of the Clean Break by Israel and the United States, profits for companies like Halliburton are bound to skyrocket. The Israeli attack on Lebanon is already estimated to have resulted in $2 billion in damage to Lebanon's infrastructure." *WMR* previously reported that Jacobs Sverdrup has been promised a lucrative Pentagon contract to build a large U.S. airbase in northern Lebanon.

This editor reported on March 11, 2005, "Washington and Jerusalem media experts spun Hariri's assassination as being the work of Syrian intelligence on orders from President Bashar Assad. However, a number of Middle East political observers in Washington claim that Hariri's assassination was not in the interests of Assad, but that the Bush and Sharon administrations had everything to gain from it, including the popular Lebanese uprising against the Syrian occupation. Lebanese intelligence sources report that even without a formal agreement with Lebanon, the contract for the northern Lebanese air base has been let by the Pentagon to Jacobs Engineering Group of Pasadena, California. Other construction support will be provided by Bechtel Corporation.

"Jacobs Engineering and Jacobs Sverdrup are currently contracted for work in Saudi Arabia for Aramco, Iraq for the U.S.

occupation authority, Bosnia, Turkey, Syria, Lebanon, Israel, Jordan, Yemen, Oman, and the United Arab Emirates. The Lebanese air base is reportedly to be used as a transit and logistics hub for U.S. forces in Iraq and as a rest and relaxation location for U.S. troops in the region. In addition, the Lebanese base will be used to protect U.S. oil pipelines in the region (Baku-Tbilisi-Ceyhan and Mosul/Kirkuk-Ceyhan) as well as to destabilize the Assad government in Syria. The size of the planned air base reportedly is on the scale of the massive American Al Udeid air base in Qatar. A number of intelligence sources have reported that assassinations of foreign leaders like Hariri and Hobeika are ultimately authorized by two key White House officials, Deputy Chief of Staff Karl Rove and Deputy National Security Adviser Elliott Abrams. In addition, Abrams is the key liaison between the White House and Sharon's office for such covert operations, including political assassinations."

Our Lebanese sources as well as the Lebanese daily newspaper *Aldiyar* now report that a NATO base is to be built soon on the grounds of the largely abandoned airbase at Klieaat in northern Lebanon. The base will serve as the headquarters of a NATO rapid deployment force, helicopter squadrons, and Special Forces units, although the cover story prepared by the Lebanese and U.S. governments is that the base will provide training for the Lebanese army and security forces. The base was pushed by elements in the office of the U.S. Secretary of Defense and the Joint Chiefs of Staff. The Bush administration had recently warned Lebanon about the presence of "al Qaeda" teams in northern Lebanon. Before his assassination, former Lebanese Prime Minister Rafik Hariri was known to have been strongly opposed to any U.S. military bases in Lebanon, including the proposed airbase in Kleiaat.

WMR's scoop on the Kleiaat airbase received an additional confirmation on May 30, 2007 from Professor Franklin Lamb of the American University in Beirut. Lamb visited the Kleiaat airbase region and reported the following, which was published on *WMR*:

As residents of Bibnin Akkar, less than two miles from the site of the proposed U.S. base, and the Lebanese daily newspaper *Aldiyar* speculate, construction of a U.S. airbase on the grounds of the largely abandoned airbase at Klieaat in northern Lebanon may begin late this year. To make the project more palatable, it is being promoted as a "US/NATO" base that will serve as the headquarters of a NATO rapid deployment force, helicopter squadrons, and Special Forces units.

The base will provide training for the Lebanese army and security forces fighting Salafi, Islamist fundamentalists and other needs.

The Pentagon and NATO HQ in Belgium have named the project, which will sit along the Lebanese-Syrian border, using this vast area "as a base for fast intervention troops." It is to be called "The Lebanese Army and Security Training Center."

Kleiaat, a nearly abandoned small airport, was used by Middle East Airlines for a period for commuter flights between Beirut and Tripoli. Residents of the area report than during the Civil War (1975-1990) a commuter helicopter service was also operated due to road closures.

The proposed base was measured by this observer to be roughly two and one-half miles down the beach from Nahr al-Bared Palestinian Camp. Both share pristine Mediterranean beachfront. Kleiaat is an expanse of gently undulating sandy dunes covered with long prairie grass and brush.

Due to opposition from Lebanon's anemic environmental movement, that argues that the pristine area should be left to its many varieties of birds and wildlife, the local community is watching closely.

Not much activity is going on as of May 29, 2007. About 20 Quonset huts, some recently driven stakes, no evidence of heavy equipment or building material. The three-man army outpost fellows appeared bored and did not even ask for ID as I toured the whole area on the back of a fine new BMW 2200cc motorcycle courtesy of one of the local militia sniper guys who until two days ago was firing into Nahr al-Bared, when the Lebanese army stopped him after the PLO leadership complained.

On June 14, 2007, *WMR* had a follow-up story on the Lebanon airbase:

*W*MR was the first to report on the Bush administration's plans to build a NATO base in northern Lebanon near the Syrian border. We have now learned that in April, U.S., German, and Turkish officers surveyed the Kleiaat airport in northern Lebanon, near Tripoli, the scene of recent fighting between "al

Qaeda"-linked Fatah al-Islam guerrillas and Lebanese army units newly supplied with weapons from the United States.

The assassinated Lebanese Prime Minister Rafik Hariri was known to be strongly opposed to the planned American base in Lebanon. Although the neocons convinced the United Nations to convene an international tribunal that would accuse Syria of being behind the assassination of Hariri, the recent car bomb assassination of anti-Syrian Member of Parliament Walid Eido in Beirut represents yet another attempt to lay the blame for that and several other car bombings, including the one that killed Hariri, at the door of Damascus.

WMR has previously reported that these car bombing assassinations are being carried out by Mossad units, using disaffected former members of Syria's intelligence apparatus in Syria with the support of covert operations personnel supplied by the Bush administration.

Thanks to the efforts of independent observers on the ground in Lebanon, the State Department's "misinformation" office had been proven to be a disseminator of myths and falsehoods.

***

The most important sign that there was a degree of success in starting to publish regularly on the Web through *WMR* on a meager shoestring budget came when *WMR* began scooping the *Washington Post* on stories. For example, on July 18, 2005, *WMR* had the following story:

*W*MR scoops the *Washington Post*. *WMR* reported on nepotism involving MZM, Inc. and the National Ground Intelligence Center (NGIC) on June 29. Today, the story made the *Post*.

This was our report on June 29: "Conflict of interests charges swirled around NGIC even before MZM eased out Battelle as the prime contractor for the agency. NGIC insiders claim that NGIC management was equally close to both MZM and Battelle. The insiders cited one case where the son of a senior NGIC manager, whose work experience largely consisted of being a waiter and bartender, was hired by MZM as a senior manager. They also pointed to the wife of an NGIC senior official being employed as a secretary for Battelle and MZM. The NGIC insiders emphasize that such employment of relatives violate the Code of Federal Regulations (CFR)."

***

Another topic on which *WMR* went where the *Washington Post* dare not tread was the extraordinary renditioning of mostly Arab and Muslim prisoners by the CIA. Although the *Post* reported that prisoners had been kept in secret cells in Eastern Europe, *WMR* provided detailed evidence, based on its military and intelligence sources, on the locations of the bases (the *Post* refused to do this at the onset of its reporting) and the methods used to detain prisoners. On November 11, 2005, Veterans Day, *WMR* reported the following:

Although the *Washington Post* failed to report on the details of CIA (now Pentagon-run) "black" interrogation sites in eastern Europe, *WMR* is able to report on the particulars of the covert operation. According to a well-placed intelligence source who served in eastern Europe, prisoners from Iraq and elsewhere have been flown from airport to airport in eastern Europe on board C-130 planes, placed in what were described as "dog-sized" cages. The covert operation became fully operational after the disclosures of prisoner abuse at Abu Ghraib, Baghdad and Camp Bucca, Umm Qasr, Iraq. The "crated" prisoners were either removed from the C-130s for interrogation at Soviet-era detention centers that were in various states of repair or were kept on board the aircraft and subjected to brutal interrogation by U.S. and/or contractor personnel, who, in some cases, were ex-members of the Soviet KGB, Stasi, and other eastern European security services. C-130s are used because of their take-off and landing capabilities on short air strips located in remote regions.

The source, who spoke on a condition of anonymity, witnessed the ground work being laid for the "black sites" in a number of countries and locations. These include the Taszar airbase in south-central Hungary, near the town of Pecs; Lv'iv, Ukraine; Szczynto-Szymany, Poland; Skopje, Macedonia; Mihail Kogalniceanu airbase in Romania; Tbilisi, Republic of Georgia; Shkoder, Albania; Burgas, Bulgaria; and the Markuleshti air base in Moldova.

Crating prisoners hearkens back to the Vietnam War when the U.S. used "tiger cages" installed by the French on Con Son island off Vietnam to hold political prisoners. The U.S. used the tiger cages to detain and torture suspected Viet Cong sympathizers. Many of the prisoners were merely innocent Buddhists and anti-war activists. The flying of caged prisoners from airport to airport on chartered C-130s is yet another indication of what military judge advocate general (JAG) lawyers have cited as the Bush administration's penchant for placing prisoners in "law-free zones."

WMR's initial report on the locations of many of the secret prisons in Europe was later confirmed in an official Council of Europe report.

WMR continued to report on the secretive aspects of the CIA's and the Pentagon's worldwide aviation business. On October 8, 2007, *WMR* reported on comments made by *Washington Post* editor Leonard Downie at a Society of Professional Journalists meeting in Washington on October 6, 2007:

> On withholding stories, Downie said that the *Post* agreed to withhold the locations of the CIA's secret prisons in Eastern Europe. He said the Bush White House wanted the entire story on the CIA prisons, written by Dana Priest, killed on grounds of endangering national security. On the advice of *Post* lawyers, Downie said he agreed to kill only the countries and locations hosting the prisons in Eastern Europe because it "would've exposed secret operations elsewhere."

Unlike the *Washington Post*, *WMR* does not believe that tassle-loafered and briefcase-wielding lawyers have any place near the news or editorial rooms.

On February 24, 2006, *WMR* published the following report on mysterious U.S. aviation activities in Afghanistan:

> WMR can now report further on the mysterious aircraft sighted on remote runways in Afghanistan. According to U.S. intelligence sources, the aircraft have been flying around Afghan tribal leaders and warlords and questionable "cargo." Afghan and U.S. intelligence sources report that opium production is at an

all-time high in Afghanistan and that President Hamid Karzai, the U.S. viceroy for Afghanistan, who has no real political power outside of Kabul, is handsomely profiting from the heroin trade.

The plane in question is a Beech 200, Model 65-A90-1, Serial number LM-64. Although the tail number (ends in 8A) is new, its former tail number was N70766 and the owner was Pactec (still seen on the plane's tail), a California-based non-governmental organization that claims to help humanitarian groups install satellite terminals and other high-tech communications systems in remote locations like Afghanistan and Pakistan. The history of the plane shows that it was exported from the United States to Mali and then re-exported to Afghanistan. At the present time, however, the Beech 200 as well as another similar plane are operated by Air Serv International. The planes are based in Kabul.

Air Serv is a Mission Aviation Fellowship (MAF) corporation that was formed in 1985 at the height of U.S. covert involvement in Central America. PacTec's directorship interlocks with MAF. Air Serv is billed as "not religious by charter" and can "operate in areas where MAF may be restricted." MAF was particularly active in Honduras and Guatemala where it coordinated its activities closely with the Interdenominational Foreign Mission Association and Evangelical Foreign Missions Association, which included other organizations linked to CIA activities, including World Vision and Trans World Radio.

***

War crimes by Americans in war is something that goes against the grain of all the patriotic hype instilled by the government and its media friends. For that reason, when Americans commit war crimes the story is treated as an anomaly. Based on sources in the U.S. military in Iraq and stateside, I reported on U.S. war crimes in Iraq early on and provided the following commentary on June 2, 2006:

As reported by *WMR* on May 30, there are now further widely confirmed reports of U.S. war crimes committed against innocent Iraqi civilians. In addition to the Nov. 2005 Haditha massacre of civilians, including women and children, there is now a report that U.S. troops massacred civilians in the town of Ishaqi in March of this year. Ishaqi is 10 miles north of

Balad. The Bush White House and Pentagon have responded to these war crimes by ordering specialized training for U.S. troops before they deploy to Iraq.

In addition to U.S. political and military leaders, international law provides for the indictment of propagandists who stoke the flames of hate by supporting war crimes and the unlawful actions of governments during wartime. William Joyce (nicknamed "Lord Haw Haw"), an Irish-American broadcaster for Nazi Germany, was hanged for treason on 1946. Mildred Sisk (nicknamed "Axis Sally"), an American who had broadcast messages to Allied troops on Radio Berlin, was convicted of one count of treason following the war. U.S. citizen Iva Toguri D'Aquino ("Tokyo Rose"), a broadcaster for Japanese radio during World War II, was convicted of treason. She was pardoned by President Gerald Ford in a deal that involved Ford's Chief of Staff, Dick Cheney.

Ferdinand Nahimana and Jean-Bosco Barayagwiza, broadcasters for Rwanda's Radio Milles Collines, were indicted by the International War Crimes Tribunal for Rwanda for airing anti-Tutsi messages in 1994. Broadcasters like Bill O'Reilly, Sean Hannity, Glenn Beck, Michael Savage, Rush Limbaugh, and other venal broadcasters who are acting on behalf of the Bush administration in defending war crimes committed by U.S. forces in Iraq, may find themselves subject to future International Criminal Court investigations.

It might have been suspected that in the process of exposing the crimes of the Bush administration, an administration that many Americans consider worse than Richard Nixon's, the potential for being spied upon was great. On January 12, 2006, I reported the following on *WMR*:

Informed intelligence sources have told this editor that he has, since October 2005, been under an active federal criminal investigation as part of the Bush administration's probe of leaks about illegal NSA surveillance of U.S. citizens.

To reiterate what I've stated before: I refuse to cede my First Amendment rights and will not cooperate with ANY grand jury asking questions about sources, and I will refuse to turn over notebooks or other materials to any investigators, warrant or not. I'm willing to become a political prisoner rather than succumb to the fascist thugs in the Bush administration.

WMR is working on a number of investigations involving The Carlyle Group, the Fellowship Foundation, and illegal surveillance. We will continue to publish until the Bush administration makes their move to shut us down. Again, your support has helped us to gain enough of a media presence to make the Bush administration nervous.

Not only was there the threat of government surveillance, but there were threats of lawsuits looming over our modest attempt to report the truth from Washington.

Threats of lawsuits are used by those who want to suppress an independent press. The misuse of the courts by war profiteers and other ne'er-do-wells plagued me, talk-radio host Randi Rhodes, and independent investigators like Daniel Hopsicker. Drew Pearson was sued a number of times by the powerful who hoped to silence the "Washington Merry Go Round." Jack Anderson, his successor, was even more of an irritant. On June 13, 1991, Watergate felon and Nixon bagman G. Gordon Liddy told Anderson on CNBC that there were plans by the Nixon White House to have Liddy assassinate him, "The rationale was to come up with a method of silencing you through killing you." Liddy said the plan was stopped by senior White House officials. So, there are worse things than being sued by people upset about your reporting.

When a top Republican operative informed me in 2007 that Karl Rove, from his position at the White House, had authorized an illegal investigation of me and Florida-based journalist John Caylor, I was not surprised. Finding my apartment "tossed" on one occasion, I had no illusions about who was pissed off and why.

With the specter of a fascist government hanging overhead, I carried a poster at one large anti-war march in Washington that contained the famous words of German Pastor Martin Niemoller about speaking out against fascism:

In Germany they came first for the Communists and I didn't speak up because I wasn't a Communist.

Then they came for the Jews and I didn't speak up because I wasn't a Jew.

Then they came for the trade unionists and I didn't speak up because I wasn't a trade unionist.

Then they came for the Catholics and I didn't speak up because I was a Protestant.

Then they came for me— and by that time no one was left to speak up.

Not only were Niemoller's words true in his Germany in the 1930s; they gained a renewed meaning in George W. Bush's and Dick Cheney's America in 2005.

When will they come for you?

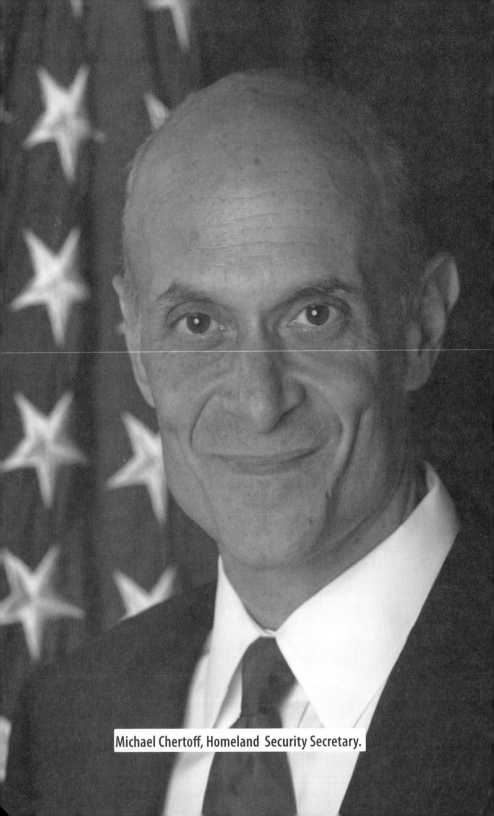

Michael Chertoff, Homeland Security Secretary.

Chapter 7

2006: The Mid-term Election

It was not always a given that the United States and America would have a close relationship....
> —George W. Bush, June 29, 2006 at the White House welcoming
> ceremony for Japanese Prime Minister Junichiro Koizumi

With 2006 being such an important political year for the future of the country, there was a need for more fiscal belt tightening in order to keep *WayneMadsenReport* up and running. With gasoline prices creeping higher and higher it was time to bid farewell to my 1988 Honda Accord. In April 2006, the Washington, DC charity for the mentally disabled, Melwood, towed away the car and I began studying the Washington Metrobus schedules. With a relatively advanced public transportation system, there was no reason to have a car inside the beltway, and it was a great way to save on expenses.

WayneMadsenReport also received generous donations from readers across the country, readers who also believed that it was important to keep the independent news channels open through the "iron curtain" the corporate media had established around the beltway.

Many Americans saw the election of 2006 as a watershed event in the history of the nation. If the opposition Democrats did not gain control of the Congress, the very future of the country was in question.

The Bush regime's concept of "perpetual war" was straight out of George Orwell's *1984*. I wrote about the Bush's global war strategy on March 17, 2006:

Yesterday, the Bush regime unveiled its "National Security Strategy of the United States of America." The 49-page strategy identifies additional nations that are considered enemies of, and, therefore, threats to the United States. The strategy reserves the right for the United States to preemptively attack these nations.

Time magazine's Matt Cooper (of Scooter Libby infamy) laughably argues the White House document is only theoretical and not binding. Similar neocon doctrine was used to justify the U.S. invasion and occupation of Iraq. Few U.S. troops in the field in Iraq and Afghanistan would argue the neocon policy is "theoretical."

Nations identified as threats to the U.S. may be worthy of invasion so their "despotic" governments can be replaced with "democracies," a code word for a sudden influx of depleted uranium weapons and bunker-buster bombs, pedophiliac and sado-masochistic jailers and interrogators, "Christian" missionaries, private mercenaries and brigands, political show trials of vanquished political leaders, looting of museums and treasuries, embedded "prostitute" journalists, and infrastructure "repair" (U.S. military base construction) companies like Halliburton and Bechtel. These nations include Iran, North Korea, Zimbabwe, Myanmar, Cuba, Belarus, and Syria. There are also warning shots in the report fired at China and Russia.

I then quoted from Orwell in *1984*:

The Party said that Oceania had never been in alliance with Eurasia. He, Winston Smith, knew that Oceania had been in alliance with Eurasia as short a time as four years ago. But where did that knowledge exist? Only in his consciousness, which in any case must soon be annihilated. And if all others accepted the lie, which the Party imposed — if all records told the same tale — then the lie passed into history and became the truth. "Who controls the past," ran the Party slogan, "controls the future: who controls the present controls the past." And yet the past, though of its nature alterable, never had been altered. Whatever was true now was true from everlasting to everlasting. It was quite simple. All that was needed was an unending series of victories over your memory. "Reality control," they called it; in Newspeak, "doublethink."

The Bush regime and the neocons call it "perception management"

In early 2006, I attended a strategy meeting at George Mason University in Fairfax, Virginia. The subject was whether Jim Webb, a former Navy Secretary under President Reagan who had switched back to being a Democrat after being a Republican, should declare his candidacy for the U.S. Senate and challenge incumbent Republican George Allen, a former congressman and Governor of Virginia. Webb, who was not present at the meeting but had his representatives there, maintained that Allen was too strong and he would likely lose. My opinion was that Allen was vulnerable due to his past ties with various neoconfederate causes, including Confederate racist groups. Little was known then about Allen's racist past.

Fortunately, Webb did declare his candidacy, and, as I predicted, Allen's racism surfaced. During the campaign, Allen referred to a Webb campaign assistant, an Asian Indian-American born and raised in Virginia, as a "macaca," a racist French term used for Africans or, more generally, people of dark complexion. Allen's Achilles' heel was racism and after his "macaca" comment and discoveries of other racist incidents in his past, Webb defeated Allen. Webb's victory gave the Democrats their razor-thin one-seat majority in the Senate.

***

Trying to overthrow a fascist regime on $15 a day may have had limited success in the United States, but there was good news from overseas concerning the roll-back of the American empire. I wrote about these developments in *WMR* on June 29, 2006:

W*MR* is elated that our truth-reporting has resulted in several European countries that hosted secret CIA prisons and facilitated rendition flights of kidnapped prisoners being called on the carpet by the Council of Europe and European Union. WMR reported details of these prisons and flights.

In addition, we congratulate Nepal's resistance leaders, Prachanda, Baburam Bhattarai, and Krishna Bahadur Mahara on their accession to political power in Kathmandu. The Bush administration's stooge, Gyanendra, who overthrew the previous King and his family in a U.S.-inspired and supported coup, fraudulently disguised as a "soap operatic" massacre by a lovesick Crown Prince, is now relegated to mere figurehead status.

WMR reported on this coup and our reports were confirmed and republished by the Nepal Communist Party and Nepalese newspapers. This editor looks forward one day to meeting Nepal's former rebel leaders in Kathmandu rather than in a remote mountain hideout, as was once the original plan. Nepal's new government should immediately expel U.S. ambassador James Moriarty, who continues to support the King and the royalists against the wishes of the Nepalese people.

WMR's other investigative reports are also helping the political opposition to Bush stooge dictators in The Gambia, Rwanda, Kazakhstan, Uganda, Equatorial Guinea, Angola, and Chad.

There was another aspect to truth reporting. After years of investigating various aspects of the 9/11 attacks, I announced at a 9/11 fifth anniversary Truth event at New York City's famed Cooper Union, a few blocks from the site of the destroyed World Trade Center, that after much deliberation I had come to the conclusion that 9/11 was a carefully coordinated covert and highly-compartmented operation by elements within and outside of the U.S. government to bring about a fascist coup in the United States.

Too many dots had connected. The evidence that 9/11 was an inside job was overwhelming. The lies of the administration had been exposed. On March 3, 2006, I wrote about some major connected dots, particularly those linking Homeland Security Secretary Michael Chertoff to individuals connected to 9/11:

M ichael Brown, the former head of FEMA, deserves credit for blowing the whistle on the "agenda" of Homeland

Security Secretary Michael Chertoff. For years, a handful of prosecutors, FBI agents, and investigative journalists have stressed the connections between Russian-Israeli mafia tycoons, weapons and diamond smugglers, and terrorist networks associated with "al Qaeda" and affiliated organizations.

Yet, it is the much-maligned Brown, a one-time GOP operative and "golden boy," who has taken the initiative to call for Chertoff's firing and a complete overhaul of the Homeland Security Department. Even in these strange times, this is an amazing turn of events and begs the question of what Brown knows about Chertoff and his connections to Dubai and covering up terrorist investigations. Brown is in the unique position of being aware of Dubai's major role in horse racing (and possibly money laundering) and being briefed on various maritime and other terrorist threats as head of FEMA. Which means that Brown may have enough information to be very dangerous to the Bush crime family.

Chertoff is a long-time GOP political hack and neocon operative. He was the Special Counsel for the Senate "Whitewater" Committee from 1994 to 1996, a costly effort to create a political scandal for President Clinton and Hillary Clinton where there was no scandal. Hillary Clinton, to her credit, cast the lone vote against Chertoff's confirmation as a federal judge in 2003. There is one thing that Hillary Clinton and Michael Brown agree on — they both despise Chertoff. And with good reason.

Chertoff was the Assistant Attorney General for the Criminal Division of the Justice Department in the lead-up to and aftermath of the 9/11 attacks. It was Chertoff who ordered the FBI not to pursue Mossad cells discovered to be operating alongside the hijacker cells in northern New Jersey. With FBI and other field law enforcement reports on suspicious Israeli office "mover" activity in the New York-New Jersey area in the months prior to 9/11, Chertoff failed to order an investigation of why Zim-American Israeli Shipping Company suddenly terminated its lease of offices on the 16th and 17th floors of the North Tower of the World Trade Center, forfeiting a $50,000 deposit a week prior to 9/11 and moving its operations to Norfolk. Zim's parent company, Zim Israel Navigation Co., is half owned by the Israeli government. Norfolk's port operations are due to come under Dubai Ports World ownership if the buy-out deal is approved.

Therefore, it is no surprise that Zim's chairman wrote to Senator Clinton offering high praise for Dubai Ports World and

169

revealed that Zim and Dubai Ports are "strong business partners." Zim's chairman also revealed that Zim's ships use Dubai ports but under different flags other than Israeli.

Chertoff also failed to investigate the presence on the 33rd floor of the North Tower of the Trade Center of the Yemen Import Company, an office that, like Zim Shipping, had been cleared of all its personnel in the weeks prior to 9/11, leaving only an answering machine and fax in place.

As Assistant U.S. Attorney, Chertoff also declined to prosecute Dr. Magdy Elamir, an Egyptian-born neurologist in Jersey City who was implicated in an FBI/ATF arms trafficking investigation code named Operation Diamondback. It turned out that Elamir was Chertoff's client in a fraud case brought against Elamir's HMO by the state of New Jersey.

NBC's *Dateline*, on August 2, 2002, referred to a 1998 foreign intelligence report obtained by the network, "The report alleges that an H.M.O. owned by Dr. Elamir in New Jersey was 'funded by ben [*sic*] Laden' and that in turn Dr. Elamir was skimming money from the H.M.O. to fund 'terrorist activities.'" New Jersey investigators discovered that $15 million in funds from Elamir's HMO were unaccounted for and *Dateline* determined that some of the funds were transferred to off-shore bank accounts. Chertoff represented Elamir at the time the money was shifted to the off-shore bank accounts.

The weapons smugglers targeted by Diamondback also included those who were smuggling nuclear components to the A.Q. Khan network. It was this network that was a prime focus of Valerie Plame Wilson and her Brewster Jennings & Associates covert CIA operatives. On January 14, 2005, *Dateline*'s Chris Hansen interviewed ATF agent Dick Stoltz, the supervisor of Diamondback:

In the summer of 1999, a group of illegal weapons dealers were meeting at a warehouse in Florida, their conversations recorded by federal investigators. One of the men, from Pakistan, was seeking technology for nuclear weapons. Whom did he say he was working for?

Dick Stoltz: "Dr. Abdul Khan."

Chris Hansen: "A.Q. Khan."

Dick Stoltz: "A.Q. Khan."

(Former federal undercover agent Dick Stoltz was posing as a black market arms dealer.)

Hansen: "Did you realize what you had at the time?"

Stoltz: "No. We didn't."

But now he does — because A.Q. Khan is considered, by some, to be the most dangerous man in the world. Why? Because

Dr. Khan has peddled nuclear weapons technology to some of the countries the United States considers most dangerous, and some accepted his offers.

Undercover federal agent Dick Stoltz says there's evidence Khan's operatives were at work here in the U.S., like a man who asked if Stoltz could supply heavy water, an ingredient used to make plutonium for nuclear bombs. Stoltz: "He said that Dr. Khan was handling the negotiations behind the scene, as far as — the heavy water."

Chertoff, in a major conflict-of-interest, abused his authority to cover up the involvement of his client in the Diamondback probe.

Other than the Homeland Security Secretary's complete incompetence during Hurricane Katrina, why would someone like Michael Brown have special animosity towards Chertoff? Perhaps Brown's past job as Commissioner of the International Arabian Horse Association (IAHA) had something to do with his sudden call for Chertoff's firing in the wake of the Homeland Security chief's approval of the Dubai Ports World deal to take over operations at 21 U.S. ports. Close Bush family friend, the Emir of Dubai, Sheikh Mohammed bin Rashid al Maktoum, is an avid horse racing fan and owner (as was the Emir's late father). Dubai is the venue for an annual thoroughbred racing event where millions of dollars change hands in betting. Horse betting in Dubai is believed by law enforcement officials to be a major conduit for money laundering in the region — something that must have been known to Brown as the oversight authority for the IAHA. In what could be the most dramatic outcome of the Bush criminal scandal, Brown's experience with the IAHA may prove embarrassing to Chertoff and the Bush criminal cartel as Dubai comes under sharper focus.

Dubai is also an important diamond center. And that brings us to Osama bin Laden's connections to the Israeli diamond trade. The following was sent to *WMR* by a journalist source who was in Peshawar, Pakistan in the weeks following U.S. intervention in Afghanistan. The information comes from a Taliban member who escaped into Pakistan:

"Osama left Afghanistan in a party of 26 people, mostly his family members, on November 4 [2001].

"He left from the 'south' [possibly to southern Iran].

"This may surprise you, but you must understand the nature of business. A business partnership is based on years of trust, and it is totally separate from political or national loyalties.

"Osama, when he realized that he was trapped between the Northern Front and the U.S. forces, called on an old business partner, who flew in his jetliner, and ferried Osama to Africa.

"Osama was a rich man, a millionaire, but spent a lot on the Afghan war and reconstruction. While he was in Africa in exile, the Israelis approached him to take over the diamond business from the Lebanese in West Africa. (Background: Muslims provide the strong arm for the raw diamond trade in West Africa, and it required a respected and tough Muslim like Osama to wrestle the trade away from the Shi'ites from southern Lebanon. The Israelis could not stand the thought of their Antwerp diamond industry financing suicide bombers in south Lebanon.)

"With the diamond trade under his control, Osama became a billionaire (repeat), a billionaire ... The diamonds were sent to the Russian mafiyah, who then sold to Antwerp.

"Antwerp, btw, was where the shoe bomber and countless other "terrorists" were financed and where A.Q. Khan money was being wired to New York via Hassidim diamond merchants.

"For building materials and equipment, bin Laden's construction family routinely dealt with Jewish businessmen through Yemen. Since Saudis could have no direct dealings, the bin Ladens used Yemenis, who lived alongside Jews in their Yemeni homeland. This is how Osama's father became so big.

"Inside Afghanistan, the Taliban were not anti-Jewish, because the Pashtun tribe is one of the "lost tribes of Israel." Our customs and names are identical to those of the Jews. So there was no problem in fighting the Soviet occupation and then Shiite enemy, and Osama led this fight."

In fact, this communique from Peshawar is born out by the story of Ambuy Gem Corporation president Yehuda Abraham, who was arrested at his New York "Diamond District" office in 2003 for his involvement in a Russian shoulder-mounted missile launcher smuggling ring involving a British national with ties to the Viktor Bout smuggling ring, Hemant Lakhani, and a Malaysian national believed to have ties to Jemaah Islamiya, the al Qaeda affiliate in southeast Asia. Bout's smuggling network was partly based in Dubai. Abraham is a Bukharan Jewish native of Afghanistan who spoke Pashto and Urdu. A well-placed Israeli source told *WMR* that Afghan-born Jews are so rare, Abraham would "have most certainly been used as an agent by Mossad."

But Abraham, like Zim Shipping, had special dispensation under the Arab boycott of Israel. A U.S.-Israeli dual national,

Abraham maintained a diamond store in the lobby of the Sheraton Hotel in Jeddah, Saudi Arabia. His primary clientele: the Saudi royal family. It was also discovered that Abraham was operating a "hawalah" — an Islamic money transfer network — from his diamond business. It was that hawalah that was used to transfer money from the weapons sales out of the United States. Moreover, Osama bin Laden's diamond courier who fenced West African diamonds into the Hassidim-run Hatton Garden, London diamond district went by the very non-Muslim-sounding name of "Cyril Jacob." A former Mossad chief told this editor in 2002 that if one wanted to find the source for most of al Qaeda's funding, one needn't look any further than West Africa's diamond trade and "the six biggest U.S. banks in New York."

In addition, Osama bin Laden is reported to own a fleet of merchant ships, something that makes the Dubai Ports World deal and Chertoff's endorsement of it even more suspect. Some of these ships reportedly are registered to China White Lines and involve Sicilian mafia business fronts.

In April 1993, Rashid bin Maktoum, the then-Crown Prince of Dubai opened a jewelry equipment manufacturers trade show in the emirate— the show highlighted the equipment needed for stone cutting and other jewelry-making processes. Soon, Dubai rivaled Antwerp and Tel Aviv as a major diamond processing center — a business in which bin Laden is now heavily invested.

Dubai Ports World and Zim Shipping, Michael Chertoff and Osama financiers and A.Q. Khan smugglers, New York and London Hassidim diamond dealers and al Qaeda and affiliated terrorist organizations are connecting more dots.

***

In my previous book, *Jaded Tasks: Brass Plates, Black Ops & Big Oil*, a number of suspicious deaths of Americans who were opposed to the Bush administration's policies were investigated in detail. Since *Jaded Tasks*' publication in June 2006, the suspicious deaths have continued unabated:

December 28-31, 2006 — California attorney and journalist Paul Sanford, Michael Newdow's attorney who argued before the US Supreme Court why "Under God" should be excised from the Pledge of Allegiance, but who is best remembered for asking

173

Bush Press Secretary Scott McClellan in 2005 why the leaking of CIA agent Valerie Plame Wilson's name by the White House should not be considered an act of treason, died suddenly at the Embassy Suites Hotel in Seaside, California on Christmas Eve.

For over a decade, this reporter has been cited as a modern-day Osiris in trying to alert the world to the suspicious deaths of journalist colleagues — from Danny Casolaro and Paul Wilcher to Gary Webb and Dale Solly. Unfortunately, there is now again reason to believe that a journalist's death may have not been what is being reported. The suspicious deaths of opponents of the Bush Crime Family, from journalists and intelligence agents to businessmen and other private citizens, have reached epidemic proportions.

According to police who spoke to the *Monterey Herald*, Sanford, who was married with two children, "probably" jumped between 9 and 12 floors above the hotel's atrium to his death in what is being called a "suicide." Odd behavior for someone who had just bought his mother's home in picturesque Pebble Beach, where he planned to retire in the future. Sanford, an advocate for progressive causes, was a strong believer in the U.S. Constitution who always carried a copy with him. In 2005, Sanford represented a Santa Cruz homeless man who was cited by police for violating a city ordinance against using "profane or abusive" language in soliciting for money. The man had a sign in his straw hat that read "Fuck the Pigs." By pigs, the man meant the police. City prosecutors later dropped the charges.

Sanford's friends expressed disbelief that he would put his family through such a trauma resulting from a suicide.

Sanford was not checked into the hotel but often met contacts at the neighboring Chili's Restaurant. His car was parked next to the Embassy Suites. Police had no clear evidence to rule Sanford's death a suicide other than some hotel cleaners' statements that he was seen pacing an upstairs hallway prior to his death.

WMR also reported in follow-up stories on the "suicide" of U.S. Army Colonel Ted Westhusing in Iraq, eg.:

January 23, 2006 — More details emerge on Col. Ted Westhusing's "suiciding" in Iraq. Days before his supposed suicide by a "self-inflicted" gunshot wound in a Camp Dublin, Iraq trailer, West Point Honor Board member and Iraqi police and security forces trainer Col. Ted Westhusing reported in e-mail to the United States that "terrible things were going on in Iraq." He also said he hoped he would make it back to the United States alive. Westhusing had three weeks left in his tour of duty in Iraq when he allegedly shot himself in June 2005.

It is noteworthy that after Westhusing's death, two top Army generals, both responsible for training Iraqi forces, General Dave Petraeus, the Commander of the Multi National Security Transition Command Iraq (MNSTCI), and Maj. Gen. Joseph Fil, the Commander of the 1st Cavalry Division, were quickly transferred without much fanfare to Fort Leavenworth, Kansas and Fort Hood, Texas, respectively.

Informed sources report that Westhusing was prepared to blow the whistle on fraud involving US Investigations Services (USIS), a Carlyle Group company, when he died. He had also discovered links between USIS principals and clandestine events involving the Iran-Contra scandal of the Reagan-Bush I administrations. Westhusing has also linked USIS to the illegal killing and torture of Iraqis. USIS personnel whom Westhusing was investigating had the keys to his trailer. In addition, Westhusing's personal bodyguard was given a leave of absence shortly before the colonel's death.

The U.S. Army's official report on Westhusing's death contained a number of falsehoods, according to those close to the case. Most importantly, the Army report stated that Westhusing had electronically communicated an interest in obtaining hollow point bullets. The bullet that killed Westhusing was a hollow point. However, the Army's statement was false, according to an informed source. In addition, the Army combed Westhusing's service record and interviewed a number of colleagues in order to concoct a story that would make suicide appear plausible.

California Democratic Senator Barbara Boxer is reportedly trying to get the Senate to investigate Westhusing's death. However, with the Republicans in firm control, it appears that murder of senior U.S. military officers is also something the GOP is more than willing to cover up.

***

It would not be the first cover-up of a murder in a combat situation. In July 2007, it was revealed that the "friendly fire" death of National Football League star Pat Tillman in Afghanistan in 2004 was anything but what the Army had claimed. Tillman, who had expressed outrage over Bush's decision to invade Iraq and made his thoughts well known to friends and family, was shot by three bullets fired from an M-16 at 10 yards away or less. The Army covered up the incident and Bush claimed executive privilege in refusing congressional requests for documents about the killing of Tillman. In addition, Army forensic specialists expressed skepticism about the Pentagon's report on Tillman's death. Adding to suspicions was the Army's order to burn Tillman's diary and body armor.

On August 1, 2007, *WMR* reported on further details concerning the Tillman death:

Three former high ranking Pentagon officials and one active duty general testified under oath on August 1 before Rep. Henry Waxman's Government Oversight and Government Committee on the April 22, 2004 death in Afghanistan of NFL star-turned-U.S. Army Ranger Pat Tillman. All four witnesses, including former Secretary of Defense Donald Rumsfeld, defaulted to the commonly-used and overly-lawyered phrases by Bush administration officials testifying before Congress: "I don't recall" and "I have no recollection of that."

What was witnessed on August 1 concerning the Pentagon's failure to inform the Tillman family and the public about the facts concerning the death of Tillman was an exercise in obfuscation and rampant amnesia by individuals who at one time ran the U.S. war efforts in Afghanistan and Iraq.

Even ranking Republican member Tom Davis used the dreaded "conspiracy" word to describe the Pentagon's handling of the Tillman case. Davis said, "There are no good answers to the necessarily tough questions raised about how the facts of this friendly-fire incident were handled, by whom and when. Testimony from our previous hearing, and the results of six separate Army investigations, all show the tragic truth can only fall somewhere between screw-up and cover-up, between rampant incompetence and elaborate conspiracy. And once you're descending that continuum, it almost doesn't matter whether the failure to follow Army regulations about updated casualty reports and prompt family notification was inadvertent, negligent or intentional."

The facts brought forward in today's hearing strongly suggest that the Tillman matter was handled by a cover-up that was intentional.

Rumsfeld testified he does not remember when he learned that the Tillman death was a possible fratricide. Rumsfeld's memory certainly seems to be foggy, at best. Rumsfeld said he recalled that he first learned about the fratricide angle on or about May 20, 2004, from his civilian assistant Robert Rangel, who had been informed about it by Rumsfeld's military assistant, Army Colonel Steven Bucci, who had heard about the Tillman fratricide in Iraq, from where Bucci had just returned. It is important to note that Tillman was killed in Afghanistan but details of the Tillman killing were known by some U.S. military personnel in Iraq before Rumsfeld claimed he knew about it. Democratic Rep. Diane Watson of California pointed out that Rumsfeld had often repeated "I don't recall" during his testimony.

The Tillman family was not notified about the fratricide until May 26, 2004.

Rumsfeld also said that he did not recall informing the White House, known for its micro-managing of almost every facet of the Afghanistan and Iraq campaigns, including the Abu Ghraib and Jessica Lynch cover-ups, about the Tillman fratricide. More amazingly, Rumsfeld testified that he first learned of Tillman's death in the press in April 2004.

Former Joint Chiefs of Staff Chairman General Richard Myers said he regretted that the Army "did not do its duty" in the Tillman case and revealed that the Army did not follow its own regulations. However, Myers claimed that he was not in the chain of command for the Tillman matter since it was an Army issue and he served in a joint command activity answerable to the Defense Secretary and National Security Council. Myers said he did not recall talking to the White House about the Tillman matter, although he conceded that public affairs channels may have circulated information about the fratricide between the Pentagon and White House. Brown also said he did not inform the White House about Tillman.

Lt. Gen. Philip Kensinger, the former commanding general of the U.S. Army's Special Forces Command, was formally censured yesterday by Army Secretary Pete Geren for his "failure of leadership" in the Tillman investigation. Kensinger appears to be the White House's and Republicans' scapegoat for the Tillman matter. Kensinger refused to accept a subpoena to testify before the House committee today and his current whereabouts, according to Committee Chairman Waxman, are unknown. Waxman said that U.S. Marshals were unsuccessful in locating Kensinger or serving the subpoena. An independent panel is considering whether to recommend that Kensinger be busted from three stars to two stars as punishment. The star removal was strongly supported by California Republican Rep. Darrell Issa, someone whose record includes car theft.

There was much discussion of an April 29, 2004, "P-FOR" or "Personal For" message sent by then-Major General Stanley McChrystal, commander of the Joint Special Operations Command and Afghan Task Force, to Commander of U.S. Special Operations Command General Bryan "Doug" Brown, General Kensinger, and Commander of U.S. Central Command Gen. John Abizaid, both headquartered in Tampa, Florida. Abizaid was an "action" addressee on the P-FOR and Kensinger and Brown were "Info" addressees, similar to a cc: addressee. The Tillman P-FOR, a high priority, sensitive, and rare message sent to the commanders and which was not for general distribution, stated that there was a strong likelihood of fratricide in the Tillman death. Rumsfeld testified that he did not recall seeing the P-FOR.

However, the P-FOR from McChrystal said that it was important to let the Defense Secretary and President know about the possibility of fratricide before they made an incorrect and potentially embarrassing statements concerning the death. Abizaid testified that he told Myers that it was "important to let the leadership know" about the P-FOR. Abizaid said he was referring to Rumsfeld and Bush. Abizaid testified that he did not inform the White House about the details of Tillman's death.

The P-FOR was sent four days before the memorial service for Tillman at which the public was told Tillman died as the result of "enemy fire."

Abizaid testified that on April 28, 2004, the day before the P-FOR was sent by McChrystal, Tillman's platoon leader told him that Tillman was killed by enemy fire. However, on the evening of April 22, Tillman's team member Private First Class Bryan O'Neal, reported that he suspected fratricide in Tillman's death. That statement appears in the Army 15-6 report required for all hostile combat deaths. However, someone, whose identity is yet unknown, re-wrote O'Neal's statement to reflect that "Corporal Tillman was killed by the enemy."

However, O'Neal's original statement had been altered to suggest Tillman's death was from enemy fire. O'Neal testified earlier about the alteration before Waxman's committee.

Even after the McChrystal P-FOR was sent to Abizaid and Brown, the Army announced that Tillman would be awarded the

Silver Star at his memorial service in May 3, 2004. The Silver Star citation for Tillman said the honor was awarded for "gallantry in action against an enemy of the United States." In answer to a question from Democratic Rep. William "Lacy" Clay from Missouri, Rumsfeld said he did not know who awarded the Silver Star because the Secretary of Defense does not involve himself in that process. Rumsfeld and Myers said the decision was solely that of the Army. Brown and Abizaid also said they did not know who awarded Tillman the Silver Star. Clay informed the witnesses and the committee that the Silver Star for Tillman was awarded by the President of the United States.

Waxman suggested the White House was interested in spinning the Tillman death because it wanted to shift public opinion away from April revelations about prisoner abuse at Abu Ghraib to something it could hype: the heroic death of a brave and well known American soldier at the hands of the Taliban and al Qaeda in Afghanistan.

Waxman then asked the most famous question in Washington when it comes to scandals: "What did the White House know and when?" Waxman thought it odd that during the time of Tillman's death from what was thought to have been enemy fire, 97 White House officials sent and received hundreds of e-mails regarding Tillman. Waxman said that weeks later, after friendly fire was admitted, there were no e-mails from the White House concerning Tillman.

However, both Waxman and Tom Davis agreed that further evidence about the Tillman death may be gleaned from personal e-mail accounts from the field in Afghanistan. Today, the committee requested the U.S. Army Criminal Investigation Command and the Pentagon's Inspector General to inform the committee if "subjects and witnesses were asked about the use of personal e-mail accounts to communicate about the Tillman matter, whether such communications were obtained and reviewed ... and, if not whether [CID and the IG] intend to secure and review them now."

Waxman and Davis wrote to the two Defense activities that the committee had "received information from a former Department of Defense official that information from the field was often transmitted to DoD officials through personal e-mail accounts."

Ohio Democrat Dennis Kucinich asked Rumsfeld if he ever coordinated press strategy with the White House concerning the war and specifically mentioned the contractor, the Rendon

Group, which has been at the forefront of drafting and distributing pro-war propaganda on behalf of the Pentagon. Rumsfeld denied he discussed press strategy on the Tillman case with the White House but conceded that Rendon and other contractors had Pentagon contracts to develop press strategies. Kucinich maintained that the Pentagon had outsourced the management of the news to contractors like the Rendon Group and that it was Defense Department strategy to cover up incidents like the Tillman, Abu Ghraib, and Jessica Lynch cases. Rumsfeld said there was no evidence of a cover-up in any of the cases mentioned by Kucinich.

However, a White House-to-Pentagon e-mail released by the committee strongly suggests that there was a willful attempt to cover up the Tillman fratricide in order to maximize positive spin. An e-mail was sent from White House staffer Jeanie S. Mamo to the Pentagon's Public Affairs chief Larry DiRita on April 23, 2004, a day after Tillman's death and after PFC O'Neal's report that fratricide was likely involved. Also, by April 23, suspected fratricide was also known by Tillman's other Alpha Company Rangers, including 1SG Fuller, CSM Birch, Maj. Scott, Col. Nixon, Maj. Hodne, LTC Bailey, and CPT Saunders.

Mamo's e-mail to DiRita says that Larry Yeager, a "terrific" reporter for *Sports Illustrated*, needed to talk to someone at the Pentagon regarding Tillman. Yeager's e-mail was also forwarded to DiRita. It requested Mamo to help him on what would be an "awesome piece" in *Sports Illustrated.* The Mamo e-mail strongly suggests a close relationship between Yeager and the Bush White House. It states Yeager "had a one-on-one interview with President Bush and knows Gov. Bush [Florida Governor Jeb Bush] as well." Mamo also states that Yeager wrote a story about Qusay and Uday Hussein and "their torture of Olympic athletes" and "has since been back to Iraq to write a follow-up on the reorganization of the Olympic team." As if to signal to DiRita that Yeager was a trusted embedded journalist, she adds, "Don gets it." The Defense Department even redacted from the disclosed e-mail Yeager's phone numbers at the Manhattan offices of *Sports Illustrated*, which is owned by AOL Time Warner.

One person who apparently was not as "in" as the *Sports Illustrated* reporter was General Bantz Craddock, Rumsfeld's senior military assistant. On July 27, 2007, Craddock, who as Commander of U.S. Southern Command in Miami, oversees the operations at Guantanamo Bay, told the Waxman committee about being kept out of the loop by DiRita and Rumsfeld's other close advisers: "I will also tell you there could have been discussions and meetings that I would not have been privy to because occasionally that happens. The fact of the matter is — and I'll just tell you that DiRita and I occasionally got into a bit of a dither over the fact that I felt that he was not informing me of military issues or that he felt I was usurping his authority to deal with political issues."

Craddock gave a picture of Rumsfeld and his civilian advisers keeping senior military officers out of the loop, something that has been confirmed to this journalist by other senior officers who served in the Pentagon under Rumsfeld. Craddock told the committee that Rumsfeld's office never contacted him for details about the Tillman killing.

The picture that is being developed from the Waxman hearings is that the death of Pat Tillman was advertised as an enemy combat death in order to create favorable spin for the White House and Pentagon and help both organizations recover from Abu Ghraib. Tillman's memorial service, Silver Star award, and *Sports Illustrated* "awesome" article were all part of a carefully designed spin, likely involving the Rendon Group and other professional contract spinmeisters, as suggested by Kucinich.

If the White House and Pentagon were able to cover up the details of the aftermath of Tillman's death, what could they have been prepared to do after they were informed that the star recruit was keeping a diary and was prepared to speak out against the Iraq war after his enlistment?

On August 1, 2007, *WMR* provided more details on the Tillman death:

At least 30 people knew about the Tillman fratricide before Donald Rumsfeld said he was informed about it. General Bantz Craddock, Rumsfeld's chief military assistant, told the House Committee on July 27, 2007, that he heard about the Tillman fratricide from his next-door neighbor in Fort Myer, General Jim Lovelace. Rep. Elijah Cummings of Maryland said Tillman's mother, Mary Tillman, said Rumsfeld's contention that he did not know about Tillman until much later was "not credible."

Cummings asked Rumsfeld if he believed there was a cover-up. Rumsfeld responded that "no one in the White House suggested there be a cover-up." Richard Myers said the White House, Joint Chiefs of Staff or Office of the Secretary of Defense were not involved in a cover-up. John Abizaid and Doug Brown also denied a cover-up.

Abizaid said he did not receive the P-FOR until May 6, 2004, although it was sent on April 29. On April 23, Abizaid said he was phoned by McChrystal and was told that Tillman had been killed. Abizaid said the P-FOR was sent to Tampa, CENTCOM's headquarters, but was not re-transmitted to Abizaid in the Middle East until May 6. Abizaid said he then called Myers and told him that Tillman had been killed by friendly fire.

Myers testified that he did not remember Abizaid's phone call and said he never saw the P-FOR. Myers also said that when he was informed of the incident he "was not sure" that fratricide was "common knowledge." Myers also said he could not recall whether he informed Rumsfeld of the fratricide.

Rumsfeld said that although he remembered drafting a letter to the Tillman family, he could not recall when he learned of Tillman's death. Although President Bush was to refer to the Tillman death in a May 1, 2004 speech, Rumsfeld said he could not recall discussing Tillman with the White House.

On August 9, 2007, there was a follow-up on *WMR* to the Tillman story. It concerned Bush's faulty recollection of the matter:

George W. Bush, like Donald Rumsfeld, Richard Myers, and John Abizaid, all in the chain of command during the cover-up of the Pat Tillman's shooting death in Afghanistan, cannot recall when he first heard that the death was from "friendly-fire" and not enemy action.

Bush, in saying he does not recall when he heard about Tillman's friendly fire death, is also either admitting his chain of command in April and May 2004 was totally broken down or that it was engaged in a massive cover-up extending up the chain of command from Afghanistan through Qatar (CENTCOM deployed theater headquarters), Tampa's CENTCOM's permanent headquarters, the Pentagon, and ultimately to the White House.

On April 29, General Stanley McChrystal sent a high priority and classified "Personal For" message to Central Command chief Abizaid warning him that Tillman's death may have been from friendly fire and that Abizaid and others high up in the chain of command should brief Rumsfeld and Bush before they made public statements on the Tillman death. McChrystal specifically mentioned preventing Bush from being embarrassed as a result of his making any public statements about Tillman's death, the first one being on May 1 in which Bush spoke of Tillman's heroic death in combat with the enemy.

***

One of the most "radioactive" stories (pun intended) was the November 2006 radiation poisoning in London of dodgy ex-Russian intelligence agent Alexander Litvinenko. *WMR* was one of the few media outlets not buying the group-think being pushed by the neocons regarding either Litvinenko's intentions or his poisoning.

I immediately got the word from European journalists and intelligence sources to look beyond the corporate media reports concerning the Litvinenko case, and concentrate on Litvinenko's right-wing network of supporters and interlocutors.

Thanks to *WMR*'s sources in the Italian media and intelligence community, we reported the following on December 30, 2006, concerning the circuitous network with which Litvinenko was involved — a network that extended into the United States:

WMR's well-placed Italian sources report that the Mario Scaramella-Alexander Litvinenko polonium-210 poisoning and right-wing political operation has been tied by Italian prosecutors to activities in southern Florida, particularly in the Miami area.

Scaramella's interrogation by magistrate Pietro Saviotti at the Regina Coeli in Rome has yielded evidence that Scaramella forged fax documents he claimed were from Litvinenko and were to be handed over to the Italian Parliament's Mitrokhin Committee, a Silvio Berlusconi contrivance designed to link top Italian progressive politicians to information obtained from KGB archival materials. Scaramella's documents, said to have originated from Litvinenko, were written by Litvinenko in the first person. Italian prosecutors have determined that Scaramella paid Litvinenko to write the false "KGB" fax documents and that they never originated with the KGB.

Scaramella has reportedly been linked by Italian investigators to Filippo Marino, who is involved in the security business. One of his companies, Securitydirector LLC, is registered at PO BOX 190487, Miami Beach, FL 33119-0487. It has also been discovered that the Italian Consulate in Miami was used as a major base of operations by Scaramella. In fact, all of the forged documents passed by Scaramella to the Mitrokhin Committee were authenticated and officially marked by the Italian Consulate in Miami....

Also of note is the British government's connection to Scaramella and Litvinenko. Not only were traces of polonium-210 discovered in the office of Britain's deputy ambassador at the UK embassy in Moscow, but Britain's Deputy Consul in Naples, Frederick Brian Keever, signed a false passport for Alexander Litvinenko with a fictitious identity: Edwin Redwald Carter. Keever also allegedly countersigned a document prepared by Litvinenko concerning a meeting with a Russian Mafia member who worked for the Russian Federal Security Bureau who was to have transported a "nuclear suitcase" from Moscow to Zurich for onward shipment to the Middle East. The document, "authenticated" by the British authorities, also ended up in the Mitrokhin Committee archives in the Italian Parliament.

The Russian media is reporting on a link between the Boris Berezovsky-Litvinenko-Scaramella link and a retired Major in one of the "western intelligence services." The major, born in one of the Baltic republics, targeted Soviet military advisers stationed in a number of Third World nations. After leaving the service, the officer, who is now said to be 50 years old, obtained a law degree and became a private businessman. He is now reportedly the right-hand intelligence aide to Berezovsky and has helped plan anti-Russian and anti-Vladmir Putin insurrections in Chechnya, Kalmykia, Karelia, Andijan in Uzbekistan, Georgia, Ukraine, Kyrgyzstan, and Moldova. Berezovsky, an Israeli citizen, also reportedly had a hand in helping to foment the Israeli-U.S.-inspired anti-Syrian "Cedar Revolution" in Lebanon. Russian-Israeli Mafia fingerprints, as well as those of the Mossad, have been discovered in several car bombings of Lebanese politicians, with the aim to place the blame on Damascus.

Meanwhile, Berezovsky's former Yukos co-owner Leonid Nevzlin, arrived at Newark, NJ from Israel on December 24. Russia and Interpol have arrest warrants out for Nevzlin. Russian authorities requested American authorities to arrest Nevzlin and send him to Russia. With the strong links between the Bush administration and the Russian-Israeli mafia, there is little chance of Nevzlin being brought to justice in Russia.

It was clear that *WMR's* reporting on the Litvinenko-Berezovsky connection was having an effect. Not only did WMR hear from Reuters about our stories, but there was obvious consternation in official Washington about our reports. People close to the Bush administration were getting hot under the collar.

The neocons targeted Vladimir Putin in the same manner they had singled out other nationalist-minded and progressive leaders. On December 18, 2006, I pointed to the anti-Putin maneuvering:

The mainstream media continues to report "KGB" activity in Italy surrounding the activities of Alexander Litvinenko colleague Mario Scaramella. The "KGB" bogeyman is being used in the efforts to damage Italian Prime Minister Romano Prodi and other Italian leftist politicians. The "KGB menace" is also being used in reports of Scaramella's illicit smuggling activities in the independent Republic of San Marino. It is clear that the now clearly established Litvinenko link between two leading neocon media "perception management" czars: deposed Russian media magnate Boris Berezovsky and defeated Italian Prime Minister and media mogul Silvio Berlusconi is a major influence in the clumsy attempt to drum up a bogus "KGB" campaign against European leftist politicians, as well as Russian President Vladimir Putin.

The bogus nature of the KGB charges is as clear as day. The Soviet-era KGB (Komitet Gosudarstvennoy Bezopasnosti, or Committee for State Security) came to an end on November 6, 1991. It was succeeded by the Russian Federal Security Bureau for domestic security functions and the Sluzhba Vneshney Razvedki (SVR) for foreign intelligence operations. It has been a neocon plan, aided by the American Enterprise Institute and their operatives inside the Polish government and the *Washington Post*, to raise the specter of a renewed Russian menace and return to Cold War polemics. Berezovsky and his exiled friends in Israel, now tied to the Litvinenko affair, are eager to cause problems for Putin at home and abroad. And based on the success of the neocon media in creating the perception that Saddam Hussein was a clear and present danger, they see the opportunity of doing the same thing to Putin. However, the former KGB Colonel is wise to the neocon antics and he has marshaled his own media interests to ensure the neocons to not succeed.

On January 3, 2007, *WMR* ran a follow-up story on Scaramella and company:

Italian suspect in the Litvinenko affair, Mario Scaramella, in addition to claiming he was a professor of environmental law at Externado University and the University of Nuestra Senora del Rosario in Bogota, Colombia from 1996 to 2000, has a Colombian link through his association with Incident Management Group (IMG) of Miami. IMG counts a number of former U.S. intelligence officers in Colombia, in addition to Scaramella's colleague Filippo Marino, among its ranks of consultants. In addition, IMG chief, Louis Palumbo, while with Kroll Associates at his Miami vantage point, reportedly tracked the activities of Colombia's drug cartels, including the Medellin Cartel. At Kroll, Palumbo also reportedly worked closely with Avram Shalom, a former member of Israel's Shin Beth domestic security service. Shalom was fired after a scandal involving the massacre of Palestinian civilians. Shalom then joined Kroll.

In 2005, *WMR* reported the following link between the Medellin cartel and the Saudi financiers of 9/11: "In 1999, the Drug Enforcement Administration (DEA) broke open a major conspiracy involving a Saudi prince's Colombian cocaine smuggling from Venezuela to support some 'future intention' involving Koranic prophecy. The DEA operations were contained in a 'Declassification of a Secret DEA 6 Paris Country Office' memorandum dated June 26, 2000, a date which coincided with the height of Israeli art student and 9/11 hijacker activity in the United States. In June 1999, 808 kilograms of cocaine were seized in Paris. At the same time, the DEA was conducting a major investigation of the Medellin drug cartel called Operation Millennium.

"Through an intercepted fax, the Bogota Country Office of the DEA learned of the Paris cocaine seizure and linked the drug smuggling operation to the Saudis. The DEA investigation centered around Saudi Prince Nayif al Saud, whose alias was El Principe (the Prince). Nayif's full name is Nayif (or Nayef) bin Fawwaz al-

Shaalan al-Saud. In pursuit of his international drug deals, Nayif traveled in his own Boeing 727 and used his diplomatic status to avoid customs checks. The DEA report stated Nayif studied at the University of Miami, Florida, owned a bank in Switzerland, speaks eight languages, was heavily invested in Venezuela's petroleum industry, regularly visited the United States, and traveled with millions of dollars of U.S. currency. Nayif is also invested in Colombia's petroleum industry.

"Nayif was also reported to have met with drug cartel members in Marbella, Spain, where the late Saudi King Fahd and the Saudi royal family maintained a huge palatial residence. The report states that when a group of cartel members traveled to Riyadh to meet Nayif, "they were picked up in a Rolls Royce automobile belonging to Nayif, and driven to the Riyadh Holiday Inn hotel. The next day they were met by Nayif and his brother [believed to be named Saul [sic] [His twin brother is Prince Saud. Nayif's older brother, Prince Nawaf, is married to King Abdullah's daughter].)… The second day they all traveled to the desert in terrain vehicles [hummers]. During this desert trip they discussed narcotics trafficking. UN [The DEA informant] and Nayif agreed to conduct the 2,000 kilogram cocaine shipment, which would be delivered to Caracas, Venzuela, by UN's people, where Nayif would facilitate the cocaine's transport to Paris, France. Nayif explained he would utilize his 727 jet airliner, under Diplomatic cover, to transport the cocaine. "The Boeing 727 was operated by Skyways International, a Saudi-owned airline with past connections to the mysterious James Bath, George W. Bush's Texas Air National Guard friend and later Arbusto and Harken Energy investment pass-through between the Saudis and Bush. These investors included Salem bin Laden, Osama bin Laden's late older brother who was killed in a 1988 plane crash in Texas. Bath was the registered agent for Salem bin Laden.

"According to the DEA Report, Nayif, asked by a DEA informant why he sold drugs, responded that "the world is already doomed and that he has been authorized by God to sell drugs. Nayif stated that 'UN' [the DEA informant] would later learn of Nayif's true intentions for trafficking narcotics although Nayif would not comment further."

WMR also reported the following nexus between the drug cartels and the 9/11 hijackers:

"On April 10 [2006], Mexican police, acting on a tip from Interpol, seized a DC-9 aircraft carrying 5.5 metric tons of cocaine with an estimated street value of $100 million.

"The DC-9 (registration number N900SA) made an emergency landing at Ciudad del Carmen in Campeche state. A Falcon aircraft that arrived at Ciudad del Carmen from Toluca airport in Mexico state in advance of the arrival of the DC-9 was also seized. The cocaine was contained in 128 suitcases. The Mexican police later claimed the unidentified DC-9's pilot managed to escape … however, the police did arrest the co-pilot.

"The DC-9 was painted in the familiar blue and white colors of the US Transportation Security Administration with a official-looking seal with an American eagle bearing the inscription: 'Sky Way Aircraft — Protection of America's Skies.' [The U.S.-registered plane was en route from Caracas (Venezuela) which, according to French intelligence, is a known hub for cocaine shipments from Colombia to Saudi Arabia. The registered owner of the aircraft is: Royal Sons Inc., 15875 Fairchild Drive, Clearwater, Florida.]

"On April 5, 2006, the plane flew from St. Petersburg/Clearwater International to Simon Bolivar International in Caracas. 'Sky Ways' has also been linked to the Saudi government and Bush family/CIA activities. Royal Sons, the name of which may indicate the involvement of Saudi princes, such as the cocaine-transporting Prince Nayif, also maintained an office at 224 East Airport Ave., Venice (Florida), at the same time lead hijacker Mohamed Atta and Marwan al-Shehhi were training at Huffman Aviation, which was located nearby at 400 East Airport Avenue.

"There is evidence that Mohamed Atta and Marwan al-Shehhi were drug couriers for the Latin American and Florida drug cartels, especially via their links with jailed GOP mobster Jack Abramoff. Atta, al-Shehhi, and other hijackers were guests aboard Abramoff's Sun Cruz gambling boat in Florida less than a week before 9/11. In late June 2001, Atta was busy gambling away some of his suspicious source of income in Las Vegas.

"The following is from an AP story from Sept. 26, 2001: 'Sun Cruz Casinos has turned over photographs and other documents to FBI investigators after employees said they recognized some of the men suspected in the terrorist attacks as customers…. Names on the passenger list from a Sept. 5 cruise matched those of some of the hijackers… Two or three men linked to the Sept. 11 hijackings may have been customers on a ship that sailed from Madeira Beach on Florida's Gulf coast.'"

I have always contended that the 9/11 attack on the United States involved elements of organized crime, including the Russian-

Israeli, Latin American, and Italian mafias. The Litvinenko case, involving dangerous radioactive substances, may have ultimately involved another "false flag" terrorist attack, perhaps a so-called "dirty bomb." It was clear that someone or some country derailed the false flag attack. Russian President Vladmir Putin was blamed for the murder of Litvinenko. I believe that President Putin, a KGB veteran himself, may have prevented a dirty bomb attack, an event that would have handed the neocons yet another reason to wage war, perhaps a war that would soon include military action against the Russian Federation.

The Miami connection was also of interest. On January 9, 2007, *WMR* published the following on the Miami link:

> *WMR* previously cited the links between Alexander Litvinenko colleague Mario Scaramella, now under arrest in Italy, and a 22-year CIA veteran based in Miami named Louis Palumbo. Palumbo's Miami-based security firm, Ackerman & Palumbo, the forerunner of Incident Management Group (IMG), which has been linked to Scaramella and his colleague Filippo Marino, was founded in 1977, just after George H.W. Bush's stint as CIA director.

Recently-released CIA documents point to the presence in Miami of a major CIA front company operation that for some time involved George H.W. Bush's Zapata Petroleum and Zapata Offshore. In fact, internal CIA memos from 1975, written at the time Gerald Ford selected Bush to succeed the late William Colby as CIA director, cite a number of Bush-affiliated front companies in which CIA veteran Thomas J. Devine was also involved. These include Zapata; the Wall Street investment firm of Train, Cabot and Associates; and CIA proprietary firms using the cover names WUSALINE and WUBRINY/LPDICTUM.

The minute Bush was nominated as CIA director by Ford, Miami was restored as a major center for CIA proprietary operations. The CIA's Miami station, code-named JM/WAVE, was responsible for planning the 1961 Bay of Pigs invasion of Cuba, an operation that involved Bush and Zapata. After Bush's one year stint at Langley, not only did Miami draw Palumbo, Ted "Blond Ghost" Shackley (who was to assist Bush in the 1980 October Surprise negotiations with Iran in Paris), and other CIA officers but Ackerman & Palumbo hired a senior Foreign Service officer who had been First Secretary of the U.S. Embassy in Paris at the time Bush was in Paris hammering out the "no hostages for arms deal."

WMR carried a report to this effect on December 21, 2006:

As previously reported by *WMR*, there is additional information coming forth that the Litvinenko poisoning incident in London may have been part of a radioactive dirty bomb plot gone awry or prevented thanks to the intervention of agents of the Russian Federal Security Bureau (FSB). According to a RIA/Novosti report from Moscow, nuclear physicist Alexander Borovoi of Russia's Kurchatov Institute and a former consultant to the International Atomic Energy Agency (IAEA) in Vienna has stated, "The worst part of the [Litvinenko] story is that it was like a rehearsal for a dirty bomb. The incident shows that something dangerous is cooking in the terrorist kitchen, with menacing ideas and plans that can generally be described as a crime … Litvinenko or one of his close friends have somehow got hold of polonium … From them we can trace a connection to those whose dream is to get hold of a dirty-bomb terrorists."

There is also unfolding information about links between the potential dirty bomb plotters and a group of shadowy cultist neo-Nazis and Fascists in Italy, some with links to the Italian SISMI military intelligence, "Islamic" front organizations in Italy and Britain, the extreme right-wing anti-Arab Kahane movement in Israel, and Russian-Ukrainian-Israeli Mafia mobsters operating from Italy, Israel, and Britain.

WMR has previously reported on terrorist attacks, including the London transit bombings, that were blamed on "al Qaeda" but were strongly linked to former neo-Nazis in Britain, Italy, Germany, and Switzerland who converted to Islam.

On January 12, 2007, *WMR* published additional details on Scaramella:

The Italian newspaper *La Repubblica* is reporting on more details of the police investigation of Neapolitan right-wing intelligence operative and swindler Mario Scaramella. The paper is reporting on the contents of a computer file on Italian Prime Minister Romano Prodi confiscated in Scaramella's office. The file was created in September 2006, during the consolidation of the Prodi government following the election campaign earlier in the year that brought down rightist Prime Minister and neocon Silvio Berlusconi. The document reveals that all of Prodi's associates were suspected of being Russian agents. The reporters on the story are Carlo Bonini and Giuseppe D'Avanzo, the same two journalists who uncovered details of the Nigergate fraudulent documents used by George W. Bush to justify his invasion and occupation of Iraq.

The Scaramella computer file claim that Bonini and D'Avanzo, Gen. Giuseppe Cucchi (chief of CESIS — Comitato Esecutivo per i Servizi di Informazione e Sicurezza that coordinates both the Italian services SISMI and SISDE — and an adversary of ex-Italian intelligence chief Nicolo Pollari), and Milan magistrates Armando Spataro and Guido Salvini were all said to be Russian agents, "according to SVR [Russian Foreign Intelligence Service] sources." All those who helped expose the Nigergate fraud are labeled in the seized computer file as Russian agents or Russian-manipulated operatives. The Scaramella file claims, "Russian SVR considers as its serious enemies those involved in the Nigergate and Abu Omar scandals, like the then-head of SISMI and his faction (Marco Mancini, Gustavo Pignero, Nicolò Pollari)."

Further information obtained by *La Repubblica* shows that the neocon apparatus was trying to taint Italian officials and journalists as Russian agents much in the same manner as bogus Iraqi documents were used to attack anti-war politicians in Europe as paid agents of Saddam Hussein. The paper said that during a court hearing pause after rejecting Scaramella's request for bail, Sergio Rastrelli, Scaramella's lawyer and cousin, stated, "I asked my client who the source of this [computer] file was and he said that the information concerning Prodi came from Yevgeni Limarev, the son of an SVR general who had been a "covert" consultant for the Mitrokhin Parliamentary Committee that was trying to taint a number of Italian officials as Russian agents. Reached by phone by *La Repubblica*, Limarev stated: "I am not the source. But I am not surprised. This is another fabrication by Scaramella. If tomorrow they would link my name to the dossier on the death of Pinochet, I wouldn't be surprised."

State attorney Carlo Saviotti stated in the hearing: "The documents confiscated from Scaramella prompt me to say that this investigation is only the beginning. On behalf of whom, in September 2006, did Mario Scaramella receive this dossier? And who paid for it?"

Italian law enforcement has discovered the couriers who supplied Scaramella with cash were employed by Battistolli Group, a security firm, that among other services, provides transportation of foreign currency and security for international jewelry shows, including the Jan. 2007 JEW.INT (Jewelers' International) Showcase in New York; Feb. 20-22, 2007 Fashion Jewels and Accessory Fair in Dubai, the March 6-10 International Jewelry Show in Hong Kong, the May31-June 3, 2007 International Jewelry Show in Moscow, the October 24-28, 2007, and the Mideast Watch and Jewelry Show in Sharjah, UAE. Law enforcement has tracked terrorist financial deals to a number of international jewelry shows where diamonds and other precious gems are fenced for cash to purchase weapons and other materials, including radioactive materials.

The bottom line is that the neocons are trying to play the old Joe McCarthy card — if you try to expose the machinations of the right-wing networks that worked with leading neocon interests in Washington, London, and Tel Aviv, you are a Communist agent.

Further description of the Russian-Israeli-Italian-British-U.S. private intelligence network and its nefarious activities is provided in Appendix B.

***

Diamonds once again figured in a neocon network of agents and influence peddlers. Diamonds had been used before to finance the activities of other terrorist groups and networks, including "al Qaeda." But none of this was being reported by the corporate media. On January 11, 2007, I commented on this blackout in the news about the neocon false flag network:

A recent article in the *New York Times*-owned *International Herald Tribune* is trying to paint Alexander Litvinenko associate Mario Scaramella, now under arrest in Italy, as a phony, a virtual "magliaro napoletano" who sells St. Peter's Square to unwary American tourists, who, through his charm or guile, managed to establish formal relations with Filippo Marino, the Florida-based associate of CIA veteran Louis Palumbo; CIA Milan station chief Robert Seldon Lady, now wanted by Italian police with a number of other CIA agents for kidnapping an Egyptian Muslim cleric from a Milan street in 2003; NATO headquarters in Brussels; the International Maritime Organization; the U.S. Environmental Protection Agency; various universities; and the Fucino Space Center in Italy.

The spin from the corporate media does not mention Scaramella's role in an interwoven network of right-wing and neocon operations in Italy and elsewhere that were part and parcel of various criminal conspiracies to bring down progressive politicians and get the United States into a war in Iraq.

The corporate media will continue to steer public attention away from the right-wing/neocon network that was exposed in the Litvinenko affair. As previously stated by *WMR*, all roads in the false flag operations experienced by the world since 2001 are leading to Rome and beyond there, to London, Washington, and Jerusalem.

What was extremely noteworthy in the Litvinenko case was the speed at which London and Washington sought to separate the Litvinenko investigation in London from the Scaramella investigation in Italy. On December 25, 2006, *WMR* ran a report on this anomaly:

The enigmatic Italian self-described environmental "security" expert and alleged weapons smuggler and colleague of various right-wing European operatives Mario Scaramella was arrested on Dec. 24 by Italian police in Naples upon his return from a medical examination in London. Scaramella was immediately transported to Rome. As previously reported by WMR, Scaramella's links to various right-wing "intelligence" groups in Italy and abroad have also placed him in the middle of an attempt by former Italian Prime Minister Silvio Berlusconi and his Russian-Israeli Mafia friends to tarnish current Italian Prime Minister Romano Prodi as a "KGB agent." Russian President Vladimir Putin was a collateral target of Russian-Israeli mobster Boris Berezovsky.

The activities of Scaramella and his colleagues are now under a criminal investigation by the Rome prosecutor's office.

The reaction of British and U.S. authorities are also suspicious. Scotland Yard claims that Scaramella's arrest by Italian authorities had nothing to do with the poisoning death of ex-KGB agent Alexander Litvinenko with polonium-210. The FBI, which is also involved in the Litvinenko case, had no comment on the arrest of Scaramella by Italian authorities. There are no indications that Scaramella's top-level connections inside the U.S. Environmental Protection Agency (EPA) — a key agency involved in the 9/11 "Ground Zero" probe — are under any active investigation by the FBI.

The British and American law enforcement reaction comes as no real surprise. Scotland Yard and the FBI take their orders from neocon elements who are afraid that a possible "dirty bomb" incident prior to the U.S. midterm election could be linked to their vast network in the U.S., Britain, Italy, Eastern Europe, and Israel.

With Scaramella now under arrest in Italy and all investigative roads — the forged Niger documents, the kidnapping and rendition by U.S. and Italian agents of an Egyptian Imam in Milan, dirty tricks against Prodi, the Pentagon's pre-war connections to Rome-based Iranian Mossad asset Manucher Ghorbanifar, and the U.S. assassination of SISMI deputy chief Nicola Calipari in Baghdad — now leading to Rome, Italy may hold the key to much more than Scaramella's dubious business dealings. That key may unlock the door of the identities of the actual perpetrators of the 9/11 and other terrorist attacks in London, Madrid, Beslan, Istanbul, and Casablanca."

The Litvinenko story continued to take suspicious twists and turns. On March 21, 2007, *WMR* published the following story on Menatep, the firm that was behind the Yukos empire:

Amid the hype over the radiation poisoning death of ex-Russian intelligence agent and Boris Berezovsky colleague Alexander Litvinenko last November, a little-reported story about a helicopter crash went largely unnoticed. In what may have been an indication of who and what was behind the Litvinenko poisoning and the attempts by Italian right-wing politicians to discredit both Russian President Vladimir Putin and Italian Prime Minister Romano Prodi, the activities of a mysterious firm tied to Berezovsky and his former Yukos Oil business partner, Tel Aviv-based Leonid Nevzlin, are under renewed scrutiny.

On January 2, 2007, *WMR* reported: "In another full circle between Tel Aviv and Italy, Menatep's [Group Menatep — the

Gibraltar-based firm behind Yukos since renamed GML] former chief for investment management Alexei Globuvich said, after his arrest last Spring in Italy, that Nevzlin may have tried to poison him and his family after mercury was found in his office, home, and car. Globuvich said he was a threat because he knew where Yukos and Menatep assets were located. Shortly thereafter, a Scotland Yard officer handed over to the British security firm ISC Global plans by the British government to extradite a number of Russian-Israeli exiles in Britain to Russia. ISC Global had been part of Menatep and Nevzlin was one of its chief customers.

The London offices of ISC Global, now known as RISC Management, were visited in November 2006 by Litvinenko and Russian businessmen Andrei Lugovoi and Dmitry Kovtun and traces of polonium-210 were discovered there. According to the *Sunday Times* of London, Russian police are also investigating whether the poisoning of Litvinenko and the attempted poisoning of Globuvich are connected to the radiation poisoning death two years ago of Roman Tsepov, a former bodyguard of Putin when he was deputy Mayor of St. Petersburg. Tsepov was involved in the Russian government's tracking of Yukos assets. Also of interest are connections to the June 2004 assassination of *Forbes* Russian edition editor-in-chief Paul Klebnikov, a U.S. citizen who wrote a damaging expose of Berezovsky. Three Chechen contract killers were charged in Klebnikov's murder. The same Russian-Israeli mob ring is also being looked at in the investigation of the assassination of Russian journalist Anna Politkovskaya of *Novaya Gazeta* as a way to embarrass Putin.

Attention is being drawn to a May 14, 2006 article in the *Times* of London. In March 2004, British attorney Stephen Curtis, the chairman of ISC Global, died, along with his pilot, in a helicopter crash near Bournemouth Airport. The two were on their way to Dublin. The *Times* reported a James Bond-like secret project by ISC Global, jailed Yukos tycoon Mikhail Khodorkovsky, and Nevzlin to launch an international smear campaign to discredit Putin and other members of the Russian government, including Defense Minister Sergei Ivanov, other ministers, and officials of state-owned energy companies. Doctored "compromising" photographs were to be used in the smear campaign. Also targeted by the Russian gangsters was Russian tycoon and Chelsea football team owner Roman Abramovich, who had earned the wrath of Nevzlin, Berezovsky, and others because Putin allowed Abramovich to retain his billions in wealth and travel freely to and from Russia.

According to the *Times*, Curtis, who managed a £16 billion portfolio for Menatep, was under surveillance and had been threatened in the weeks before his death. He told a relative, "If anything happens in the next two weeks then it won't be an accident." After his death, Curtis' home was found to contain a small magnet used for a bugging device. It also was revealed at the Curtis death inquest that the British attorney had been in contact with British police "on many occasions" concerning the activities of his Russian clients.

ISC was to obtain a luxury yacht, the Constellation, that would become a headquarters for exiled Russian-Israeli oligarchs (a la "SPECTRE"— SPecial Executive for Control, Terrorism, Extortion, and Revenge) wanted by Moscow for fraud. The yacht would have its own armed SWAT team and crew to repel any attacks. The yacht would be outfitted with bullet proof glass and "white noise" generators to prevent eavesdropping. Prostitutes invited on board would be specially screened by a "trusted agency." Nevzlin authorized the anti-Putin project in a 12-page dossier marked "Secret." In the document, Putin is referred to as "X." British ex-SAS commandos were to be used as personal bodyguards to protect the exiled Russian tycoons from kidnapping and extradition by Russian agents.

On January 11 this year, Yuri Golubev, 64, a Yukos cofounder, along with Khodorkovsky, and colleague of former Yukos deputy chairman Nevzlin, was found dead in his bed in London. Police ruled the cause of death as "natural causes." Our sources in Britain report that the scandals surrounding British Prime Minister Tony Blair and key members of his government are part and parcel of the fact that Britain's government has been co-opted by the Russian-Israeli mobsters, much in the same way that their American colleagues, acting through neocon proxies, have captured control of the Bush administration. The British honors-for-cash scandal, British defense contractor malfeasance, and phony intelligence about Iraqi WMDs laundered through the British government, are all results of the mobsters' control of Blair and his advisers.

Another indication that Russian-Israeli organized crime was running roughshod over U.S. law enforcement came in a December 1, 2006 *WMR* report:

While the Department of Homeland Security has placed the name of every air passenger traveling into and out of the

United States on a secret terrorist rating list based on the mining of various types of personal data and is today hyping a phony "al Qaeda" cyber attack alert directed at stock and commodities exchanges and other financial houses in the United States, the same department, headed by Michael Chertoff, is ignoring a major breakdown in U.S. national security.

On November 27, WMR reported on the case of Israeli Hazki Hen who was arrested for attempting to smuggle as much as $100 million in counterfeit $100 bills from the semi-independent enclave of South Ossetia via middlemen in Georgia and Israel. We can now report that a similar ring connected to the Russian-Israeli Mafia, involving some key participants in the Iran-Contra scandal and illegal U.S. wars in Central America in the 1980s, is traveling into and out of the United States on cleverly forged U.S. passports.

Although the U.S. passport numbers are clearly out of sequence and should be flagged by Immigration and Customs Enforcement (ICE) officials, higher-ups at the Homeland Security Department are looking the other way as unsavory characters transit in and out of the United States on the fake passports.

Major destinations for the U.S.-transiting Russian-Israeli Mafia travelers are Mexico, including the troubled states of Oaxaca and Chiapas; Nicaragua; Panama; Venezuela; Guatemala; Honduras; Costa Rica; Colombia; Ecuador; Venezuela; Paraguay; Argentina; Brazil; Chile; and Bolivia.

There is clear evidence that the Russian-Israeli criminals are involved in smuggling drugs and weapons and are engaged in money laundering and bank fraud.

Favored transit airports for the organized crime mobsters and couriers include Houston's George H.W. International Airport and Miami International Airport."

WMR ran an interesting postscript to the Litvinenko affair on December 28, 2006:

The British media is reporting on the close connections between Russian-Israeli mobster Boris Berezovsky and his coterie that attempted to blame Russia's government for the polonium-210 poisoning of ex-KGB agent Alexander Litvinenko and a top-shelf public relations firm that has shilled for various right-wing politicians for a number of years.

The source of Litvinenko's "death bed" photo, which was shopped successfully to the world's media, was Bell Pottinger, a

British public relations firm headed by Tim Bell, also known as Lord Bell of Belgravia. Bell is a former Saatchi & Saatchi public relations guru who became Margaret Thatcher's top spin doctor who is now closely linked to top public relations spinmeisters in Tony Blair's "New Labor" Party machine.

Bell, who is the top PR handler for Berezovsky, has also counted among his clients the late Chilean dictator Augusto Pinochet, South Africa's National Party (the party of the apartheid regime) (Bell's pro-apartheid PR counterpart in Washington during the 1980s was none other than Jack Abramoff), Thatcher's African mercenary-imbued son Mark Thatcher, the government of Saudi Arabia, News Corporation's Rupert Murdoch, Berezovsky's patron Boris Yeltsin, Sultan Hassanal Bolkiah of Brunei, "Friends of Alexander Litvinenko," and the "democracy" campaign in Iraq in association with Dubai-based Bates PanGulf and the media consultants, Balloch & Roe.

Litvinenko's and Berezovsky's Italian interlocutor, Mario Scaramella, now under arrest by Italian authorities, is linked to a number of right-wing Italian politicians, including neo-Fascists and former Italian Prime Minister and media mogul Silvio Berlusconi.

In the neocon world, it was only the perceptions that mattered, not the truth.

***

There was another interesting story from Italy that hit the press in 2007. The story involved the smuggling of arms from and to Iraq. *WMR* highlighted the story on August 14, 2007:

The Italian media is abuzz with emerging details of a major Italian arms smuggling operation involving Iraq and Libya, as well as offshore "brass plate" and other companies in Malta, Dubai, Bulgaria, Amman, and Cyprus.

The investigation of the arms smuggling network was unearthed by Italian anti-mafia prosecutor Dario Razzi and stems from an investigation started in 2005 of drug smuggling.

It should be noted that the former neocon government of Prime Minister Silvio Berlusconi also had links to international mobsters, most notably Russian-Israeli fugitive tycoon Boris Berezovsky and his network that worked to discredit, through bogus intelligence, the current Prime Minister Romano Prodi.

Four Italians have been arrested on weapons smuggling charges and a fifth, Vittorio Dordi, a diamond dealer, is being sought in the Democratic Republic of Congo.

Italian police confiscated 100,000 Russian-made AK-47s and 5000 Russian PKM machine guns bound for Iraq. The Nouri al-Maliki government claims the weapons were for the Iraqi police in Anbar province. The Bush administration is denying any knowledge of the transaction.

Recently, U.S. Government Accountability Office (GAO) auditors discovered that 110,000 AK-47s and 80,000 pistols were unaccounted for after the United States distributed them to Iraqi military and police services from 2004 to 2005. There is a strong possibility that some of these weapons ended up on the international black market and ultimately in the hands of the Italian and Russian-Israeli mafias. Turkey has complained that U.S. arms sent to Iraq have ended up in the hands of Kurdish PKK guerrillas operating in northern Iraq and Turkey.

The broker for the weapons destined for Iraq from Italy is Al Handal Trading Company, a Dubai-based firm with close connections to scores of mercenary private military companies operating in Iraq. According to the Associated Press, e-mail intercepted by the Italians points to Iraqi middlemen claiming the operation had the support of the Pentagon.

A Malta-based firm called MIR Ltd. acted as the weapons broker, along with Al Handal, a company cited by the CIA as being involved in the Iraq-United Nations "Oil-for-Food" scandal. Al Handal, owned by Jordanian national Waleed Noori al-Handal and his parent Al Thuraya Group, also maintains an office in Amman. Waleedal-Handal claims the Italian-Iraqi weapons deal had the support of the Pentagon and his "friends" in the U.S. military hierarchy in Iraq. Al Handal's web site claims the firm has "built up a network of operations throughout most of the Middle East, Europe, North Africa, and Central Asia."

The weapons smuggling deal commenced during the time when Donald Rumsfeld served as Secretary of Defense. The Italians have already indicted U.S. military members and intelligence agents in the rendition kidnapping of an Egyptian imam from a Milan street and have also indicted a U.S. Army enlisted man for the shooting death in Baghdad of Italian deputy intelligence chief, General

Nicola Calipari during his mission to rescue kidnapped Italian journalist Giuliana Sgrena.

On June 13, 2005, *WMR* reported on incidents in which private contractors in Iraq had engaged in firefights with U.S. military units, including one gun battle between Americans working for Zapata Engineering and a Marine Corps unit. Other confrontations took place between Custer Battles armed mercenaries and U.S. military units at Baghdad airport. Blackwater USA, Triple Canopy, and Aegis Defense Services, a British mercenary firm contracted to the Pentagon, have also been accused of wantonly shooting civilians in Iraq. Rep. Jan Schakowsky (D-IL) recently said there is "no excuse" for mercenaries running around Iraq who are accountable to no one. A number of employees of private mercenary companies have revealed shocking stories about their colleagues shooting innocent civilians in Iraq.

The Italian investigation into weapons smuggling into Iraq is likely to expand to include the culpability of the Pentagon and Bush White House in the affair.

London and Rome were not the only cities to experience intrigue involving mysterious deaths. On June 15, 2006, *WMR* reported,

The Chesapeake Bay is becoming to Washington, DC what the Jersey Pine Barrens were for the New York and Philly mobs — a place where people simply disappear. The latest victim of the "Chesapeake Triangle" is Philip Merrill, the publisher of the Annapolis-based Capital-Gazette Newspapers (publisher of the *Annapolis Capital* and *Maryland Gazette*) and the *Washingtonian* magazine. Last Sunday, Merrill's sailboat, the Merrilly, was found drifting with the engine running off Breezy Point in Calvert County, Maryland. Although Merrill's wallet was found on board, there was no sign of Merrill, an experienced sailor who, after an extensive search, was declared dead. A witness who found the drifting Merrilly said there was some blood found in the back of the boat.

Washington has experienced similar inexplicable losses in the Bay. On Sep. 26, 1978, retired CIA Deputy Director for Strategic Research John A. Paisley's sailboat was found moored off Solomon's Island, Maryland, south of where Merrill's boat was found. Later, Paisley's body was found in the nearby Patuxent River, his submerged body tied to diving weights. Although Paisley was shot through the head, police ruled it a suicide. Paisley was involved with the electronic intercept programs of both the CIA and NSA and may have had important information on the assassination of President John F. Kennedy that he was about to impart to the House Select Committee on Assassinations.

On April 28, 1996, former CIA Director William Colby, who was cooperating with John DeCamp, a Republican State Senator in Nebraska and a former CIA colleague in Vietnam, in investigating a national pedophile ring said to involve George H.W. Bush and reported in the *Washington Times*, went missing at his home at Rock Point on Cobb Island in Charles County, southwest of where Paisley's boat was found. After Colby's canoe was found adrift, his body was later discovered on the shoreline of the bay. Colby, a veteran of CIA missions in Southeast Asia and elsewhere, was said to have lost his footing and drowned.

Local police never ruled out foul play in either the Paisley or Colby cases.

Now we have Merrill disappearing under similar circumstances. Merrill outwardly was connected to many neoconservative organizations. He served on the advisory council of Frank Gaffney's ultra-neocon Center for Security Policy; the Defense Policy Board alongside such arch-neocons as Richard Perle, James Woolsey, and Ken Adelman; set up the neocon Center for Strategic Studies under his Defense Policy Board neocon colleague Eliot Cohen; and was appointed as the President of the U.S. Export-Import Bank by President George W. Bush and was sworn in by his friend Dick Cheney, who recommended him for the EX-IM Bank position. Merrill was also described in yesterday's *Washington Post* editorial as someone who took on "diplomatic and intelligence missions for the government over the years."

However, Merrill also was very much part of the traditional Washington foreign policy establishment, having served as Assistant Secretary General of NATO, a participant in Law of the Sea and disarmament conferences, philanthropist for the environmental Chesapeake Bay Foundation and the University of Maryland journalism college, and a trustee of the chic Aspen Institute. Merrill served intermittently as a Senior Intelligence Analyst for South Asia at the Department of State from 1961 to 1968.

WMR has learned from an informed source who knew Merrill for a number of years that while Merrill headed the EX-IM Bank from 2002 to 2005, the bank routed a significant amount of money to entities associated with the Russian-Ukrainian-Israeli mafia — the shadowy network that his been linked to fugitive Marc Rich, his one-time lawyer "Scooter" Libby, Jack Abramoff, Adam Kidan, and various Russian oligarchs who are now exiled in Israel to avoid extradition for their various crimes. The EX-IM Bank under Merrill's tenure also financed U.S. reconstruction projects in Coalition Provisional Authority-occupied Iraq, programs that resulted in the loss of billions of U.S. taxpayers' funds. Merrill had also supported using future Iraqi oil and natural gas revenues to finance Halliburton and Bechtel oil industry infrastructure projects in the occupied country. In May 2003, Merrill told a congressional committee that the locking of Iraqi revenues for future U.S. projects had "real merit."

WMR's suspicions about Merrill's death proved correct. On June 21, 2006, *WMR* reported,

The body of Maryland publisher Philip Merrill was discovered Monday in the Chesapeake Bay near Poplar Island with a gunshot wound to the head and weighed down with an anchor. Merrill's body was discovered 11 miles from where his boat was found last week. As with Paisley, investigators concluded Merrill committed suicide by shooting himself in the head with a shotgun.

Investigators ruled Merrill's death a suicide even before an autopsy was performed, An experienced medical examiner told *WMR* that bodies found in the water rapidly lose toxicological and other critical evidence, including the presence of drugs in the bloodstream.

WMR was the first to speculate that Merrill's death was more than an accident, as reported last week by the mainstream media. *WMR* learned that while Merrill, a close friend of Vice President Dick Cheney and financial backer of a number of neoconservative organizations, was the head of the U.S. Export-Import Bank, the bank made a number of dubious loans to the U.S.-run Coalition Provisional Authority (CPA) in Iraq and a successor agency known as the Trade Bank of Iraq. In November 2003, $500 million in credit was extended to the Trade Bank of Iraq by the U.S. Export-Import Bank. Much of the money was used to facilitate U.S. "exports" to Iraq, which was actually used to pay major U.S. contractors operating in the occupied country.

A 2005 audit report by the Office of the Special Inspector General for Iraq Reconstruction concluded that "the CPA did not establish or implement sufficient managerial, financial and contractual controls to ensure that funds were used in a transparent manner." The report stated that $8.8 billion allocated to the CPA was unaccounted for.

***

It was clear that in the lead-up to the November elections in 2006, the Bush administration was trying desperately to keep the "war on terror" alive as a fear factor to influence American public opinion. Perhaps the most ridiculous attempt to continue the fear campaign was the case of the "Liberty City Seven" in Miami. I wrote about this on June 25, 2006 for *WMR*:

> This editor will be appearing on Al Jazeera this morning talking about the hype over the recent "terrorist" apprehensions in Miami, Toronto, and London. These appear to be yet additional neocon inspired "crises" to push their all-too-evident agendas.
>
> The case of the "Liberty City Seven," a group of self-employed youths of mainly Haitian descent, is yet another example of the propaganda of the neocons creating new bogeymen. The barrage of fear mongering was best represented by agenda-laden cable news polemicists like Steven Emerson, Joel Mowbray, Sean Hannity, William Kristol, Ann Coulter, and Byron York, to demonize yet another sector of American society, this time Miami's Haitian and non-Cuban Caribbean community. First, it was the Arabs and Muslims, then, it was the turn of the Hispanics, now, it is the Haitians. Tomorrow, it will be sub-continental Indians, then, Native Americans, and Chinese and Koreans. "Homeland security," that awful Teutonic phrase, is being used to establish an apartheid South African-style racial regime in the United States under the cover of "counter terrorism" and "homeland security."
>
> The Liberty Seven are said to have run a "temple" in an old warehouse in the desperately poor Liberty City section of Miami. The seven, who gave out bottled water to people in the wake of Hurricane Wilma last year and sold shampoo and hair tonic on the street, studied Islam, Christianity, and Judaism. That is a far cry from being members of al Qaeda or Black Muslims, which

was claimed by the mainstream media. It is clear the neocons are now looking for Fallujahs and Ramadis right here in the good old USA. Liberty City was perfect for the neocon agenda. It is poor, ethnic, and populated by those who the neocons despise — legal and illegal Haitian immigrants.

The Liberty Seven appear more like a self-styled Caribbean ersatz religious sect than an "al Qaeda" affiliate. The group seems to be a milder and smaller version of Philadelphia's M.O.V.E. group, which, because of their odd "back to nature" beliefs, drew the ire of their neighbors. M.O.V.E. was ultimately shattered by violence created by itself and an overreaction by the Philadelphia police in 1985. It is interesting to note that Miami's current police chief, John Timoney, was appointed Philadelphia's police chief by then-Mayor Ed Rendell.

Rendell was a chief prosecutor against M.O.V.E. and Timoney was a proponent of attacking the headquarters of "subversive" groups during major conferences and political conventions. Timoney called the anti-globalist Ruckus Society "a cadre of criminal conspirators" who "go in and cause mayhem." In 2000, Timoney raided the Ruckus Society warehouse and confiscated wire and gasoline-soaked rags. Immediately, Timoney charged Ruckus with planning terrorist acts, even though the materials were used to construct large puppets used in protests during the Republican National Convention. Timoney did not care that Ruckus was supported by the Ted Turner Foundation, the Ben and Jerry's Foundation, Body Shop International, and Patagonia, Inc., hardly terrorist groups.

Now Timoney is in Miami, and seven Miami residents belonging to a religious order calling itself the "Seas of David" find themselves charged by the Justice Department with conspiring to blow up the Sears Tower in Chicago and the FBI Building in Miami. It is clear that these not very smart Seas of David members were entrapped in an FBI sting. It is doubtful that they could bring down any building. They were not even interested in obtaining explosives from the FBI informant who posed as an "al Qaeda" representative — they merely wanted a video camera and boots. It is also suspicious how the charges against the Liberty Seven were announced.

Attorney General Alberto Gonzales made the announcement of the arrest at a heavily-covered Washington, DC news conference in the same manner as John Ashcroft's announcement of the arrest of "dirty bomber" Jose Padilla in June 2002. FBI Director Robert

Mueller chose a suspicious outlet to discuss the case — the *Larry King Show* on CNN. Meanwhile, the neocon-run Fox News, NBC, and CNN were all speaking of a derailed violent Islamist Jihad plan to launch a terror attack worse than 9/11. All this was false. The Seas of David, which number no more than 50 adherents, is a quasi-Christian group, with elements of Caribbean animism and voodoo. It has been linked to the Chicago-based Moorish Society Temple of America, a group that combines Islam with the teachings of Jesus. Hardly the Islamist Jihadi group ballyhooed by the droning neocon commentators who receive their talking points from Israeli-influenced propaganda outlets in Washington, New York, Boston, and Jerusalem.

Even with evidence that the Republicans, under the aegis of master "election engineer" Karl Rove, had, once again, fixed an election to assure continued control of the Senate, a massive Democratic turnout coupled with dissatisfaction with Republicans over two October sex scandals — the House male page scandal involving Florida Representative Mark Foley and the gay prostitute affair involving fundamentalist Christian leader Rev. Ted Haggard — ensured a Democratic win, albeit razor-thin in the Senate.

***

On November 8, 2006, the day after the election, it turned out that Connecticut's Democrat-turned-Independent Senator Joe Lieberman would hold the Democrats hostage by possessing the 51st vote needed by either party for the majority in the Senate. I wrote the following on *WMR* the "morning after":

Connecticut's re-elected Senator Joe Lieberman has been cast into the role of a pivotal deal maker in a split Senate. Although Lieberman, who lost his party's primary, says he intends to caucus with the Democrats, there are already signs that Lieberman is negotiating a special deal with such GOP-elected officials as New York Mayor Michael Bloomberg. The wild card is Lieberman's inflated ego, which may prompt him to name himself as a larger-than-life "bridge" between the Democratic Senate and White House.

Jon Tester has been declared the winner in Montana and Jim Webb remains ahead in Virginia, although George Allen says he will challenge the vote count.

The Democrats shut out the Republicans in the House and Senate. No incumbent Democrats lost, including two vulnerable House members in Georgia who squeaked out small margins over their Republican opponents. It was likely that Karl Rove engineered Bush's last minute visits to Georgia to avoid a shut-out, but that strategy was not successful.

The Democratic win in the Congress had immediate effects. As Democrats relished their victory, Secretary of Defense Donald Rumsfeld submitted his resignation. It was a sign that even the tone-deaf Bush White House knew that the unpopular war in Iraq had cost their party control of Congress.

Chapter 8

2007 to 2008: Bush Reduced to Lame Duck & Bush Fatigue Sweeps the Nation

Not that I don't love all of America, but rednecks who think they're the real America should read a history book once in a while. George Washington, Thomas Jefferson, Franklin, Madison — the whole lot of them were well read, erudite, European thinking children of the Enlightenment, and they would have had absolutely nothing in common and less to say to a cowboy simpleton like George Bush.

— Bill Maher, July 20, 2007

With polls in mid-2007 showing the Republicans at their lowest popularity in recent years, there was hope that things would turn around in 2008. The world, stunned for many years by the Bush-Cheney coups of 2000 and 2004 and America's "Reichstag fire" of September 11, 2001, began to wake up from its hypnotic spell and rally to action.

The Bush perception managers and their media pals had lulled a majority of Americans into believing the Iraqi war was "someone else's" war. However, as the number of military funerals increased in many small towns across America, the American people demanded action. They began to hold their elected officials accountable for their actions or inaction. By the summer of 2007, large percentages of the American people were in favor of impeaching Bush and Cheney.

As early as 2005, I was writing about the effects of the Iraq War that most of the corporate media were ignoring. On July 16, 2005, I wrote the following on *WMR*:

According to a knowledgeable U.S. Army medical source, the U.S. Army Institute for Surgical Research's Burn Center at Fort Sam Houston, Texas, near San Antonio, is handling some of the worst U.S. military casualties from Iraq.

Although the Pentagon spinmeisters steer politicians and journalists to Walter Reed Army Medical Center and Bethesda Naval Medical Center inside the Washington Beltway to see the numerous recovering amputee veterans from Iraq, Fort Sam Houston is an entirely different matter. The wounded at the Sam Houston Burn Center suffer from severe and painful life-threatening burns, the source said, adding, "You've got guys down there at Sam Houston lying in comas ... their families, including young children, sit by their bed sides every day waiting ... its an awful thing to see."

Perhaps President Bush may want to take time off from clearing brush off his "ranch" to take a spin over to Sam Houston to see for himself what his senseless war has done to these soldiers and their families."

With the conviction of Cheney's former Chief of Staff "Scooter" Libby over his obstruction of justice and perjury in the investigation of the leak of Valerie Plame Wilson's covert identity, there were also nascent signs that the grip that AIPAC had on U.S. politicians and policymakers was beginning to slip. This was a subject of a *WMR* report on March 7, 2007:

From inside the halls of Congress to the offices of Democratic politicians around the country there is increasing criticism of the stranglehold the American Israel Public Affairs Committee (AIPAC) and its political allies have on the Democratic Party's agenda and political message. *WMR* has spoken to a number of Democrats off the record and the story is much the same: Democratic leaders, from House Democratic Caucus Chairman Rahm Emmanuel to Senators Hillary Rodham Clinton and

Dianne Feinstein — pursuant to dictates from pro-Israeli political interests — are curbing debate on the withdrawal of U.S. troops from Iraq, impeachment, and generally, any strong or effective reaction by the Democrats to the Bush administration's and the neocons' disastrous war in Iraq. In various congressional districts, the Democratic Congressional Campaign Committee (DCCC) is bypassing progressive Democratic candidates and replacing them with "centrist" and less anti-war candidates for the 2008 election.

Criticism within the Democratic Party of AIPAC is carried out very quietly. The consequence for any Democratic politician who is identified as speaking ill of the powerful lobby group is a political death sentence. However, from Washington DC to California, the message is much the same — AIPAC and its allies are wearing down the patience of a number of Democrats who see the organization as a Republican and neocon Trojan Horse within the Democratic Party. Next week, AIPAC will be holding its annual convention at the Washington, DC Convention Center. The gathering is bound to create more angst among Democrats — with both Democratic presidential frontrunners, Hillary Clinton and Barack Obama, tripping over themselves in seeking AIPAC campaign support.

The schism within the Democratic Party appeared when House Speaker Nancy Pelosi refused to allow ranking member of the House Permanent Select Committee on Intelligence Jane Harman of California to become chairman. Pelosi was backed by powerful House Defense Appropriations Committee chairman John Murtha. That set off a battle for the House Majority Leader position between Murtha and Steny Hoyer of Maryland. Hoyer handily won the election while Pelosi supported Murtha. Hoyer's sister, Bernice Manocherian, has served as an executive president of AIPAC.

The controversy about Harman arose after she attempted to interfere in the Justice Department's investigation of AIPAC for espionage. Harman's links to AIPAC sank her chances of becoming HPSCI chair. Harman reportedly agreed to work with Republican chairman Peter Hoekstra to avoid an investigation of the cooked up pre-war intelligence on Iraq in return for the Bush administration going easy on the investigation of AIPAC officials Steve Rosen and Keith Weissman, both later indicted for receiving highly classified documents from Israeli Pentagon spy Larry Franklin. After the Libby trial, the next major bombshells are expected to come from the Rosen and Weissman trial, set for June 4. The AIPAC conference next week will undoubtedly be readying for public relations spin for June's "perfect storm" — sentencing for Libby is scheduled for June 5, the day after the Rosen and Weissman trial commences.

The last straw for some Democrats is quiet but firm backing from AIPAC-allied politicians and special interests for a presidential pardon for convicted former Vice President Chief of Staff Irving Lewis "Scooter" Libby. Even as Libby was being found guilty, the Libby Legal Defense Fund announced a new member had joined its advisory committee. He is Charles Heimbold, Jr., former Chairman and CEO of Bristol-Myers Squibb Company and a former U.S. ambassador to Sweden. Advisory Committee Chairman Mel Sembler, the former U.S. ambassador to Italy whose fingerprints are found on the transmittal of the bogus Niger documents from Italian hands to the Bush administration — one of the incidents that led to CIA Leakgate — said the following about the conviction of Libby: "Scooter is a good man and a distinguished public servant who has been wrongly accused."

Other Libby Defense Fund advisory committee members who continue to support the convicted felon include Mary Matalin, former aide to Dick Cheney and wife of Democratic Party insider and Hillary Clinton supporter James Carville; former Education Secretary William Bennett; former HUD Secretary Jack Kemp; former Attorney General Edwin Meese III; former Senator Don Nickles; former Rep. Bill Paxon; former Clinton Middle East envoy Dennis Ross; former Senator Alan Simpson; Hollywood straphanger and former Senator [and Republican presidential hopeful for 2008] Fred Thompson; and former CIA Director James Woolsey. The one question that can be asked of all these and other Libby Advisory Committee members is: "Why do they hate America so much?"

On November 15, 2006, *WMR* ran a more detailed report on the schism between Pelosi and Harman:

There is word that Nancy Pelosi has very good reasons to prevent ranking House Permanent Select Committee on Intelligence (HPSCI) member Jane Harman from succeeding Peter Hoekstra as Chairman of the intelligence oversight committee. Informed sources report that Harman may be implicated in the larger FBI investigation of the America Israel Public Affairs Committee (AIPAC) and its receipt of classified Pentagon and CIA documents from convicted former Pentagon intelligence official Larry

Franklin. The investigation, according to a senior government source, involves the passing of "bags" of classified documents to Israeli intelligence assets who penetrated the Pentagon's Office of Special Programs. One such transfer of "bags" of documents was witnessed occurring between Franklin and an important official of the OSP at the Rockville, Maryland Metro parking lot. The involvement of Israeli agents, AIPAC officials, and Pentagon employees in the illegal transfer of sensitive classified documents to Israel was a matter of grave concern for the HPSCI, yet Harman never indicated the gravity of the situation to the House Democratic leadership, according to informed sources.

***

Following the Democratic takeover of Congress, there was another massive anti-war march in Washington in January 2007. Unlike previous marches, there was a noticeable stand-down of security forces around the Capitol Building. The marchers — a cross section of America, old, young, white, African American, Asian American, Hispanic, labor, men, women, church groups, Jewish and Muslim groups, and veterans — could still feel the ominous nature of the Bush's security force. On January 25, 2007, I wrote about the "psyops" used by the Pentagon to deter a large turnout for the march:

First, the corporate media attempted to ignore the January 27 anti-war march on Washington. As the Internet and progressive talk radio spread the word about the march and groups around the nation began to mobilize their members to participate in it, the Bush administration — now armed with all sorts of Defense Advanced Research Projects Agency (DARPA) "non-lethal" toys — decided to stage a test of an anti-crowd microwave weapon, code named "Sheriff," in a demonstration for the media at Moody Air Force Base in Georgia.

On January 24, the military demonstrated its Active Denial System (ADS) millimeter wave directed energy beam in a test designed for the media, and hence, the public. Using enlisted airmen, acting as "rioters," as "guinea pigs," a beam was directed at them from a parabolic antenna located 500 yards away atop a Humvee. The wave heated the skin of the "rioters" to 130 degrees,

211

creating the feeling in the targets that they were being burned alive, scattering them in the process. The military pointed out that the beam can penetrate winter clothing (which will be worn by those participating in Saturday's march) and 1/64th of an inch under the skin. As with any electronic weapon, it is clear that the "juice" can be turned up on Sheriff to cause more than a nasty skin burn, including internal organ damage, blindness, and death.

The weapon was developed under a contract awarded by the Pentagon's non-lethal weapons program office at the Quantico, Virginia Marine Corps Base to Raytheon.

The public testing of such a weapon by the military just prior to what may be the largest anti-war march in Washington since the Vietnam War is a clear message by the Pentagon to marchers that the millimeter wave technology exists and is deployable. Psychologically, most people find the idea of being burned alive frightening and this Pentagon "show and tell" was an obvious ploy to scare away marchers, especially those planning to bring their families.

However, marchers should keep in mind that a Humvee is no match against hundreds of thousands of marchers and that any attempt to use such a weapon would have one shot before an angry crowd descended on the vehicle and rendered it useless as both a weapon and a vehicle.

No sooner had I published the above article, than I heard from a technology expert who said not to worry. The Bush ray gun could be defeated. I wrote about the simple way to defeat Bush's "death ray" on the eve of the march, January 26, 2007:

According to a technology expert who is familiar with the Raytheon Active Denial System (ADS), tested January 24 at Moody Air Force base in Georgia, the millimeter microwave directed beam weapon can be defeated by a crowd of people using aluminum- or gold-coated Mylar to conduct the beam to ground or even direct it back to the Humvee housing the ADS system. Although the Humvee is shielded, any law enforcement or military personnel standing near the Humvee would get a burning taste of their own medicine if the directed beam were reflected back to its source or to a crowd of police. In addition to aluminum or gold coated Mylar, Mylar reflective space blankets, aluminum coated windshield heat protective screens, and more sophisticated and precise corner cube retro-reflectors or Luneburg spheres can all be used to reflect the millimeter wave beam back to its source.

The source we spoke to also revealed that the ADS technology has already been used in Iraq against civilian rioters even though the Pentagon claims it will not be deployable until 2010. The source added that even if the ADS Humvee is present at the anti-war march in Washington tomorrow, Raytheon would not permit its use because of liability issues stemming from potential eye damage and human rights violations. However, *WMR* has learned that Raytheon is offering the ADS technology to police departments and as a component of home security alarm systems.

***

War and new weaponry was the mainstay of the Bush administration and its military-industrial complex friends. However, *WMR* was able to expose another weapons program, one involving the smuggling of old weapons from an old war, the Southeast Asian conflict on the 1960s and 1970s. *WMR* reported the following on March 2, 2007:

Israel has been a major, albeit covert, player in Southeast Asia since Israeli multi-billionaire tycoon Shaul Eisenberg began supplying weapons to Cambodia's genocidal Khmer Rouge regime in the 1970s. Eisenberg, a close business partner of China's military, was also an early arms supplier to Khmer Rouge leader Pol Pot. Eisenberg was active with Asia's Jewish community during World War II, not as a compatriot of the Allies but as a close intelligence and business partner of Japan's Imperial government, which was allied with Nazi Germany and Fascist Italy in the Axis Alliance.

Escaping Nazi-controlled Europe, Eisenberg settled in the Far East, making his primary bases of operation Japanese-occupied Shanghai and Japan itself. In Shanghai, Eisenberg, along with Imperial Japanese military intelligence units, formed units of future Jewish terrorist groups — the Irgun and the Shanghai Betar. Betar was founded to battle the British for control of Palestine in the 1930s by the Polish Zionist Yakob Jabotinsky, a supporter of Italian Fascist leader Benito Mussolini, and the ideological godfather of later neoconservative oracle Leo Strauss.

The Japanese taught the Jewish paramilitary forces in Shanghai, including some who escaped from Joseph Stalin's Jewish Autonomous Region creation in the Soviet Far East on the Chinese border, how to disrupt colonial occupiers' logistics and command and control elements, strategies that had been successful against the British, Dutch, French, and American colonial authorities in Asia. The Irgun and Betar gangs would eventually use the knowledge gained from the Japanese in their terror campaign against British and Arab forces in Palestine following World War II. Eventually, Irgun and Betar veterans would form the present-day Likud Party, now headed by Binyamin Netanyahu, a noted extreme right-winger.

After the war, Eisenberg began selling war surplus material, including iron and steel scrap. Married to a Japanese woman, Eisenberg established the Israel Corporation, a huge holding company, which, during the 1970s, began to secretly export Israeli military equipment and weapons to China. Under a Panama-based company called United Development, Inc., Eisenberg also began exporting weapons to Central America's most insidious dictatorships, including that of Anastasio Somoza in Nicaragua. Eisenberg's vast holdings eventually included Israel Aircraft Industries and Zim Israel Navigation Company.

As the United States faced imminent defeat in the Indochina War at the hands of the Vietnamese, Laotian, and Cambodian Communist-nationalist forces, Eisenberg wasted no time in cashing in on America's defeat and the new power alignments in Southeast Asia. He began selling weapons from his new business partner — China — to the Cambodian forces of Khmer Rouge leader Pol Pot. After the defeat of the U.S.-backed military government of General Lon Nol, installed after Richard Nixon's National Security Adviser Henry Kissinger, a close friend of Eisenberg, ordered the CIA to overthrow Cambodian head of state Prince Norodom Sihanouk, Cambodia fell victim to a bloody civil war between Vietnamese troops backing Pol Pot's one-time ally Hun Sen and the Chinese-backed "Democratic Kampuchea" government of Khmer Rouge leader Pol Pot.

It was no mistake that the Gerald Ford administration and Secretary of State Kissinger backed the Khmer Rouge. Kissinger and Ford's long-time Michigan financial backer, industrialist Max Fisher, were both financially and ideologically linked to Eisenberg. Ford's supposed "grand moment" — the repatriation in 1975 of the crew of the U.S. "merchant" (spy) ship, the SS *Mayaguez*, from

Khmer Rouge forces was a Kissinger- and Eisenberg-designed ruse to build up Ford's support in the face of the American military defeat in Southeast Asia. That ruse came at the cost of 41 Marines and countless Cambodian military forces and civilians.

Kissinger authorized Eisenberg to begin a discreet program to modernize China's armed forces with $10 billion in Israeli and U.S.-designed weapons, re-exported through Israel. The reason — neoconservative to its roots — was to have China counteract Soviet military power in Asia and beyond.

As a result of Eisenberg's Israel-China military alliance, Pol Pot's Khmer Rouge forces were amply supplied by Israel and China. Logistics were no problem since Eisenberg's Israel Corporation owned a 49 percent share in Zim Shipping, the world's third largest shipping company. Although Eisenberg died from a sudden heart attack in Beijing in 1997, the weapons smuggling activities of his friends in Mossad and Zim Shipping continue to plague Southeast and South Asia.

Under a United Nations, European Union, and Cambodian government weapons buy-back program, Cambodia is striving to eliminate the proliferation of small arms, including AK-47s and grenade launchers and mortars, among the Cambodian population. However, the storage program for the collected weapons has been an ongoing problem for the Cambodians, as cited in an EU report that stated there were four major problems with the program:

1. No formal mechanisms for registering numbers, types and condition of weapons;

2. No records of any of the above;

3. Weapons stored alongside various types of explosives including mines, mortars, grenades and ammunition;

4. Weapons stored in buildings without adequate security.

Storage facilities with so-called "enhanced security" were constructed in Phnom Penh (several facilities), Battambang, Pailin, Banteay Meanchey, Siem Reap, Banteay Srei, Preah Vihear, and Kampong Thom. The suspicions about Israeli involvement in smuggling stored Khmer Rouge and other weapons were heightened in 1999 after a mysterious fire destroyed the Cambodian military weapons storage facility at the Ream Naval Base near Sihanoukville. According to a New Zealand intelligence officer in Cambodia, the depot was destroyed by an Israeli squad after it was revealed they were smuggling weapons from the facility to guerrilla groups throughout Southeast Asia, including the small "Free Vietnam Movement" battling Vietnam's central government and Hmong guerrillas battling Laotian government forces. The Vietnamese became even more suspicious about the role of the depot after weapons from the Ream warehouse were seized by Cambodian and Vietnamese police at the Bavet border checkpoint. The weapons were destined for guerrillas of the Free Vietnam Movement.

WMR visited Phnom Penh, Cambodia and discovered that the Mossad and Cambodian criminal syndicate allies continue to obtain bought-back Cambodian weapons from Cambodian government warehouses and are selling them to guerrilla groups throughout Asia, including Sri Lanka's Tamil Tigers, anti-Laotian Hmongs, the small anti-Communist Free Vietnam Movement, and Burmese tribal guerrilla groups.

WMR photographed a number of Zim shipping containers portside along the Mekong River in Phnom Penh. From this and other port facilities, including the port of Sihanoukville, bought-back Cambodian weapons, some originally provided to the Khmer Rouge by Eisenberg and the Chinese, are making their way to insurgent groups around Asia, possibly including Iraqi guerrillas battling U.S. forces in Iraq.

Not far from Zim's Mekong port facilities in Phnom Penh sits a quiet and unassuming Mossad surveillance station. From this vantage point, Israeli operatives keep a close eye on Mekong river traffic and any "new players" who arrive into town. With new oil deposits being discovered in contested waters of the Gulf of Thailand, border skirmishes in the region are likely to increase, driving up the demand for small arms in the region. The cached weapons in Cambodia stand to make Israeli intelligence a handsome profit.

Recently, the U.S. ambassador to Sri Lanka, Robert Blake, was injured in a Tamil Tiger mortar attack on a Sri Lankan military helicopter transporting him and other Western envoys. Italian ambassador Pio Mariani was also injured in the attack. Although Israel has been supplying weapons and training to Sri Lanka's government to be used against the Tamil Tigers, it has been playing a double game in also supplying Cambodian weapons to the Tamils.

On September 28, 2005, the Zim Asia collided with a Japanese fishing vessel, killing seven Japanese sailors aboard the fishing vessel. The collision occurred 25 miles off the Nosappu Cape in northern Japan. What followed was the arrest in Haifa of the Zim Asia's captain, Moshe Ben David, and the Serbian second captain and Bulgarian lookout man for negligence and failure to save the lives of the Japanese fisherman, a violation of international maritime law. Israeli police confiscated documents from Zim's headquarters. The presence of a Zim ship in northern Japanese waters near North Korea once again heightened concerns about the activities of the shipping company in weapons smuggling.

If Cambodia is any measure of Israel's true intentions, it is clear that Israel's double game seeks to destabilize world and regional peace by selling to adversarial sides in civil and other wars and reaping huge profits as a result.

GOP Sex Scandals

One of the factors that sent the Republicans reeling was the constant involvement of their party leaders at all levels — federal, state, and local — in sordid sex scandals. The "party of family values" became a poster for hypocrisy. *WMR* was at the forefront of reporting on the so-called "Washington Madam" scandal involving not only implicated Republican politicians but also the scandal's links to the firing of a U.S. Attorney in Maryland.

WMR was the first to report on Dick Cheney's involvement with the Pamela Martin & Associates escort firm. On June 4, 2007, *WMR* reported,

Vice President Dick Cheney remains at the center of the "Washington Madam" scandal. While he was President and CEO of Halliburton, Cheney split his time during the mid and late 1990s between Dallas and his home in McLean, a residence described by someone familiar with escort visits to be a "modest townhouse."

We visited the secluded townhouse sub-division in posh McLean, Virginia and found Mr. Cheney's former 6613 Madison of McLean home and, indeed, it is a "modest townhouse," by McLean standards. In 1994, Cheney, the former Secretary of Defense, was 53 years old.

217

WMR's report on Cheney opened a floodgate of additional information from knowledgeable sources, including some of Cheney's old "neighbors" at the nearby headquarters of the CIA in Langley, a small town adjacent to McLean.

On June 7, 2007, *WMR* had a short follow-up on Cheney:

W*MR* has learned that among the clients of Pamela Martin & Associates escort service were a number of Pentagon associates of Dick Cheney when he served as Secretary of Defense during the George H.W. Bush administration."

On July 16, 2007, *WMR* ran the following story:

W*MR* has learned that Vice President Dick Cheney used an alias while he was President and Chief Executive Officer of Halliburton. On occasion, Cheney traveled under the alias of "Bruce Chiles" (phonetic spelling, there is a slight possibility that the name may have also been spelled "Childs"). Cheney's middle name is Bruce. *WMR* has previously reported that some sex escorts knew him by the name "Richard," with no last name used.

Cheney may have used "Bruce Chiles" for both business and pleasure purposes. Cheney, while at Halliburton, engaged in business with Iran and Libya via Halliburton Products & Services Ltd. of Dubai, a foreign subsidiary incorporated in the Cayman Islands. "Chiles" may have also been used to identify Halliburton's then-CEO in dubious deals with nations like Nigeria.

A few days later, on July 20, *WMR* reported additional details on Cheney and the escorts:

W*MR* has received yet additional confirmation that Vice President Dick Cheney was involved with the phone solicitation of escorts from Pamela Martin & Associates, the Washington escort firm that is currently making the news after a federal judge permitted the firm's phone records to be released.

Shortly after being confirmed as Vice President by the Supreme Court, and after he had obtained Secret Service protection, Cheney, who was living at his McLean, Virginia townhouse, took his dog to the McLean Animal Hospital at 1330 Old Chain Bridge Road, not far from his residence off Dolly Madison Boulevard, near CIA headquarters.

According to well-placed U.S. intelligence sources, Cheney forgot his cell phone at the hospital. After Cheney had discovered his cell phone was missing, the Secret Service entered the hospital and clamped a security cordon on the building. No one was permitted to leave or enter as Secret Service agents combed the building for the lost cell phone.

The Secret Service also demanded to know who had accessed and exited the hospital in the meantime and set out to interrogate those who had left the facility.

Eventually, the cell phone was found. However, we have learned that the reason for Cheney being worried was that stored in the cell phone's memory was the number of Pamela Martin & Associates (PMA) and the phone number of at least one escort.

In fact, we have been told by intelligence sources that one female Department of Agriculture official, who received a political appointment from the Bush administration, was chewed out by Cheney for not returning his cell phone call shortly after his inauguration in January 2001. The female had received a message that the Vice President had phoned and wanted her to call back. Thinking that it was a joke, the Agriculture official ignored the message.

Soon, she received word that Cheney was irritated over not being phoned back and the female official phoned the White House switchboard and asked to speak to Cheney. Eventually, she made contact with Cheney, who told her that she should have known his personal cell phone number since he and she had used it before to talk to one another. It is known that several PMA escorts were educated and professional working women in the Washington area.

WMR previously reported that Cheney used PMA services while chief of Halliburton and that at least one phone call was made to the service from the Bush-Cheney 2000 Transition office in McLean, which had previously served as a Halliburton office.

ABC News, which had obtained part of Pamela Martin's phone list from the firm's proprietor, Deborah Jeane Palfrey proceeded to quash the story after the network received tons of pressure from the Bush administration.

On July 9, 2007, *WMR* provided more details on the Washington sex scandal, studiously ignored by the corporate media:

Deborah Jeane Palfrey, the proprietor of Pamela Martin & Associates (PMA), the sexual fantasy escort firm that provided introductions for some of Washington's most politically powerful men to female escorts, maintains she was unfairly singled out for prosecution because of the moral zealousness of the Justice Department and other federal law enforcement agencies.

An examination of the phone records of PMA from the mid 1990s to about 1997 reveals that calls were placed by the agency mostly to land line phones at offices, homes, and hotels. Calls were also placed by PMA to the escorts, who were independent contractors for the firm. Towards the end of the 1990s and the new decade, more cell phones were used to make calls and landline use drastically tapered off.

As cell phone numbers became more portable, the records from 2001 to 2006 show a number of non-Washington area cell phone numbers increasingly used to phone PMA from the Washington DC area, particularly numbers from Georgia (Atlanta), Texas (San Antonio), West Virginia, North Carolina (Raleigh), South Carolina (Columbia), Illinois, Florida (West Palm Beach), and California (La Jolla and Poway).

Poway, just north of San Diego, was the headquarters of ADCS, Inc. and its subsidiaries. ADCS was the company headed by Brent Wilkes, a key GOP figure involved in the scandal that sent San Diego Republican Congressman Randy "Duke" Cunningham to prison for various felonies, including bribery. Cunningham was also linked to the use of prostitutes on his MZM, Inc.-supplied yacht, the "Duke-ster," Cunningham's party boat located in the Washington Marina. MZM was headed by GOP contributor Mitchell Wade, who pleaded guilty to paying bribes to Cunningham in February 2006.

Wade stated to federal investigators that he had an arrangement with Shirlington Limousine, which had an arrangement with an escort service to transport prostitutes to suites at the Watergate Hotel and the Westin Grand paid for by Wilkes. The suites often hosted "poker parties," at which Cunningham, former CIA Director Porter Goss, Goss' House Intelligence Committee staffer Brant "Nine Fingers" Bassett, and Goss' Executive Director Kyle "Dusty" Foggo were reportedly in attendance.

There are several calls between PMA and a Poway cell phone number in January 2006, just three months before the Shirlington Limousine-Wilkes-Wade-Cunningham story hit the newspapers. Palfrey maintained a residence in Escondido, also the home town of Cunningham, during this time frame. Palfrey does recall that someone using the first name of "Brett" or "Brent" did phone the agency on occasion from the San Diego area.

Cunningham resigned from Congress in November 2005 after pleading guilty to receiving bribes from Wilkes and Wade.

WMR has determined that the PMA escort business was, in addition to several other notable Washington hotels, centered on two hotels close to the White House: the St. Regis Hotel and the Capitol Hilton, which are across the street from one another on 16th Street, a few blocks north of the White House.

The nexus of the prosecution of Jeane Palfrey and the Cunningham-Wilkes-Wade-Shirlington Limousine case is noteworthy. Palfrey's case also involves the sacked U.S. Attorney for Baltimore, Tom DiBiagio, who was investigating Republican Governor Bob Ehrlich's staff for use of prostitutes and other corruption. DiBiagio was fired by the Justice Department for pursuing the case against Ehrlich. U.S. Attorney for San Diego Carol Lam was fired, in part, for her aggressive prosecution of Cunningham and his cronies.

The prosecution of Palfrey as part of a vendetta by Justice against those involved in major investigations of GOP corruption involving escorts may be a large part of the reason U.S. Judge for DC Gladys Kessler permitted Palfrey to release her phone records.

Louisiana Republican Senator David Vitter and State Department Agency for International Development director Randall Tobias were two of the most notable clients of Pamela Martin & Associates "outed" in the sex scandal, however, the corporate media ensured the story died with these two top Republicans.

***

On October 9, 2007, *WMR* ran a story about Idaho Senator Larry Craig, who pleaded guilty to charges of lewd conduct in a Minneapolis Airport men's room earlier in the year:

W*MR* has obtained an e-mail from Dan Whiting (press secretary to Idaho Senator Larry Craig), to an *Idaho*

Statesman reporter. The e-mail is dated September 25, 2007. Whiting uses past Democratic support for Craig in defending the Senator over the incident in a Minneapolis Airport men's room that resulted in Craig's guilty plea for disorderly conduct after he engaged in a repertoire known to be a means to signal someone an interest in having homosexual contact.

The e-mail to Idaho Statesman reporter Todd Gillman, who covered the Craig story, states that "the Idaho Statesman started its investigation no later than the middle of last November. Mike Rogers, the activist blogger, started harassing Sen. Larry Craig's office about his 'sources' in August 2004."

Whiting then goes on to dig deeper into the conspiracy against Craig. "Because Dan Popkey is a prominent journalist in Idaho, especially among news and political geeks, it was noticed that he wasn't producing his twice-weekly column. Because he called so many people about the rumors, word quickly spread that this is what he was working on. Consequently, every media outlet in Idaho would ask me periodically about it."

Craig's press secretary then asks, "Is 'news' media simply a means to escalate the old political rumor mills? . . . When does a reporter cross the line between conducting due diligence and helping to spread a rumor by lending credibility to the rumor simply by asking about it?"

Whiting then uses Democrats to defend past allegations against Craig. "I reference the Califano Report from the 1982 [Congressional] page scandal. The CBS reporter who broke the 'story,' and came to then Rep. Craig's office and accused him of being involved, was rebuked by Califano for helping to lend credibility to the page's story. [Joseph Califano was the Secretary of Health, Education, and Welfare under President Jimmy Carter, but was fired in a Cabinet reshuffle in 1979]. According to the Report, then Rep. Patricia Schroeder's office didn't believe the page's story, but when the reporter asked about it, they decided to ask the DOJ to investigate. I quote from a column by Califano in the *Washington Post* (10/4/2006), 'The big surprise came when the two pages who CBS had put on its evening news show recanted. They testified under oath that they had lied and that CBS reporter John Ferrugia had put words in their mouths.'"

What Whiting does not say is whether the pages had been threatened by the powerful political forces involved in the 1982 scandal unless they recanted their stories. Whiting, interestingly, notes that Ferrugia is now a reporter in Colorado and "is credited with breaking the story about sexual misconduct at the Air Force Academy."

When a reporter covers sexual perverts for a number of years, he or she develops a sense for who is lying and who is telling the truth. What Califano and Whiting fail to realize is that in saying CBS News got the page story wrong they are suggesting that CBS News' Roger Mudd, the anchor, also got it wrong, in addition to the entire CBS News staff.

Whiting ends his e-mail by asking, "what is more important ó political rumors or issues of the day? Why is so much time spent on the salacious, controversial, etc. and seemingly so little on the depth of the issues?"

The simple answer is that it was Craig's Republican Party that delved into the salacious when they went after President Bill Clinton's sexual affairs. Craig even called Clinton a "naughty . . . a nasty, bad, naughty boy." Craig obviously does not understand that when you go to the toilet in a glass men's room, you shouldn't throw stones, and will not admit that he was also a "naughty . . . a nasty, bad, naughty boy," both in 1982 and 2007.

The corporate media treatment of the GOP escort sex scandal, as compared to how the same media treated the allegations against President Clinton by women, must serve as a classic example of the dangers inherent in allowing almost complete control of the media by one political party. *WMR* dared to tread where the corporate media dared not go. It is one reason why people, en masse, began turning away from newspapers and television and to the Internet for their news.

Beyond the U.S. Attorneys firings

*W*MR went beyond the headlines of Bush's firings of a dozen U.S. Attorneys around the country after his 2004 re-election, concentrating attention on some less well-known cases involving U.S. Attorneys. On August 16, 2007, *WMR* reported:

*W*MR has previously reported on the mysterious December 2003 death of Assistant U.S. Attorney for Maryland Jonathan Luna.

WMR reported on May 14, 2007: "A husband and father of two, Luna had departed in his vehicle, strangely leaving his cell phone on his desk at his office, and drove a circuitous route through Delaware, New Jersey, and then Pennsylvania before he was found in a creek near the Pennsylvania Turnpike in Denver, Pennsylvania, stabbed to death 36 times, supposedly with his own pen knife. Federal authorities leaned toward a suicide but local investigators treated the death as a homicide."

In 2004, DiBiagio claimed he was being pressured to stop his investigation of Ehrlich's staff for links to gambling (particularly the gambling interests of jailed Maryland/DC GOP lobbyist Jack Abramoff), prostitution, and other corruption and filed a threat report with the FBI. The *Washington Post* and *Washington Times* then reported that Luna was fearful that DiBiagio was going to fire him, which led to Luna's "suicide." It is a charge DiBiagio strongly denied. DiBiagio told the *New York Times* that the pressure from Ehrlich's office and the Justice Department served "to intimidate my office and shut down the investigations." Maryland Democratic Senator Ben Cardin has asked for an investigation of DiBiagio's firing.

The investigation of Ehrlich's office's role in the prostitution investigation has been linked to police misconduct in Baltimore surrounding the use by former Baltimore Police Commissioner Ed Norris of Deborah Jeane Palfrey's Pamela Martin & Associates escort service, which ensnared a number of top Republicans, including Louisiana Senator David Vitter and Assistant Secretary of State Randall Tobias. The Baltimore prostitution connection may also be linked to the use of escorts by then-New York Mayor Rudolph Giuliani.

Luna's mysterious death has not been an isolated incident among federal prosecutors during the George W. Bush presidency.

On September 9, 2003, the former U.S. Attorney for Eastern Texas, Michael Bradford, who served for seven years until April 2001, was found dead near his car in a wooded area in Hardin County, Texas. Bradford was 51 and was appointed U.S. Attorney on the advice of Texas' longtime Congressman Jack Brooks, a no-nonsense investigator of administration scandals, Republican and Democrat. As U.S. Attorney, Bradford successfully sued several large oil companies to recover $400 million in royalty payments due the federal government. Bradford suffered a gunshot wound to his head, and police found a shotgun near his body. Police ruled the death a suicide.

Bradford's replacement, Wes Rivers, served as U.S. Attorney for East Texas for seven months until being downgraded to Assistant U.S. Attorney in Tyler, Texas. Rivers prosecuted several drug cartel leaders. Last month, Rivers died suddenly of a brain aneurysm while vacationing with his family on the Bolivar Peninsula, near Galveston. Rivers was 56.

During the evening of October 11, 2001, Tom Wales, 49, the Assistant U.S. Attorney for Washington state, was shot through a window in his basement. The assailant fired the shots from Wales' back yard. Wales later died in the hospital. The FBI investigation, code named "SEPROM" [Seattle Prosecutor Murder], remains unsolved. John McKay, the U.S. Attorney for Western Washington, who pressured both the Justice Department and FBI to more vigorously investigate Wales' murder, was, like Maryland U.S. Attorney Tom DiBiagio, fired by U.S. Attorney General Alberto Gonzales for asking too many questions and not being seen as a "loyal Bushie."

In 2004, two female federal prosecutors in Texas, who were prosecuting cases involving Medicare fraud by Novation LLC and other medical care providers, were found dead from suspicious causes. Federal prosecutor in Fort Worth, Thelma Colbert, was found dead in her swimming pool on July 20, 2004, while Assistant U.S. Attorney Shannon Ross was found dead in her home on September 13, 2004. The Tarrant County medical examiner ruled Colbert's death an accident. The Dallas County medical examiner determined Ross' death was from "natural causes."

By the summer of 2007, I told several colleagues about a new syndrome suffered by many journalists and others who followed the Bush administration: moral indignation fatigue. How much more could a person take in trying to grasp the dishonesty, corruption, and pure evil of the Bush crime family and their cronies?

... And Then Came Blackwater

Although there are over 120 private security companies active in Iraq, Blackwater USA is the most controversial and, with its right-wing roots, the most politically-connected to the Bush administration. By mid-2007, Blackwater and its contracts with the State Department had come under intense congressional scrutiny. *WMR* had been on the story from the very beginning.

On September 29, 2005, for example, *WMR* reported the following:

Blackwater USA represents a return to "Praise the Lord and Pass the Ammunition." According to a knowledgeable political insider in Washington, the private military contractor Blackwater USA has close ties to the Christian Right. The Prince Group, the McLean, Virginia-based parent company of Blackwater, recently hired Joseph E. Schmitz as its Chief Operating Officer and General Counsel. Previously, Schmitz was the Inspector General of the Department of Defense. Schmitz was a Special Assistant to Attorney General Edwin Meese III, who is both an official of the dominionist Christian Fellowship Foundation and a Heritage Foundation Fellow who recently authored a blueprint for rebuilding New Orleans and Louisiana. Perhaps not coincidentally, Blackwater USA and its sister company Presidential Airways, have been providing security for petrochemical industry and other installations damaged by Hurricane Katrina

Joseph Schmitz is active in the Washington, DC Lawyers' Chapter of the right-wing Federalist Society, the same group with which the new Chief Justice John G. Roberts was affiliated. Schmitz is also a member of the Sovereign Military Order of Malta.

Schmitz was accused of covering up several investigations into fraud, waste and abuse within the Rumsfeld Pentagon. He is the son of the late GOP far-right congressman (and segregationist American Independent Party presidential candidate) John G. Schmitz. Joesph Schmitz's sister is former Washington State schoolteacher Mary Kay Letourneau, who was jailed for child rape after having sex with her 12-year old sixth grade student. After Letourneau was released from prison in 2004, and after she had two children with the student, she and the boy, Vili Fualaau, married. Their sexual relationship began in 1996, when Letourneau was 34.

John G. Schmitz was himself discovered to have had an affair out of wedlock with one of his Santa Ana College political science students. In 1982, a 13-month old infant boy, who was the product of Schmitz's relationship with a German national, was rushed to an Orange County, California hospital with a hair so tightly tied in a square knot around the boy's penis, it was almost severed. Child abuse charges were later dropped against the German college student, and the infant was restored to her custody.

Joseph Schmitz is not the only connection between Blackwater and right-wing GOP politicians. Blackwater's CEO and co-founder is Michigan-based Erik D. Prince: ex-US Navy SEAL, heir to an auto parts fortune, former intern for President George H.W. Bush, and contributor, through a Virginia entity called Prince Household LLC, as well as the aforementioned Prince Group, to such right-wing Republicans as recently indicted Tom DeLay, Peter Hoekstra and North Carolina Rep. Sue Myrick (appointed to the Joint Congressional "Review" panel for Hurricane Katrina relief). Hoekstra, the current House Permanent Select Committee on Intelligence (HPSCI) chairman, has been pressuring the CIA to accept more intelligence from HPSCI sources. The close connection between Hoekstra and Blackwater, a company that advertises its own intelligence gathering services, should be of significant concern to non-politicized and career U.S. intelligence professionals.

Erik Prince's sister Betsy, who is chairman of the Michigan GOP, is married to Dick DeVos, the son of Amway founder Richard DeVos, a member of the board of the conservative and Christian Dominionist Council for National Policy (CNP), an umbrella organization where he rubs shoulders with such leading right-wingers as Jack Abramoff, Howard Ahmanson, the Leadership Institute's Morton Blackwell, Focus on the Family's James Dobson, Coral Ridge's Dr. D. James Kennedy, Edwin Meese III, Pat Robertson, Richard Viguerie, and Paul Weyrich. The DeVos family has used corporate entities such as the Windquest Group, DP Fox Ventures, and Alticor, Inc. to funnel many thousands of dollars to conservative GOP politicians and their PACs, including Restoring the American Dream board member Sue Myrick, South Dakota Sen. John Thune, and Louisiana Rep. Bobby Jindal.

Blackwater maintains the largest private military training facility in the United States. Located on an abandoned U.S. military base at Moyock, North Carolina on the edge of the Great Dismal Swamp near the Virginia border, Blackwater's Security Consulting subsidiary attracts military and paramilitary trainees from around the country and the world. Former Chilean and Honduran military personnel have been trained at Moyock prior to deployment to Iraq. What is even more attractive for the Bush administration and Blackwater is the fact that, as a private company, Blackwater is far removed from potential oversight via government inspectors general [or at least some of them, see below], Freedom of Information Act requests, the Government Accountability Office (GAO), and snooping reporters.

Iraqi insurgents killed and mutilated the bodies of four Blackwater mercenaries near Fallujah, Iraq in April 2004, an act that triggered a massive U.S. military response that laid waste to the "city of mosques." Recently, Blackwater mercenaries have been patrolling the streets of New Orleans along with other mercenaries from the United States and Israel.

After the apparently wanton slaughter of innocent Iraqis by Blackwater bodyguards in September 2007, public and congressional pressure on the administration forced additional disclosures. On November 14, 2007, *WMR* reported,

In testimony today before the House Committee on Oversight and Government Reform, State Department Inspector General Howard "Cookie" Krongard at first denied that his brother, former CIA Executive Director Alvin B. "Buzzy" Krongard, had any relationship with Blackwater USA. The State Department IG changed his testimony however, after the committee produced documents proving that Buzzy Krongard had been invited to join Blackwater Worldwide's Advisory Board, and had accepted the invitation, and was actually in attendance at a Blackwater Advisory Board meeting in Williamsburg, Virginia, mere hours before Howard Krongard's testimony.

Howard Krongard first stated that he had no way of knowing whether his brother accepted the Blackwater invitation, and after the committee produced an e-mail from Blackwater CEO Erik Prince thanking Buzzy Krongard and other advisory board members for accepting the invitation, Howard Krongard changed his testimony again, and said that after speaking to his brother during a hearing break, he learned that Buzzy was, in fact, in Williamsburg at the Blackwater meeting the prior day. Howard Krongard then stated before the committee that he was officially recusing himself from all matters dealing with the current investigations of Blackwater.

According to a report by the committee's Democratic majority, Blackwater is under Justice Department investigation for the smuggling of weapons to Iraq, in addition to the FBI and Justice Department investigations of the shooting deaths of 17 Iraqi civilians on September 16, 2007. The FBI has already determined that 14 of the deaths were unjustified. It is believed that some of the smuggled weapons have ended up in the hands of the Turkish Kurdistan Workers' Party (PKK) and other insurgent groups in Iraq.

After Howard Krongard expressed his belief that his brother had not accepted the Blackwater invitation to serve on its advisory board, chairman Henry Waxman informed the State Department official that committee staff had contacted the conference hotel in Williamsburg and they confirmed that Buzzy Krongard was a guest. Howard Krongard said his brother was at home when he phoned him during an early afternoon break during the hearing.

Howard Krongard, a graduate of Harvard Law School and a former General Counsel for the accounting firm Deloitte Touche, did not seem to understand that his brother's relationship with Blackwater was a major of conflict of interest, since the State Department Inspector General has oversight authority over State contractors, including Blackwater.

A number of Howard Krongard's senior staff told the committee in interviews and sworn testimony that Howard Krongard repeatedly interfered in investigations, squashing some and, in some cases, caused the shredding of critical evidentiary documents. Howard Krongard has also been accused by Justice Department officials of blocking their investigation of alleged Blackwater arms smuggling to Iraq.

Trying to obfuscate the committee's line of questioning was California Republican Darrell Issa (a past defender of Blackwater in a committee hearing involving testimony by Erik Prince), who attempted to compare the debacle over the building of the grandiose U.S. embassy in Baghdad to the construction of the Capitol Visitors Center in Washington. Issa may have his own conflict of interest with Blackwater.

The committee produced a June 10, 2007 e-mail from Blackwater President Gary Jackson to Erik Prince regarding the selection of advisory board members for Blackwater's Worldwide Advisory Board. It suggests an honorarium of $2500 for members for regular meetings, with expenses, and double that amount for "emergency" meetings. Jackson indicates that Prince's top selections for the board were Buzzy Krongard and retired Army Major General David Grange, a frequent CNN commentator. Jackson's e-mail also states, "I think we should try to find someone from big business, a successful American businessman with military background if possible and maybe a former politician: someone *like Issa from California* [emphasis added]."

229

On November 16, in an article subtitled "The 'Cookie' Crumbles," *WMR* cited the following communication from the House committee:

On Wednesday, November 14, 2007, the full Committee held a hearing entitled, "Assessing the State Department Inspector General." At this hearing, Inspector General Howard J. Krongard testified that his brother, Alvin "Buzzy"Krongard, told him that he was not on the board of Blackwater USA and had no connections to Blackwater. Yesterday, in response to a letter from the Committee, Buzzy Krongard called the Committee staff and said that contrary to Howard Krongard's testimony, he did tell his brother about his relationship with Blackwater.

The information from Buzzy Krongard raises serious questions about the veracity of Howard Krongard's testimony before the Committee.

The committee's communication contained a memo from chairman Waxman which cited possible perjury on the part of Howard Krongard:

On November 15, I sent a letter to Buzzy Krongard requesting an interview and documents relating to his communications with Howard Krongard about Blackwater. After receiving the letter, Buzzy Krongard called Committee staff and provided information that differed significantly from Howard Krongard's testimony.

Buzzy Krongard stated that Howard Krongard called him specifically to ask about any relationship he had with Blackwater "in preparation for his testimony" to the Committee. Buzzy Krongard stated, "He asked me whether I had any financial interest or any ties to Blackwater, and so I told him, 'I'm going on their Board.'" According to Buzzy Krongard, "He responded by saying, 'Why would you do that?' and 'Are you sure that's a good idea?'" Buzzy Krongard then said, "I told him that was my decision, not his, and that we just differed on that."

Buzzy Krongard stated that during the Committee hearing, he was at home watching it live. He listened to Howard Krongard's prepared opening statement. Then, he heard Howard Krongard offer spontaneously the comment that his brother had no connection to Blackwater. Buzzy Krongard said, "You could have blown me over." During the hearing, he attempted to reach Howard Krongard by telephone. Before he could reach him, Buzzy Krongard received a call from Howard Krongard and explained again that he was a member of the Board.

On December 7, a date already commemorated to infamy, Howard Krongard announced his resignation as Inspector General of the State Department.

And as 2007 drew to a close, it appeared that some Democrats like Waxman were more than fed up with the usual Bush administration lies, and more than willing to chase the weasels to their dens. Would they? The rest of us could only wonder what the next outrage would be.

Wayne Madsen in Oregon during Northwest promotional tour for his book, *Jaded Tasks*.

Afterword

The political trek from 2000 to 2007 was a long slog with many pitfalls and disappointments. By 2007, however, with calls for the impeachment of Bush and Cheney at an all-time high, there appeared to be finally a light at the end of the tunnel. The Internet permitted a coalescing of progressive and anti-war forces that would have been impossible in the past. People around the world, through the Internet, became aware that "globalization = corporatism + planet-wide fascism."

But there were also danger signs. Neocons, if anything, are most dangerous when they are cornered. That is why they, like Nazis and racists, must be marginalized as a fringe and dangerous political grouping, unworthy of attention or representation in legislatures.

On a speaking trip through northern California in August 2007, I saw that the old spirit of the American people to fight against oppressors like the Bush-Cheney clique was still present. However, so were the fringe supporters of the right wing and the neocons.

The people must also take back their public airwaves and conduits for information from the propagandists and perception managers who seek to enforce a dangerous "group-think" on the world's population. The announcement that News Corporation's neocon chief Rupert Murdoch was acquiring the *Wall Street Journal* in August 2007 (there were also rumors that Murdoch was also going to try and buy the *New York Times*), thus adding the financial world's newspaper-of-record to his other vast media holdings, was seen as a sign that the global neocon movement was not seeing a reduction of power but, in fact, was gaining more power and influence.

After the neocons seized control of France in 2007, President Nicolas Sarkozy's Finance Minister, Christine Lagarde, told the French to abandon their "old national habit" of thinking too much. Lagarde, a product of neocon training while serving as an executive of the Chicago law firm Baker and McKenzie, in the city that spawned the neocon movement in the University of Chicago political science classes of Professor Leo Strauss, an admirer of national socialism, said, "There is hardly an ideology that we [the French] haven't turned into a theory ... This is why I would like to tell you: enough thinking, already. Roll up your sleeves." Lagarde was merely paraphrasing the sign above the Auschwitz concentration camp: "Arbeit macht frei" — "work brings freedom."

Globalization is nothing more than corporate exploitation of the poor, and the increasingly marginalized middle class, on a global scale. The working class serving the interests of a powerful elite is not a new idea, it is an ancient construct that has been repackaged thanks to a complicit media and a bought-and-paid-for academic community. Honest intellectualism and humanitarianism, as far as the neocons are concerned, spawn dangerous notions that threaten the elites and the oligarchs. Talk of environmentalism, Communism, socialism, ecumenicism, and sustainable living standards, by 2007, became subversive activities worthy of total information surveillance.

However, by 2007, poll numbers in the United States and elsewhere were showing that a sense of frustration and indignation was sweeping some countries that had been taken over by global corporatist and neocon interests. The defeat by the progressive Democratic Party of Japan of the pro-business Liberal Democratic Party in the election for the Diet's House of Councillors, the upper house, and the failure of the pro-U.S. Prime Minister, Shinzo Abe, to step down, pointed to the trouble facing neocons globally and their determination to hold on to power at all costs.

It was clear by 2007 that there was a popular resistance against corporatist fascist forces at all levels in all states and nations on all continents. But as this book goes to press, there is another ominous trend. The cause of liberty and freedom in the United States and other countries is losing ground, and losing it rapidly.

The Democratic Congress became known as a facilitator and collaborator for Bush administration actions and policies rather than a constitutionally-mandated resistance body. House of Representatives Speaker Nancy Pelosi maintained that impeachment of Bush and Cheney were "off the table" and her policy on that issue was echoed by a majority of Democrats. Meanwhile, Democrats in the Senate and House not only voted to fund an extension of Bush's unpopular war in Iraq but voted to give Bush enhanced electronic surveillance authority — all this in the face of repeated perjury before the Congress by then-Attorney General Gonzales over past illegal domestic surveillance by the Bush administration.

With the election of the Democratic Congress in 2006, the light at the end of the tunnel grew brighter. However, after the new Congress continued to support the fascist policies of the Bush administration in terms of support for the Pentagon, increased electronic surveillance, permitting the administration to use spy satellites for domestic intelligence gathering, withdrawing the threat of impeachment, and other outrageous policies of appeasement, the light, once again, grew dimmer.

As for *WMR*'s shoestring and modest attempt to make a difference in an age of mega-media corporations, there were some signs of success. Although they would dare not admit to it, *WMR* was often consulted by the corporate media, including the *New York Post, New York Daily News*, Bloomberg News, CBS News, MS-NBC, Fox News, and a host of others. Sometimes, a person can invent a new mousetrap.

The best sign of success was the number of inquiries from students at some of the country's best journalism schools asking about summer internships at *WMR*. With that kind of interest, it was clear that *WMR* was headed in the right direction

However, it will take millions of people around the world spending $15 a day, and more than a few new "rat" traps and Web sites, to turn the tide against the corporate fascist grip that is seizing control of the entire planet.

Appendix A

Excerpts from hearings of South African Truth and reconcilliation Commission

September 11, 1998:

MR BIZOS: When you became a security policeman at the Security Police Headquarters what year was that?

MR WILLIAMSON: During 1980 Mr Chairman,

MR BIZOS: During 1980? And when did you attend the first Sanhedrin meeting?

MR WILLIAMSON: Mr Chairman, I would imagine relatively soon.

MR BIZOS: Thereafter?

MR WILLIAMSON: Probably in the first, sometime in the first quarter of 1980 or mid 1980.

MR BIZOS: And how often did the Sanhedrin meet?

MR WILLIAMSON: The Sanhedrin was — I think there were basically two Sanhedrins. One was a more in depth one on a weekly basis but I think, if I'm not wrong Mr Chairman, that's what was termed the Sanhedrin and then we had a daily meeting as well.

MR BIZOS: The daily meeting which was a junior Sanhedrin?

MR WILLIAMSON: I would — yes I think, but here I stand under correction but I think it could be the junior Sanhedrin.

MR BIZOS: The junior Sanhedrin, yes, very good. Now tell us who were the ex official members of the main Sanhedrin?

MR WILLIAMSON: Mr Chairman as far as I know this was a meeting of the staff officers of security headquarters which would then be the commander, the deputy commander.

MR BIZOS: No, just give us names from 1980 to 1984 please when you attended the main Sanhedrin meetings?

MR WILLIAMSON: I would imagine 1980, certainly General Coetzee.

MR BIZOS: Did he preside over the main Sanhedrin?

MR WILLIAMSON: At times.

MR BIZOS: Regularly?

MR WILLIAMSON: Yes.

MR BIZOS: Yes and who else would be there regularly?

MR WILLIAMSON: The deputy who at that time was Brigadier du Preez.

MR BIZOS: Du Preez, yes?

MR WILLIAMSON: And then group heads and some section heads.

MR BIZOS: Give us the group heads that were there at the time please, from 1980 to approximately 1984. There may have been changes we understand but the familiar faces on the main Sanhedrin?

MR WILLIAMSON: Mr Chairman, I'd have to get some type of an organogram or something to get all the names but I'd say obviously my group head, Brigadier Goosen, would be there.

MR BIZOS: Brigadier Goosen would be there, yes?

MR WILLIAMSON: And then as I said, if I go down the passage ...[intervention]

MR BIZOS: Let me help you. Let me help you.

MR WILLIAMSON: Thank you Mr Chairman.

MR BIZOS: Colonel Heuér?

MR WILLIAMSON: Yes, possibly.

MR BIZOS: You see there's not all documents ...[intervention]

CHAIRPERSON: Sorry, can you repeat that name?

MR BIZOS: H-e-u-é-r. His initials are A.N. Heuér, Heuér, Brigadier, sometimes called Colonel or it's Brigadier. You see not all documents were destroyed. Then F.W. Schoon?

MR WILLIAMSON: That's correct, he would be there.

MR BIZOS: Yes and then B.F. Kotze, Brigadier?

MR WILLIAMSON: Yes, I'm prepared to say yes, Mr Chairman, I remember him vaguely.

MR BIZOS: You remember him vaguely, alright. Colonel later Brigadier J.C. Broodryk?

MR WILLIAMSON: Yes, he was the legal section.

MR BIZOS: Then Brigadier C.J.W. du Plooy?

MR WILLIAMSON: Yes, he was training section.

MR BIZOS: Colonel H.J.J. Smit?

MR WILLIAMSON: Yes, I think he was also in the training section in the library, I'm not sure.

MR BIZOS: Yes, we had a representative from Namibia here for the sake of completeness didn't we?

MR WILLIAMSON: In the Sanhedrin?

MR BIZOS: Yes.

MR WILLIAMSON: Yes, we had also military intelligence.

MR BIZOS: Yes, we'll come to them.

MR WILLIAMSON: We also had Railway Police.

MR BIZOS: But here H.J.J. Smit was from South West Africa — I beg your pardon, he was dealing with the South West African section?

MR WILLIAMSON: He was South West African, yes.

MR BIZOS: Yes, thank you. Yes, yes I must be careful.

Lieutenant Colonel Joubert of Group H?

MR WILLIAMSON: Ja, I — was he Church? Churches?

MR BIZOS: No, no I don't see that but everyone that was head of a group was there?

MR WILLIAMSON: Yes the group heads were there, would be there but there would also be section heads.

MR BIZOS: Section heads?

MR WILLIAMSON: At times.

MR BIZOS: And you were a section head?

MR WILLIAMSON: That is correct.

MR BIZOS: At times. How often did you attend this Sanhedrin meeting?

MR WILLIAMSON: I often attended the weekly meeting because there was something called the "Insum", the "inlightings summary" and I presented ...[intervention]

MR BIZOS: Yes so you would then — you presented that to the .... [intervention]

MR WILLIAMSON: Not the whole thing, I would present something from my side.

MR BIZOS: From your side?

MR WILLIAMSON: Which then would be ...[intervention]

MR BIZOS: So ...[intervention]

MR WILLIAMSON: Listened to by the meeting and a decision would be made as to whether this was believed by the meeting to be accurate and then it would be approved basically for transmission up the channels.

MR BIZOS: And what was the day on which the Sanhedrin met? What day of the week?

MR WILLIAMSON: I wanted to say immediately Friday, Mr Chairman, but I'm sure one of my colleagues can easily tell me.

MR BIZOS: Yes, well it doesn't matter really for my purposes at this stage, it met regularly every week?

MR WILLIAMSON: Yes.

MR BIZOS: And it was probably the most important co-ordinating meeting of the Security Police that was to be held and generally speaking it was presided over by General Coetzee or if he was not available for some reason or other, his deputy?

MR WILLIAMSON: Mr Chairman, it was presided over by General Coetzee or whoever else was at the time the commanding officer.

MR BIZOS: Yes?

239

MR WILLIAMSON: So between 1980 and the end of 1985, General Coetzee would only have presided over it ...[intervention]

MR BIZOS: Until 1983?

MR WILLIAMSON: That is correct.

MR BIZOS: Did you attend the daily Sanhedrin meetings?

MR WILLIAMSON: Mr Chairman, on occasion I attended them but that was, ja, I think I often attended.

MR BIZOS: You often attended and to which Sanhedrin meeting was the death of Ruth First reported?

MR WILLIAMSON: I have no idea Mr Chairman.

MR BIZOS: You don't remember?

MR WILLIAMSON: No.

MR BIZOS: Very well.

MR WILLIAMSON: I don't know whether it was a daily one or the weekly "Insum" meeting.

MR BIZOS: Yes. Please tell us in your own words and for as long as you like what was the main function of these Sanhedrins?

MR WILLIAMSON: Sanhedrin.

MR BIZOS: Sanhedrin, okay.

MR WILLIAMSON: It was — the name Sanhedrin was a nickname, I'm sure there was an official name but everybody referred it to Sanhedrin: "Jy moet vanoggend Sanhedrin toe gaan of more Sanhedrin toe gaan". I believe that the main purpose of the meeting in my experience was to get input from the section heads and group heads dealing with various problem areas on what had occurred either the day before or the week, in the past week, so obviously at the weekly meeting this would be a broader discussion. At the morning meeting it was just a discussion about "Last night they blew up Sasol — what happened, who went there, are there any clues" da-da da-da because — and then some type of a report was drawn up which, once that meeting had given that report, it was really a report back.

That meeting was, I would imagine, formerly reporting to the head of the Security Branch and he then would report to the Commissioner, the Commissioner to the Minister, the Minister to the Cabinet and obviously also on a weekly basis there was a document, the "Insum" was a written. I think maybe even everyday there were also — yes there was but it was on an A4 paper type of report but on a weekly basis there was a little booklet brought out, an A5 booklet type of thing which had a much more detailed basic summary of what was going on and in particular what could be expected to be going on in the next week and my responsibility from intelligence was to put my input and the people listening to the input and whichever people were there or this wasn't only a report by all of us, just to the commanding officer who would then go up to the top structures, it was also so we could each be informed from the different desks what was going on.

MR BIZOS: Yes, you told us about Sasol being blown up. What about the other way, what about the successes of the "manne" during the week or during the day against the enemy?

MR WILLIAMSON: Yes Mr Chairman, what about them?

MR BIZOS: Wasn't there a report about that?

MR WILLIAMSON: There were at times I'm sure reports about that.

MR BIZOS: No, don't say I'm sure, you were there, you attended the meetings regularly.

MR WILLIAMSON: Absolutely, I mean if there had been — how would one term it, some type of a confrontation or a shoot-out or contact yes, it was reported.

MR BIZOS: Or elimination?

MR WILLIAMSON: No. To my knowledge no clandestine operation would have been reported, no.

MR BIZOS: Why not? Particularly in the weekly Sanhedrin?

MR WILLIAMSON: Mr Chairman, I don't even know whether the question's actually really serious because you know it's just maybe, the culture is just so different but I spent all these years in this culture of intelligence in security and it was need to know and if this wasn't such a serious matter it would actually be laughable to suggest that any member of the Sanhedrin would come to the meeting and say: "General, yesterday in Maputo we blew up a car and six ANC died". It may have come as a factual report: "Yesterday there was an explosion at the corner of such and such a street in Maputo and such and such a member of the ANC is believed to have died or was injured" etc. etc. That was — a report would have just come through in that way.

MR BIZOS: Let us question you on that basis, Mr Williamson. How many reports were made either to the big Sanhedrin or the small Sanhedrin about ANC activists, who you would have called terrorists of course, were killed in the country and outside the country. How many reports of deaths were made to the main and/or subsidiary Sanhedrin?

MR BIZOS: Mr Chairman, there's absolutely no way that I could put a number to it. When it came to deaths outside South Africa in the area for which I was responsible to gather information, I for example remember specifically reporting on Joe Gwabe's death.

MR BIZOS: Yes?

MR WILLIAMSON: So it was done Mr Chairman and I used to hear from the South West Africa desk, there was a contact, so many people were killed. That was on a daily basis what was going on.

MR BIZOS: Let us just expand that, let us expand that a little. How many chief representatives of the ANC's death were reported to the Sanhedrin in your presence? We know that the Swaziland head of mission of the ANC was killed, was that reported?

MR WILLIAMSON: I didn't report it, I believe it should have been reported yes. We can accept it was reported.

MR BIZOS: No I asked, and it — we can accept that within this culture with which you were so familiar and which we are so unfamiliar with, that that would have been reported.

MR WILLIAMSON: I accept that it's one of the things that ...[intervention]

MR BIZOS: Yes, we know that the ...[intervention]

CHAIRPERSON: It would have been extremely important, certainly?

***

September 28, 1998:

MR WILLIAMSON: But my role in the Defence Force as I said, was as SO1 in charge of "ander lande" which was, I was dealing with the geopolitical implications of Soviet power, etc Mr Chairman.

MR LEVINE: A document was put to you, Exhibit W about Sanhedrin, do you have it or can I put one in front of you?

MR WILLIAMSON: I am sure I have it here somewhere.

MR LEVINE: Let me put one in front of you.

MR WILLIAMSON: We have it here Mr Chairman.

MR LEVINE: Did you coin the name Sanhedrin for the meetings?

MR WILLIAMSON: No Mr Chairman, I am sure that name existed possibly even before I was born Mr Chairman.

MR LEVINE: Mr Bizos sought to suggest that some sort of death sentences were dealt with at these Sanhedrin meetings, what do you say about that?

MR WILLIAMSON: I think as I said Mr Chairman, in my evidence, the Sanhedrin was almost a rapid fire, quick report back meeting Mr Chairman, and there was no discussion or death sentences passed Mr Chairman.

MR LEVINE: Where does the term Sanhedrin come from?

MR WILLIAMSON: Well, I at the time thought it was a Biblical term, but I have now actually seen that it is an old Rabbinical term from what I read here Mr Chairman.

MR LEVINE: If you read the first paragraph of Sanhedrin, you will see that it is a (indistinct) of the Greek, Synédrion, meaning assembly?

MR WILLIAMSON: I see that Mr Chairman.

MR LEVINE: Yes. Now, do you have any knowledge about the Jewish (indistinct) laws?

MR WILLIAMSON: No Mr Chairman, but perhaps my legal advisor can assist me in that area Mr Chairman.

MR LEVINE: It could be a very costly opinion Mr Chairman. Mr Williamson, read the last paragraph please to yourself of Exhibit W. Tell us what that sets out as being the purpose of the Sanhedrin?

MR WILLIAMSON: From in the course of Jewish history?

CHAIRPERSON: Is there any importance to be attached to the Sanhedrin point? The applicant has said that he doesn't know where it came from, and it already existed when he joined the Committee, isn't that an end to it?

MR BIZOS: Let's come back to it a little later. Let me round off this Sanhedrin situation. Do you who was responsible for naming these meetings, the Sanhedrin Meetings?

MR WILLIAMSON: For naming them, Mr Chairman?

MR BIZOS: Yes.

MR WILLIAMSON: You mean for coining the term: "Sanhedrin"?

MR BIZOS: Yes.

MR WILLIAMSON: Absolutely no idea.

MR BIZOS: Did you ever — wasn't your curiosity aroused as to why they were called Sanhedrin Meetings?

MR WILLIAMSON: Mr Chairman, as I said, you know I've absolutely no idea, I never bothered to even think about it, that was the name. You know, we called Section A,B,C,G, whatever you know, that was the name. I've got no idea. It's an Afrikaans term that even today I'm not entirely familiar with. I believe it's some type of an upper structure in, referred to somewhere in the Bible.

MR BIZOS: Well you see, whoever gave it that name was spot on for what we will suggest you were doing.

MR WILLIAMSON: Mr Chairman, I can't comment. I'm sure the term: "Sanhedrin" probably existed when I was a child, that it was even then called the Sanhedrin.

MR BIZOS: Oh, much longer than that Mr Williamson, much longer.

MR WILLIAMSON: Well the original Sanhedrin, obviously much longer but I'm talking about the Security Police Sanhedrin.

MR BIZOS: Yes. Well it must have come along, it must have been adopted when you were a bit older than a child, when they decided to become a sort of superior court.

MR WILLIAMSON: Superior?

MR BIZOS: Court.

MR WILLIAMSON: Court or Port?

MR BIZOS: Yes.

MR WILLIAMSON: No, Mr Chairman.

MR BIZOS: I want to hand in Mr Chairman, from the 1963 edition of the Encyclopaedia Britannica, Volume 19 and page 946A, what the Sanhedrin was and whoever chose the name may have known more than the witness is prepared to tell us.

"Sanhedrin, sometimes incorrectly written Sinedrium(?) ...[intervention]

ADV DE JAGER: Do you suggest the Security Police actually went to the encyclopaedia, Britannica or did they look at what or the Afrikaans ...[intervention]

MR BIZOS: No, Mr Chairman, what we are going to argue is that they chose the name. Usually people that choose a name try to find an aim which represents more or less what they are doing, and whoever did it knew what it meant, Mr Chairman.

"Sanhedrin, sometimes incorrectly written Sinedrium or Sanhedrin, the Supreme Rabbinic Court in Jerusalem during second commonwealth era. The term is a hybridization of the Greek Sinedriun meaning assembly. The term also is used for the Hieropegus in Athens".

Do you know that the Hieropegus was the highest court established by the Gods?

MR WILLIAMSON: No, Mr Chairman, I don't have your advantage in terms of Greek mythology.

MR BIZOS: That's a pity. Rabbinic sources speak of a great Sanhedrin of 71 members and smaller Sanhedrin trial courts of 23 members judging criminal cases or violations of Jewish law.

Now you will agree that the Security Police, never mind who had what knowledge, had set themselves up as the Judges of who could live and who could die?

MR WILLIAMSON: No, I can't agree to that at all Mr Chairman.

MR BIZOS: Well, they had a meeting to which reports were made, they had a Target Selection Committee and they allowed their people, like yourself, to arrange for the elimination of people. Now why do you quarrel that the name was deliberately chosen as suggested by the person who wrote the article for this encyclopaedia, Britannica.

MR WILLIAMSON: Well I don't see any reference here to the Sanhedrin passing Judgment and deciding who must live and die, Mr Chairman.

MR BIZOS: Judging criminal cases.

MR WILLIAMSON: That's not deciding who's going to live or die, Mr Chairman.

MR BIZOS: Well, in some criminal cases the decision is made as to who should live and die, and certainly during the period that you were a security policeman.

MR WILLIAMSON: Mr Chairman, I — this is very interesting information but I really have absolutely no idea who coined the term Sanhedrin, who decided it would be what the committee was called, Mr Chairman. It wasn't even a committee, it was a group. I really can't make any further statement or suggestion.

MR BIZOS: Yes. It is further described lower down:

"Dalmoedic tradition pictures the great Sanhedrin as the highest legislative and judicial court".

When a person decides that Ruth First and Jeanette Schoon must die as with a letter bomb, isn't that like a sentence of death that the highest court has the power to impose?

MR WILLIAMSON: Well Mr Chairman, I certainly — again there was never any such decision or sentence passed at any Sanhedrin that I was present at, Mr Chairman.

MR BIZOS: I'm going to put to you Mr Williamson, that your description of this fleeting communications between members is so highly improbable that the only conclusion that we will ask the Committee to draw is that the conspiracy of silence that there was at the time is continuing with you, without wanting to disclose who really decided, what preparations were made by whom, and who executed it, for the purposes of protecting your colleagues or erstwhile colleagues and more particularly, General Coetzee.

MR WILLIAMSON: Mr Chairman, all I can say is that all I can do is say what I know happened when I was involved in what happened. I cannot comment on Sanhedrins and passing of sentences, things that you know, might be something that comes from the fiction around, and by fiction I mean the writings in fiction, around spying and these types of operations.

But the reality was different Mr Chairman, and I do not believe that a conspiracy of silence — if remember the Sanhedrin and the assembly that we had ever morning and the number of people who were there and the number of different people who were there on different occasions and the number of different organizations that were there and the number of different individuals to whom they went and reported, I believe that this would have to be a rather incredible conspiracy of silence to maintain, Mr Chairman.

MR BIZOS: Well we only have now your word. And what I want to ask you before the adjournment Mr Williamson, have you got any yardstick which you can suggest to the Committee that it should use as to whether you can be believed or not, having regard to your admitted deceptions almost throughout a lifetime?

MR WILLIAMSON: Yes, Mr Chairman. All I can say is that this Committee and nobody else would have known anything about these operations if it hadn't been for me.

MR BIZOS: You're giving yourself too much credit Major Williamson.

MR WILLIAMSON: Well.

MR BIZOS: Others spoke before you and you know that.

MR WILLIAMSON: Other spoke about these operations before me?

MR BIZOS: No, about the manner in which people were eliminated, killed, brutalized, assassinated.

MR WILLIAMSON: Mr Chairman, nobody spoke about these operations before me and nobody would have known anything about these operations if it hadn't been for me.

MR BIZOS: Oh. So you had absolute faith that your colleagues would ...[indistinct] the conspiracy of silence?

MR WILLIAMSON: I don't understand how that follows what I said, Mr Chairman.

MR BIZOS: Yes. You only spoke about them when it became clear to you that you may have to go to prison for these acts unless you could manage to persuade the Committee or the Commission even before you spoke, to give you amnesty, to try to trade your information for your freedom. You didn't do it out of any sense of humanity or devoid of personal interest.

Appendix B

The links between the Litvinenko affair and the World Trade Center were also a subject of interest. On January 2, 2006, I wrote the following on these links:

Mario Scaramella, the Italian interlocutor for the poisoned Alexander Litvinenko and Russian-Israeli media/mobster tycoon Boris Berezovsky, is now under investigation by prosecutors in Rome, Naples, and Bologna for international arms smuggling, divulging official judicial secrets, conspiracy, international trafficking in radioactive materials, and the dumping of hazardous waste through unauthorized third parties. Scaramella was arrested last month by Italian police and his offices have been searched by police several times.

The Italian media is reporting on transcripts of phone conversations between Scaramella and two former U.S. intelligence officers. One conversation, reported in *La Repubblica*, is a January 25, 2006 conversation between Scaramella and a mysterious ex-CIA agent from California who uses the name "Perry." In the conversation, Scaramella stresses to Perry that his activities are not "just my activity, but the activity of the organization." It is becoming clear that the "organization" to which Scaramella is referring is a private and global intelligence organization involving former members of the KGB and Russian Federal Security Bureau (like Litvinenko), private military and intelligence companies, and ex-CIA and British intelligence officers. Scaramella discussed the political dirty "trick" they are preparing for Italian center-left leader Romano Prodi and it is clear from the conversation that Perry gives Scaramella his orders, though politely. When Scaramella goes into a tangent on his international activities, Perry merely replies, "You must work on the Italian politics." When Scaramella presents a list of the possible future options open to him, Perry very curtly suggests, "You could be part of the cabinet of the minister." But

Scaramella is pessimistic when he states, "most probably Prodi will win, even if we will launch our attack…"

The "attack" is key to the conversation. *WMR* was the first media outlet to suggest that the Scaramella-Litvinenko affair was a dirty bomb plot gone bad and that the intelligence services of Russian President Vladimir Putin may have actually derailed the plot.

Scaramella relates to Perry his conversation with then-Prime Minister Silvio Berlusconi, in which he asked the right-wing and now-indicted politician for a job, preferably at NATO or the United Nations. Scaramella claims that he was first offered a seat in the Italian parliament but declined because he feared a rough political campaign against him after he had made public his "KGB claims" against Prodi and that he "preferred a post outside Italy in an international organization."

The Italian paper *Corriere della Sera* is also reporting on a telephone conversation between Scaramella and Paolo Guzzanti, the Miktrokhin Committee's chairman on 28 January 2006, three days after the phone conversation between Perry and Scaramella that Romani Prodi was "cultivated by the KGB" and cited ex-KGB Colonel Oleg Gordievsky as his source. Guzzanti responds, "In that case he is our man?" "Yes," replies Scaramella. "That's enough. I don't want to know anything else," Guzzanti replies.

It has also been revealed that while talking to Perry, Scaramella declared that he had obtained taped testimony against Prodi from Gordievski and that the testimony was given in the presence of "Lou Palumbo," who has now been identified as a 22-year veteran of the CIA. Gordievski, who is under the protection of the British intelligence services, has since denounced Scaramella as a fraud. It is also clear that Scaramella's mission was to seek out prominent Russian exiles and defectors in order to trick them into bringing false charges against leftist politicians like Prodi.

Previously, *WMR* reported that Scaramella was linked by Italian investigators to Filippo Marino, who is involved in the security business and founded the Special Research Monitoring Center (SRMC), and claims he was a member of the elite Italian Army 131st Regiment and member of an Italian law enforcement organized crime task force targeting the mob in Naples. One of Marino's companies, Securitydirector LLC, is registered at P.O. Box 190487, Miami Beach, FL 33119-0487. According to *La Stampa*, a link has now been discovered between Marino and Hallandale, Florida-based Incident Management Group (IMG). Marino has been a senior consultant for IMG, according to *La Stampa*. IMG's Managing Partner is none other than Louis F. Palumbo, Scaramella's task master in the reported attempt to tarnish Prodi. Palumbo's bio at the IMG Web site states that in 1977, he founded the security consulting firm Ackerman & Palumbo. The Association of Former Intelligence Officers (AFIO) lists a Louis F. Palumbo of Miami Beach, Florida.

Palumbo's partners at IMG include Daniel Donohue, a former CIA clandestine services agent in Southeast Asia and India; Harley Stock, a "forensic hypnosis" expert with the FBI and U.S. Secret Service; and, perhaps most intriguingly, Christopher Hagon, a 21-year veteran of the London Metropolitan Police or "Scotland Yard."

Hagon told *La Stampa* that Marino did work as a consultant for IMG as a consultant. In fact, IMG's consultant profiles list Marino as:

"FILIPPO MARINO, SENIOR CONSULTANT, has 10 years of international experience in the areas of security and environmental crime prevention. Marino has worked on a variety of security-related assignments ranging from investigative support of judicial authorities to personal awareness training and private consulting worldwide. He is one of the founders of Special Research Monitoring Center (SRMC) and a founding member of the Permanent Intergovernmental Conference for Environmental Crime Prevention. He is currently Director of Security & Operations, for the SRMC. Marino served as an officer of the prestigious 131st Regiment of the Italian Army, and is an inspector for a law-enforcement, environmental task force against organized crime in Naples, Italy. He holds a magna cum laude B. A. in Behavioral Sciences from San Jose State University, and has obtained multiple certifications in security and protection services. He speaks fluent Italian and German."

Note that Marino's links to Scaramella's ECPP is also cited above. Also of interest is the listing of a Curtis Perry as an IMG consultant:

"CURTIS PERRY, SENIOR CONSULTANT, has 27 years experience in government and private sector security. He served for ten years in the CIA and was stationed throughout the Far East. Mr. Perry is fluent in several Chinese dialects and has access to numerous government agencies in the Philippines and throughout Southeast Asia. Previously he was employed as a Senior Consultant by the security firm of Ackerman & Palumbo and was a Managing

Director for Kroll Associates in Manila from 1992 -1996. Mr. Perry has undertaken numerous investigations for Corporate America — including those involving kidnappings, extortions and product contaminations — in the Far East and Australia."

Another IMG consultant is Robert Wager, whose bio claims he manages security for the U.S. Embassy in Bogota, Colombia. Scaramella claims to have also worked in Bogota. The bio of another IMG consultant, Ned Timmons, states, "for two years Timmons directed an international import/export corporation operating undercover in Colombia, Venezuela, Peru and Central America.... He currently serves as a consultant to the U.S. and Cayman Governments on drug trafficking matters." There is yet another Colombian link, "John Stabler, Senior Consultant, has 17 years experience in the security management and consulting profession, with 13 years of specialization in Colombia. He has designed security for plantations, mines, pipelines, piers and airfields in hostile locations in Colombia, Panama, Ecuador and Chile."

Also of interest is another "environmental" link that ties the various Scaramella-Litvinenko players under the cover of an international environmental network. An SEC EDGAR search revealed a stockholders' agreement between Harrison-Kroll Environmental Services, Inc. of Louisiana and Palumbo Partners, a Delaware corporation dated December 31, 1992, in which Kroll acquired Palumbo Partners. A Google search also revealed that former Secret Service Presidential Protective Division agent Jim Holt served as Training Director for Ackerman & Palumbo and was "one of the original directors and consultant partners with Palumbo Partners, Inc., Miami." An office of Harrison-Kroll Environmental Services is listed at 300 S. Grand Avenue, Suite 1300, Los Angeles, CA 90071.

Kroll Associates is an enigmatic "security services" company which has close links to the CIA. Not only is Kroll active in private military contracting in Iraq but it has long been associated with dubious U.S. intelligence activities at home and abroad. According to a knowledgeable source, Jules Kroll, who founded Kroll Associates in 1972, obtained needed funding for his firm from Foothill Capital in the 1980s. Foothill was deeply enmeshed in the Savings & Loan collapses in the 1980s but salvaged itself to become a part of Wells Fargo Bank. Kroll, who helped Curtis Publishing (renamed Cadence Industries after a merger) cut waste in the 1970s (and deplete the company's pension fund in the process), got his first big break when he helped locate the stolen millions of Philippine ex-President Ferdinand Marcos. He would later go after the offshore bank accounts of Haiti's Jean-Claude Duvalier and Iraq's Saddam Hussein.

According to our well-placed source, Ray Steffans (aka Ray diStefano of New Jersey), mobster Gideon Chern, and Eddie Baker of Vanguard Petroleum met in Houston in September 1983 to discuss, among other items, funding for Kroll. In December 1977, Bernard Taubenfeld, Gideon Chern and Shalom Goldburd, officials of B'nai Torah Institute affiliate Nutrition for Youth, were convicted of defrauding the government by submitting bills for food that was never served to poor children in the New York City summer lunch program. Chern's other organized crime activity in the 1980s reportedly had an important protector — former U.S. Attorney for the Southern District of New York Rudolph Giuliani. The former New York Mayor and prospective GOP presidential candidate reportedly suppressed a wealth of evidence against Chern.

Two days after the Houston meeting, a Jaguar supposedly with the body of Baker in it was found charred outside of Houston. A fire investigator later revealed that no body was found in the car at the time of the fire. Kroll, after Enron's bankruptcy, purchased Zolfo-Cooper, and thus owned Zolfo-Cooper's Steven Cooper, the attorney appointed by New York bankruptcy Judge Arthur Gonzalez to run Enron in bankruptcy. In July 2004, Marsh-McLennan bought Kroll and Associates. Marsh-McLennan is run by Jeffrey Greenberg, son of Maurice (Hank) Greenberg of AIG. Chase and Citibank notes from Kenneth Lay/Enron were purchased in May 2001 by AIG and the MacArthur Foundation.

Kroll was responsible for the security of the World Trade Center on 9/11. The firm had hired FBI top counter-terrorism agent John O'Neill as Director of World Trade Center security upon his retirement from the FBI. O'Neill died in the 9/11 attacks. Kroll also markets Identity Theft Shield, the first time Kroll has offered its services to individuals as opposed to governments and companies. As of June 30, 2006, Kroll had amassed over 560,000 customers for its Identity Theft Shield program.

The Chern link brings us back to the Russian-Israeli Mafia connections of Scaramella and company. Berezovsky's friend, former Yukos co-owner Leonid Nevzlin, is a Russian-Jewish oligarch and former President of the Russian Jewish Congress who now lives in Tel Aviv and is wanted by Russia for tax evasion

251

and corruption. As the Democrats prepare to assume control of Congress, Nevzlin is now in the United States, protected by the FBI from arrest based on previously-issued Russian and Interpol arrest warrants. This is not Nevzlin's first visit to the United States. In the summer of 2005, he appeared before the U.S. Congress' Helsinki Committee to criticize the government of Vladimir Putin. Nevzlin's sponsors were incoming House International Relations Committee chairman Tom Lantos (D-CA) and New Jersey Rep. Chris Smith. Nevzlin used the hearing to argue for the expulsion of Russia from the G-8. Another Nevzlin supporter is Arizona Republican Senator John McCain, another prospective GOP presidential candidate.

In a further example of the dubious activities of the Arlington, Virginia-based Fellowship Foundation, dubbed the "Christian Mafia" by many local residents, two of Nevzlin's wanted Yukos fellow shareholders, oligarchs Mikhail Brudno and Vladimir Dubov, who were indicted in Russia on charges similar to those brought against jailed Yukos former chairman Mikhail Khodorkovsky, were invited to have breakfast with President George W. Bush at the February 5, 2005 "National Prayer Breakfast." The annual Prayer Breakfast contrivance of the Fellowship Foundation is a ruse designed to provide a series of top-level intelligence and organized crime meetings under the sanctioning smile of "Jesus."

The person who invited Brudno, Dubov, and the jailed Khodorkovsky to the prayer breakfast was Lantos, whose wife, daughter, and son-in-law are devout Mormons. Brudno and Dubov, citizens of Israel, were assured by the FBI that it would ignore the Interpol and Russian arrest warrants, just as the FBI is ignoring the arrest warrant for Nevzlin, who is now in the United States, most likely with the acquiescence of Lantos. Lantos, who has his own connections with mob-run unions operating at San Francisco International Airport, does not seem to mind the fact that Nevzlin has been under investigation by Israeli police for illegally laundering $500 million through a Tel Aviv branch of Bank Hapoalim, Israel's largest bank. Nevzlin also took over assets of Khodorkovsky's collapsed bank, Menatep, which was also linked to money laundering involving the Bank of New York. Former Soviet President Mikhail Gorbachev supports Putin's attempt to bring the Russian-Israeli oligarchs to justice. He told Britain's *Sunday Times* that it is believed that the exiled oligarchs have hidden away $1 trillion.

Nevzlin's and Berezovsky's activities with Litvinenko are the tip of a huge iceberg of private intelligence intrigue that involves a number of wanted Russian exiles, including Nevzlin, Berezovsky, ex-Russian media magnate Vladimir Gusinsky, Mikhail Chernoy, Roman Abramovich, and Chechen "Foreign Minister" Akhmed Zakayev. Berezovsky's [and Litvinenko's] spokesman, Russian exile Alex Goldfarb, freely operates out of both London and New York. All are involved in various efforts to destabilize Russia with the help of neocons in the Bush administration and the government of Israel. However, the Israel Lobby's pressure on the U.S. media, most notably the Associated Press, *New York Times*, and *Washington Post*, ensures that the Russian exiles' links to Israel and organized crime are studiously ignored.

In another full circle between Tel Aviv and Italy, Menatep's former chief for investment management Alexei Globuvich said, after his arrest last spring in Italy, that Nevzlin may have tried to poison him and his family after mercury was found in his office, home, and car. Globuvich said he was a threat because he knew where Yukos and Menatep assets were located. Shortly thereafter, a Scotland Yard officer handed over to the British security firm ISC Global plans by the British government to extradite a number of Russian-Israeli exiles in Britain to Russia. ISC Global had been part of Menatep and Nevzlin was one of its chief customers. The London offices of ISC Global, now known as RISC Management, were visited in November 2006 by Litvinenko and Russian businessmen Andrei Lugovoi and Dmitry Kovtun and traces of polonium-210 were discovered there. According to the *Sunday Times* of London, Russian police are also investigating whether the poisoning of Litvinenko and the attempted poisoning of Globuvich are connected to the radiation poisoning death two years ago of Roman Tsepov, a former bodyguard of Putin when he was deputy Mayor of St. Petersburg. Tsepov was involved in the Russian government's tracking of Yukos assets. Also of interest are connections to the June 2004 assassination of *Forbes* Russian edition editor-in-chief Paul Klebnikov, a U.S. citizen who wrote a damaging exposé of Berezovsky. Three Chechen contract killers were charged in Klebnikov's murder. The same Russian-Israeli mob ring is also being looked at in the investigation of the assassination of Russian journalist Anna Politkovskaya of *Novaya Gazeta* as a way to embarrass Putin.

The connection of Nevzlin to the polonium and the receipt of classified British secrets is more of a reason for Russia's Prosecutor General's office to seek his extradition — but the FBI refuses to cooperate due to the orders coming from people like

Lantos, McCain, FBI Director Robert Mueller, and others who do the bidding of the Russian-Israeli mob and their Italian mafiosi underlings.

The Russian Prosecutor-General's office has stated, "A version is being looked at, those who ordered these crimes [polonium poisoning, etc.] could be the same people who are on an international wanted list for serious and very serious crimes, one of whom is ... Leonid Nevzlin."

The connections now discovered by Italian and Russian investigators between the Russian-Israeli-Italian-British-U.S. private intelligence network of former intelligence agents and billionaire mobsters suggest that the "serious crimes" committed may be more than the poisoning of Litvinenko and others with radioactive materials. The investigators are wise to pursue the links to U.S. security firms and former CIA personnel involved in pre-9/11 protection functions. The FBI cannot or will not investigate the actual perpetrators of 9/11. However, the Italian and Russian law enforcement professionals are beginning to get very close. It is a shame that American law enforcement is not interested in pursuing real leads in the biggest crime in American history.

Index

Symbols

9/11 v, 5, 15, 22, 39, 40, 44,
48-65, 69-72, 76-79, 98,
102, 107-109, 113, 128,
168-170, 186-188, 194,
205, 251, 254
60 Minutes 143

A

ABC News 87, 219
Abdullah, King 187
Abe, Shinzo 234
Abizaid, John 178, 179, 182
Abou-Enein, Youssef 109, 110
Abramoff, Jack 146, 150-153,
188, 198, 202, 224, 227
Abramovich, Roman 195, 253
Abrams, Elliott 108, 125, 147, 155
Abu Ghraib 103-107, 143, 158,
177-181
Ackerman & Palumbo 189, 190,
249, 250
Acxiom 3-5
Adelman, Ken 201
Aderholt, Robert 99
Adham, Kamal 71
African National Congress 150
Ahmanson, Howard 227
Ahmed, Fayyaz 56, 57, 87,
113-118
Ahmedinejad, Mahmoud 50
AIG 251
Air Serv International 160
Akin Gump Strauss Hauer & Feld
144
al-Ali, Sulaiman 51
Albright, Madeleine 35

Alderly Management 54
Aldiyar 155
Alexander H Finance Co 54
Alexander the Great 83
Alexander, Yonah 45
al Faisal, Turki 66, 71, 77
Al Handal Trading Company 199
al-Handal, Waleed Noori 199
Alibek, Ken (born Kanatjan Alibekov) 72, 73
Al Jazeera 88, 203
Allen, George 167, 205
Allentown Morning Call 107
Almond, Lincoln 18
al Nahayan royal family 59
al Qaeda 40, 49-53, 57-68, 70, 71,
78, 79, 82, 87, 88, 114, 148,
149, 155, 156, 169, 172,
173, 179, 190, 192, 197,
203, 204
al-Saud, Fahd 70, 187
al-Saud, Nawaf 187
al-Saud, Nayif 186-188
al-Saud, Saud 187
al-Shehhi, Marwan 188
Alt, Franz 134
Al Thuraya Group 199
Alticor, Inc 227
al Zawahiri, Ayman 68
American Enterprise Institute 113,
131, 185
American Israel Public Affairs
Committee (AIPAC) 67,
208-211
American Reporter 11, 15-17
Amin, Hafizullah 82
Anderson, Jack xi, 141-144, 162
Andromeda International 57
Andropov, Yuri 79, 81
Angueira, Alexander 55
Annapolis Capital 200
anthrax 49, 72-77, 109, 140, 145

Applebaum, Jack 41
Arafat, Yasir 69
Arbusto 187
Aristide, Jean-Bertrand 133
Armitage, Richard 34, 68
Ashcroft, John 29, 49, 98, 113,
    116, 127-132, 204
Ashe, Victor 133
Asia-Cell 114
Assaad, Ayaad 110
Assad, Bashar 154, 155
Associated Press (AP) 20, 139,
    188, 199, 253
Atheer 114
Atta, Mohamed 188
Avrakotos, Gus 69

B

Baker and McKenzie 234
Baker, Eddie 251
Baker, Howard 34
Baker, James 68, 98, 117
Baker, Susan 98
Balloch & Roe 198
Banca Svizzera Italiana 56
Banco Ambrosiano 60
Bank Hapoalim 252
Bank of America 60
Bank of Credit and Commerce
    International (BCCI) 30,
    53, 66, 70
Bank of Italy 60
Bank of New York 252
Barak, Ehud 118
Barayagwiza, Jean-Bosco 161
Barbour, Haley 132
Barrett, Gresham 99
Bassett, Brant "Nine Fingers" 220
Bates PanGulf 198
Bath, James 187
Battelle 157, 158
Bauer, Gary 97

Baxter, J. Clifford 61, 62
Beale, Howard 89
Bechtel 33, 154, 166, 202
Beck, Glenn 161
Bell Pottinger 197
Bell, Tim 20, 51, 127, 197, 198
Ben and Jerry's Foundation 204
Ben David, Moshe 216
Bennett, William 39, 210
Benson, Ralph 100
Berezovsky, Boris 184, 185,
    193-199, 247, 251-253
Bergen, Peter 70
Berger, Sandy 32
Berlusconi, Silvio 89, 90, 126,
    183, 185, 191, 193, 198, 248
Bernstein, Carl 142
bin Faisal, Turki 66
bin Laden, Osama 30, 40, 51, 52,
    63-71, 78, 85-87, 121, 149,
    171-173, 187
bin Laden, Salem 68, 187
bin Maktoum, Rashid 173
*Biological Warfare in the 21st
    Century* 75
Biopreparat 72
Black, Conrad 88, 89
Blackwater 200, 225-231
Blackwell, Kenneth 136, 227
Blair, Tony 4, 86, 89, 126, 196,
    198
Blake, Robert 216
Bloomberg News 235
Bluelake World SA 57
BMI, Inc. 51
Body Shop International 204
Bolkiah, Hassanal 198
Bolton, John x, 109-111, 114
Bonini, Carlo 191
Booyse, Wim 150, 151
Bosnia Defense Fund 66
Bout, Victor 57, 58, 172

The True History of the Bilderbergers
BY DANIEL ESTULIN

More than a center of influence, the Bilderberg Group is a shadow world government, hatching plans of domination at annual meetings ... and under a cone of media silence.

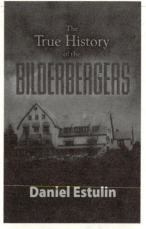

THE TRUE HISTORY OF THE BILDERBERGERS goes inside the secret meetings and sheds light on why a group of politicians, businessmen, bankers and other mighty individuals formed the world's most powerful society. As Benjamin Disraeli, one of England's greatest Prime Ministers, noted, "The world is governed by very different personages from what is imagined by those who are not behind the scenes."

Included are unpublished and never-before-seen photographs and other documentation of meetings, as this riveting account exposes the past, present and future plans of the Bilderberg elite.

Softcover: **$24.95** (ISBN: 9780977795345) • 366 pages • Size: 6 x 9

Fighting For G.O.D.
(Gold, Oil, Drugs)
BY JEREMY BEGIN, ART BY LAUREN SALK

This racehorse tour of American history and current events scrutinizes the lineage and affiliations of key players who transcend commonly accepted liberal/conservative political ideologies. In comic-book format, it examines the Neo-Con agenda and its relationship to the "New World Order." From the privatized fund- raising system enslaving politicians to evidence contradicting the conventional wisdom that the 19 hijackers took our nation by surprise to the widespread suppression of human rights, *FIGHTING FOR G.O.D.* discusses major issues confronting America's citizenry, as well as steps the populace can take not only to halt but to reverse the march towards totalitarianism.

Softcover: **$9.95**, (ISBN 9780977795338) • 64 Pages • Size: 8.5 x 11

The Oil Card
Global Economic Warfare in the 21st Century
BY JAMES NORMAN

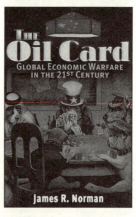

Challenging the conventional wisdom surrounding high oil prices, this compelling argument sheds an entirely new light on free-market industry fundamentals. By deciphering past, present, and future geopolitical events, it makes the case that oil pricing and availability have a long history of being employed as economic weapons by the United States. Despite ample world supplies and reserves, high prices are now being used to try to rein in China — a reverse of the low-price strategy used in the 1980s to deprive the Soviets of hard currency. Far from conspiracy theory, the debate notes how the U.S. has previously used the oil majors, the Saudis, and market intervention to move markets — and shows how this is happening again.   — Available in July 2008 —

Softcover **$14.95** (ISBN 0977795390) • 288 PAGES • Size: 5.5 x 8.5

Dr. Mary's Monkey

How the Unsolved Murder of a Doctor, a Secret Laboratory in New Orleans and Cancer-Causing Monkey Viruses are Linked to Lee Harvey Oswald, the JFK Assassination and Emerging Global Epidemics

BY EDWARD T. HASLAM, FOREWORD BY JIM MARRS

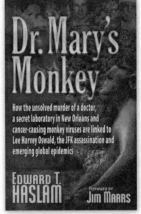

Evidence of top-secret medical experiments and cover-ups of clinical blunders

The 1964 murder of a nationally known cancer researcher sets the stage for this gripping exposé of medical professionals enmeshed in covert government operations over the course of three decades. Following a trail of police records, FBI files, cancer statistics, and medical journals, this revealing book presents evidence of a web of medical secret-keeping that began with the handling of evidence in the JFK assassination and continued apace, sweeping doctors into cover-ups of cancer outbreaks, contaminated polio vaccine, the genesis of the AIDS virus, and biological weapon research using infected monkeys.

Softcover: **$19.95** (ISBN: 9780977795307) • 385 pages • Size: 5 1/2 x 8 1/2

The Franklin Scandal

A Story of Powerbrokers, Child Abuse & Betrayal

BY NICK BRYANT

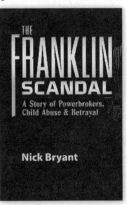

A chilling exposé of corporate corruption and government cover-ups, this account of a nationwide child-trafficking and pedophilia ring tells a sordid tale of corruption in high places. The scandal originally surfaced during an investigation into Omaha, Nebraska's failed Franklin Federal Credit Union and took the author beyond the Midwest and ultimately to Washington, DC. Implicating businessmen, senators, major media corporations, the CIA, and even the venerable Boys Town organization, this extensively researched report includes firsthand interviews with key witnesses and explores a controversy that has received scant media attention.

The Franklin Scandal is the story of a underground ring that pandered children to a cabal of the rich and powerful. The ring's pimps were a pair of Republican powerbrokers who used Boys Town as a pedophiliac reservoir, and had access to the highest levels of our government.

Hardcover: **$24.95** (ISBN: 9780977795352) • 360 pages • Size: 6 x 9
—Available January 2009—

Fixing America

Breaking the Strangehold of Corporate Rule, Big Media, and the Religious Right

BY JOHN BUCHANAN, FOREWORD BY JOHN MCCONNELL

An explosive analysis of what ails the United States

An award-winning investigative reporter provides a clear, honest diagnosis of corporate rule, big media, and the religious right in this damning analysis. Exposing the darker side of capitalism, this critique raises alarms about the security of democracy in today's society, including the rise of the corporate state, the insidious role of professional lobbyists, the emergence of religion and theocracy as a right-wing political tactic, the failure of the mass media, and the sinister presence of an Orwellian neo-fascism.

Softcover: **$19.95**, (ISBN 9780975290682) 211 Pages, 5.5 x 8.5

Sinister Forces
A Grimoire of American Political Witchcraft
Book One: The Nine
BY PETER LEVENDA, FOREWORD BY JIM HOUGAN

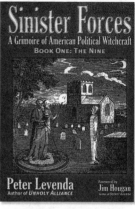

A shocking alternative to the conventional views of American history.
The roots of coincidence and conspiracy in American politics, crime, and culture are examined in this book, exposing new connections between religion, political conspiracy, and occultism. Readers are taken from ancient American civilization and the mysterious mound builder culture to the Salem witch trials, the birth of Mormonism during a ritual of ceremonial magic by Joseph Smith, Jr., and Operations Paperclip and Bluebird. Not a work of speculative history, this exposé is founded on primary source material and historical documents. Fascinating details are revealed, including the bizarre world of "wandering bishops" who appear throughout the Kennedy assassinations; a CIA mind control program run amok in the United States and Canada; a famous American spiritual leader who had ties to Lee Harvey Oswald in the weeks and months leading up to the assassination of President Kennedy; and the "Manson secret.

Hardcover: **$29.95** (ISBN 9780975290620) • 395 pages • Size: 6 x 9

Book Two: A Warm Gun

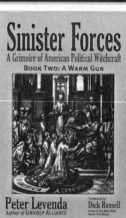

The roots of coincidence and conspiracy in American politics, crime, and culture are investigated in this analysis that exposes new connections between religion, political conspiracy, terrorism, and occultism. Readers are provided with strange parallels between supernatural forces such as shaminism, ritual magic, and cult practices, and contemporary interrogation techniques such as those used by the CIA under the general rubric of MK-ULTRA. Not a work of speculative history, this exposé is founded on primary source material and historical documents. Fascinating details on Nixon and the "Dark Tower," the Assassin cult and more recent Islamic terrorism, and the bizarre themes that run through American history from its discovery by Columbus to the political assassinations of the 1960s are revealed.

Hardcover: **$29.95** (ISBN 0975290637) • 370 pages • Size: 6 x 9

Book Three: The Manson Secret

The Stanislavski Method as mind control and initiation. Filmmaker Kenneth Anger and Aleister Crowley, Marianne Faithfull, Anita Pallenberg, and the Rolling Stones. Filmmaker Donald Cammell (Performance) and his father, CJ Cammell (the first biographer of Aleister Crowley), and his suicide. Jane Fonda and Bluebird. The assassination of Marilyn Monroe. Fidel Castro's Hollywood career. Jim Morrison and witchcraft. David Lynch and spiritual transformation. The technology of sociopaths. How to create an assassin. The CIA, MK-ULTRA and programmed killers.

Hardcover: **$29.95** (ISBN 0975290651) • 522 pages • Size: 6 x 9